Data Engineering with Scala and Spark

Build streaming and batch pipelines that process massive
amounts of data using Scala

Eric Tome

Rupam Bhattacharjee

David Radford

Data Engineering with Scala and Spark

Associate Group Product Manager: Kaustubh Manglurkar

Associate Publishing Product Manager: Arindam Majumder

Book Project Manager: Kirti Pisat

Senior Editor: Tiksha Lad

Technical Editor: Kavyashree K S

Copy Editor: Safis Editing

Proofreader: Safis Editing

Indexer: Subalakshmi Govindhan

Production Designer: Alishon Mendonca

DevRel Marketing Coordinator: Nivedita Singh

First published: January 2024

Production reference: 1160124

Published by Packt Publishing Ltd.

Grosvenor House

11 St Paul's Square

Birmingham

B3 1RB, UK.

ISBN 978-1-80461-258-3

www.packtpub.com

Contributors

About the authors

Eric Tome has over 25 years of experience working with data. He has contributed to and led teams that ingested, cleansed, standardized, and prepared data used by business intelligence, data science, and operations teams. He has a background in mathematics and currently works as a senior solutions architect at Databricks, helping customers solve their data and AI challenges.

Rupam Bhattacharjee works as a lead data engineer at IBM. He has architected and developed data pipelines, processing massive structured and unstructured data using Spark and Scala for on-premises Hadoop and K8s clusters on the public cloud. He has a degree in electrical engineering.

David Radford has worked in big data for over 10 years, with a focus on cloud technologies. He led consulting teams for several years, completing a migration from legacy systems to modern data stacks. He holds a master's degree in computer science and works as a senior solutions architect at Databricks.

About the reviewers

Bartosz Konieczny is a freelance data engineer enthusiast who has been coding for 15+ years. He has held various senior hands-on positions that helped him work on many data engineering problems in batch and stream processing, such as sessionization, data ingestion, data cleansing, ordered data processing, and data migration. He enjoys solving data challenges with public cloud services and open source technologies, especially Apache Spark, Apache Kafka, Apache Airflow, and Delta Lake. In addition, he blogs at `waitingforcode.com`.

Palanivelrajan is a highly passionate data evangelist with 19.5 years of experience in the data and analytics space. He has rich experience in architecting, developing, and delivering modern data platforms, data lakes, data warehouses, business intelligence, data science, and ML solutions. For the last five years, he has worked in engineering management, and he has 12+ years of experience in data architecture (big data and the cloud). He has built data teams and data practices and has been active in presales, planning, roadmaps, and executions. He has hired, managed, and mentored data engineers, data analysts, data scientists, ML engineers, and data architects. He has worked as a data engineering manager and a data architect for Sigmoid analytics, Nike, the Data Team, and Tata Communications.

Table of Contents

2

Part 2 – Data Ingestion, Transformation, Cleansing, and Profiling Using Scala and Spark

3

4

Part 3 – Software Engineering Best Practices for Data Engineering in Scala

8

9

Part 4 – Productionalizing Data Engineering Pipelines – Orchestration and Tuning

10

11

Part 5 – End-to-End Data Pipelines

12

13

Preface

Every company today is a data company regardless of the industry. Innovative companies use data to analyze the past, predict what will happen, and react to what is happening now. Data engineers are some of the most critical employees at companies today. They are essential for collecting, cleaning, and maintaining trusted datasets that analysts, data scientists, and reporting tools use to provide insights.

This book will teach you to leverage the Scala programming language on the Spark framework and the latest cloud technologies to build continuous and triggered data pipelines. You will do this by setting up a data engineering environment for local development and scalable distributed cloud deployments, using data engineering best practices, test-driven development, and **Continuous Integration/Continuous Delivery (CI/CD)**. You will also orchestrate and performance-tune your end-to-end pipelines to deliver data to your end users.

Who this book is for

This book is aimed at the data professional who is experienced with working with data but wants to understand how to transform raw data into a clean, trusted, and valuable source of information for their organization, using Scala, Spark, and the latest in cloud computing.

What this book covers

Chapter 1, Scala Essentials for Data Engineers, introduces Scala in data engineering, recognizing its importance due to type safety, adoption by major companies such as Netflix and Airbnb, native integration with Spark, fostering a software engineering mindset, and its versatility in both object-oriented and functional programming. The chapter covers concepts such as functional programming, objects, classes, higher-order functions, polymorphism, variance, option types, collections, pattern matching, and implicits in Scala.

Chapter 2, Environment Setup, presents two data engineering pipeline development environments. The first, a cloud-based setup, offers portability and easy access but incurs costs for system maintenance. The second involves local machine utilization, requiring a setup but avoiding cloud expenses.

Chapter 3, An Introduction to Apache Spark and Its APIs – DataFrame, Dataset, and Spark SQL, focuses on Apache Spark as a leading distributed data processing framework. It emphasizes handling large data volumes across machine clusters. Topics include working with Spark, building Spark applications with Scala, and comprehending Spark's Dataset and DataFrame APIs for effective data processing.

Chapter 4, Working with Databases, dives into relational databases' utilization within data pipelines, emphasizing efficiency in reading from and writing to databases. It covers the Spark API and building a straightforward database library, exploring Spark's JDBC API, loading configurations, creating an interface, and executing multiple database operations.

Chapter 5, Object Stores and Data Lakes, discusses the evolution from traditional databases to the era of data lakes and lakehouses, due to surges in data volumes. The focus will be on object stores, which are fundamental for both data lakes and lake houses.

Chapter 6, Understanding Data Transformation, goes deeper into essential Spark skills for data engineers aiming to transform data for downstream use cases. It covers advanced Spark topics such as the distinctions between transformations and actions, aggregation, grouping, joining data, utilizing window functions, and handling complex dataset types.

Chapter 7, Data Profiling and Data Quality, stresses the importance of data quality checks in preventing issues downstream. It introduces the Deequ library, an open source tool by Amazon, for defining checks, performing analysis, suggesting constraints, and storing metrics.

Chapter 8, Test-Driven Development, Code Health, and Maintainability discusses software development best practices applied to data engineering, defect identification, code consistency, and security. It introduces **Test-Driven Development** (TDD), unit tests, integration tests, code coverage checks, static code analysis, and the importance of linting and code style for development practices.

Chapter 9, CI/CD with GitHub, introduces **Continuous Integration/Continuous Delivery (CI/CD)** concepts in Scala data engineering projects using GitHub. It explains CI/CD as automated testing and deployment, aiming for rapid iteration, error reduction, and consistent quality.

Chapter 10, Data Pipeline Orchestration, focuses on data pipeline orchestration, emphasizing the need for seamless task coordination and failure notification. It introduces tools such as Apache Airflow, Argo, Databricks Workflows, and Azure Data Factory.

Chapter 11, Performance Tuning, emphasizes the critical role of the Spark UI in optimizing performance. It covers topics such as the Spark UI basics, performance tuning, computing resource optimization, understanding data skewing, indexing, and partitioning.

Chapter 12, Building Batch Pipelines Using Spark and Scala, combines all of your previously learned skills to construct a batch pipeline. It stresses the significance of batch processing, leveraging Apache Spark's distributed processing and Scala's versatility. The topics cover a typical business use case, medallion architecture, batch data ingestion, transformation, quality checks, loading into a serving layer, and pipeline orchestration.

Chapter 13, Building Streaming Pipelines Using Spark and Scala, focuses on constructing a streaming pipeline, emphasizing real-time data ingestion using Azure Event Hubs, configured as Apache Kafka for Spark integration. It employs Spark's Structured Streaming and Scala for efficient data handling. Topics include use case understanding, streaming data ingestion, transformation, serving layer loading, and orchestration, aiming to equip you with the skills to develop and implement similar pipelines in your organizations.

To get the most out of this book

Before starting the book, at a minimum, you should be familiar with databases and some programming languages. Possessing business domain knowledge is beneficial, as you will be able to approach the book with business metrics and key performance indicators in mind. Understanding SQL for data analysis and familiarity with programming languages such as Python, Java, or C# is recommended.

All the setup required for this book and its examples are available in *Chapter 2, Environment Setup*, and are introduced in the appropriate chapters.

If you are using the digital version of this book, we advise you to type the code yourself or access the code from the book's GitHub repository (a link is available in the next section). Doing so will help you avoid any potential errors related to the copying and pasting of code.

Download the example code files

You can download the example code files for this book from GitHub at `https://github.com/PacktPublishing/Data-Engineering-with-Scala-and-Spark`. If there's an update to the code, it will be updated in the GitHub repository.

We also have other code bundles from our rich catalog of books and videos available at `https://github.com/PacktPublishing/`. Check them out!

Conventions used

There are a number of text conventions used throughout this book.

Code in text: Indicates code words in text, database table names, folder names, filenames, file extensions, pathnames, dummy URLs, user input, and Twitter handles. Here is an example: "It specifies the structure of the data with fields such as device_id, country, event_type, and event_ts."

A block of code is set as follows:

```
val updateSilver: DataFrame = bronzeData
    .select(from_json(col("value"), jsonSchema).alias("value"))
    .select(
      col("value.device_id"),
      col("value.country"),
      col("value.event_type"),
      col("value.event_ts")
    )
    .dropDuplicates("device_id", "country", "event_ts")
```

Any command-line input or output is written as follows:

```
argo submit my-first-workflow.yaml --serviceaccount=spark -n spark-app
--watch
```

Bold: Indicates a new term, an important word, or words that you see onscreen. For instance, words in menus or dialog boxes appear in bold. Here is an example: "You can find your policy in **Shared access policies** in the left-side of the **Azure Event Hubs** service."

> **Tips or important notes**
> Appear like this.

Get in touch

Feedback from our readers is always welcome.

General feedback: If you have questions about any aspect of this book, email us at customercare@ packtpub.com and mention the book title in the subject of your message.

Errata: Although we have taken every care to ensure the accuracy of our content, mistakes do happen. If you have found a mistake in this book, we would be grateful if you would report this to us. Please visit www.packtpub.com/support/errata and fill in the form.

Piracy: If you come across any illegal copies of our works in any form on the internet, we would be grateful if you would provide us with the location address or website name. Please contact us at copyright@packt.com with a link to the material.

If you are interested in becoming an author: If there is a topic that you have expertise in and you are interested in either writing or contributing to a book, please visit authors.packtpub.com.

Share Your Thoughts

Once you've read *Data Engineering with Scala and Spark*, we'd love to hear your thoughts! Scan the QR code below to go straight to the Amazon review page for this book and share your feedback.

https://packt.link/r/1804612588

Your review is important to us and the tech community and will help us make sure we're delivering excellent quality content.

Download a free PDF copy of this book

Thanks for purchasing this book!

Do you like to read on the go but are unable to carry your print books everywhere?

Is your eBook purchase not compatible with the device of your choice?

Don't worry, now with every Packt book you get a DRM-free PDF version of that book at no cost.

Read anywhere, any place, on any device. Search, copy, and paste code from your favorite technical books directly into your application.

The perks don't stop there, you can get exclusive access to discounts, newsletters, and great free content in your inbox daily

Follow these simple steps to get the benefits:

1. Scan the QR code or visit the link below

https://packt.link/free-ebook/9781804612583

2. Submit your proof of purchase

3. That's it! We'll send your free PDF and other benefits to your email directly

Part 1 –
Introduction to Data
Engineering, Scala, and an
Environment Setup

In this part, *Chapter 1* introduces Scala's significance in data engineering, emphasizing its type safety and native compatibility with Spark. It covers key concepts such as functional programming, objects, classes, and higher-order functions. Moving to *Chapter 2*, it contrasts two data engineering environments – a cloud-based setup offering portability and easy access with associated maintenance costs, and a local machine utilization option requiring setup but avoiding cloud expenses.

This part has the following chapters:

- *Chapter 1, Scala Essentials for Data Engineers*
- *Chapter 2, Environment Setup*

1

Scala Essentials for Data Engineers

Welcome to the world of data engineering with Scala. But why Scala? The following are some of the reasons for learning Scala:

- Scala provides type safety
- Big corporations such as Netflix and Airbnb have a lot of data pipelines written in Scala
- Scala is native to Spark
- Scala allows data engineers to adopt a software engineering mindset

Scala is a high-level general-purpose programming language that runs on a standard Java platform. It was created by Martin Odersky in 2001. The name Scala stands for *scalable language*, and it provides excellent support for both object-oriented and functional programming styles.

This chapter is meant as a quick introduction to concepts that the subsequent chapters build upon. Specifically, this chapter covers the following topics:

- Understanding functional programming
- Understanding objects, classes, and traits
- **Higher-order functions (HOFs)**
- Examples of HOFs from the Scala collection library
- Understanding polymorphic functions
- Variance
- Option types
- Collections

- Pattern matching
- Implicits in Scala

Technical requirements

This chapter is long and contains lots of examples to explain the concepts that are introduced. All of the examples are self-contained, and we encourage you to try them yourself as you move through the chapter. You will need a working Scala environment to run these examples.

You can choose to configure it by following the steps outlined in *Chapter 2* or use an online Scala playground such as **Scastie** (https://scastie.scala-lang.org/). We will use Scala 2.12 as the language version.

Understanding functional programming

Functional programming is based on the principle that programs are constructed using only **pure functions**. A pure function does not have any side effects and only returns a result. Some examples of side effects are modifying a variable, modifying a data structure in place, and performing I/O. We can think of a pure function as just like a regular algebraic function.

An example of a pure function is the length function on a string object. It only returns the length of the string and does nothing else, such as mutating a variable. Similarly, an integer addition function that takes two integers and returns an integer is a pure function.

Two important aspects of functional programming are **referential transparency** (**RT**) and the **substitution model**. An expression is referentially transparent if all of its occurrences can be substituted by the result of the expression without altering the meaning of the program.

In the following example, *Example 1.1*, we set x and then use it to set r1 and r2, both of which have the same value:

```
scala> val x: String = "hello"
x: String = hello

scala> val r1 = x + " world!"
r1: String = hello world!

scala> val r2 = x + " world!"
r2: String = hello world!
```

Example 1.1

Now, if we replace x with the expression referenced by x, r1 and r2 will be the same. In other words, the expression hello is referentially transparent.

Example 1.2 shows the output from a Scala interpreter:

```
scala> val r1 = "hello" + " world!"
r1: String = hello world!

scala> val r2 = "hello" + " world!"
r2: String = hello world!
```

Example 1.2

Let's now look at the following example, *Example 1.3*, where x is an instance of `StringBuilder` instead of `String`:

```
scala> val x = new StringBuilder("who")
x: StringBuilder = who

scala> val y = x.append(" am i?")
y: StringBuilder = who am i?

scala> val r1 = y.toString
r1: String = who am i?

scala> val r2 = y.toString
r2: String = who am i?
```

Example 1.3

If we substitute y with the expression it refers to (`val y = x.append(" am i?")`), r1 and r2 will no longer be equal:

```
scala> val x = new StringBuilder("who")
x: StringBuilder = who

scala> val r1 = x.append(" am i?").toString
r1: String = who am i?

scala> val r2 = x.append(" am i?").toString
r2: String = who am i? am i?
```

Example 1.4

So, the expression `x.append(" am i?")` is not referentially transparent.

One of the advantages of the functional programming style is it allows you to apply local reasoning without having to worry about whether it updates any globally accessible mutable state. Also, since no variable in the global scope is updated, it considerably simplifies building a multi-threaded application.

Another advantage is pure functions are also easier to test as they do not depend on any state apart from the inputs supplied, and they generate the same output for the same input values.

We won't delve deep into functional programming as it is outside of the scope of this book. Please refer to the *Further reading* section for additional material on functional programming. In the rest of this chapter, we will provide a high-level tour of some of the important language features that the subsequent chapters build upon.

In this section, we looked at a very high-level introduction to functional programming. Starting with the next section, we will look at Scala language features that enable both functional and object-oriented programming styles.

Understanding objects, classes, and traits

In this section, we are going to look at classes, traits, and objects. If you have used Java before, then some of the topics covered in this section will look familiar. However, there are several differences too. For example, Scala provides singleton objects, which automatically create a class and a single instance of that class in one go. Another example is Scala has case classes, which provide great support for pattern matching, allow you to create instances without the new keyword, and provide a default toString implementation that is quite handy when printing to the console.

We will first look at classes, followed by objects, and then wrap this section up with a quick tour of traits.

Classes

A class is a blueprint for objects, which are instances of that class. For example, we can create a Point class using the following code:

```scala
class Point(val x: Int, val y: Int) {

  def add(that: Point): Point = new Point(x + that.x, y + that.y)

  override def toString: String = s"($x, $y)"
}
```

Example 1.5

The Point class has four members—two immutable variables, x and y, as well as two methods, add and toString. We can create instances of the Point class as follows:

```scala
scala> val p1 = new Point(1,1)
p1: Point = (1, 1)

scala> val p2 = new Point(2,3)
p2: Point = (2, 3)
```

Example 1.6

We can then create a new instance, p3, by adding p1 and p2, as follows:

```
scala> val p3 = p1 add p2
p3: Point = (3, 4)
```

Example 1.7

Scala supports the infix notation, characterized by the placement of operators between operands, and automatically converts p1 add p2 to p1.add(p2). Another way to define the Point class is using a case class, as shown here:

```
case class Point(x: Int, y: Int) {

   def add(that: Point): Point = new Point(x + that.x, y + that.y)

}
```

Example 1.8

A case class automatically adds a factory method with the name of the class, which enables us to leave out the new keyword when creating an instance. A factory method is used to create instances of a class without requiring us to explicitly call the constructor method. Refer to the following example:

```
scala> val p1 = Point(1,1)
p1: Point = Point(1,1)

scala> val p2 = Point(2,3)
p2: Point = Point(2,3)
```

Example 1.9

The compiler also adds default implementations of various methods such as toString and hashCode, which the regular class definition lacks. So, we did not have to override the toString method, as was done earlier, and yet both p1 and p2 were printed neatly on the console (*Example 1.9*).

All arguments in the parameter list of a case class automatically get a val prefix, which makes them parametric fields. A parametric field is a shorthand that defines a parameter and a field with the same name.

To better understand the difference, let's look at the following example:

```
scala> case class Point1(x: Int, y: Int) //x and y are parametric
fields
defined class Point1
```

```
scala> class Point2(x: Int, y: Int) //x and y are regular parameters
defined class Point2

scala> val p1 = Point1(1, 2)
p1: Point1 = Point1(1,2)

scala> val p2 = new Point2(3, 4)
p2: Point2 = Point2@203ced18
```

Example 1.10

If we now try to access p1.x, it will work because x is a parametric field, whereas trying to access p2.x will result in an error. *Example 1.11* illustrates this:

```
scala> println(p1.x)
1

scala> println(p2.x)
<console>:13: error: value x is not a member of Point2
        println(p2.x)
                   ^
```

Example 1.11

Trying to access p2.x will result in a compile error, value x is not a member of Point2. Case classes also have excellent support for pattern matching, as we will see in the *Understanding pattern matching* section.

Scala also provides an abstract class, which, unlike a regular class, can contain abstract methods. For example, we can define the following hierarchy:

```
abstract class Animal

abstract class Pet extends Animal {
  def name: String
}

class Dog(val name: String) extends Pet {
  override def toString = s"Dog($name)"
}

scala> val pluto = new Dog("Pluto")
pluto: Dog = Dog(Pluto)
```

Example 1.12

Animal is the base class. Pet extends Animal and declares an abstract method, name. Dog extends Pet and uses a parametric field, name (it is both a parameter as well as a field). Because Scala uses the same namespace for fields and methods, this allows the field name in the Dog class to provide a concrete implementation of the abstract method name in Pet.

Object

Unlike Java, Scala does not support static members in classes; instead, it has **singleton objects**. A singleton object is defined using the object keyword, as shown here:

```
class Point(val x: Int, val y: Int) {

  // new keyword is not required to create a Point object
  // apply method from companion object is invoked
  def add(that: Point): Point = Point(x + that.x, y + that.y)

  override def toString: String = s"($x, $y)"
}

object Point {
  def apply(x: Int, y: Int) = new Point(x, y)
}
```

Example 1.13

In this example, the Point singleton object shares the same name with the class and is called that class's **companion object**. The class is called the **companion class** of the singleton object. For an object to qualify as a companion object of a given class, it needs to be in the same source file as the class itself.

Please note that the add method does not use the new keyword on the right-hand side. Point (x1, y1) is de-sugared into Point.apply(x1, y1), which returns a Point instance.

Singleton objects are also used to write an entrypoint for Scala applications. One option is to provide an explicit main method within the singleton object, as shown here:

```
object SampleScalaApplication {

  def main(args: Array[String]): Unit = {
    println(s"This is a sample Scala application")
  }

}
```

Example 1.14

The other option is to extend the App trait, which provides a main method implementation. We will cover traits in the next section. You can also refer to the *Further reading* section (the third point) for more information:

```
object SampleScalaApplication extends App {
  println(s"This is a sample Scala application")
}
```

Example 1.15

Trait

Scala also has traits, which are used to define rich interfaces as well as stackable modifications. You can read more stackable modifications in the Further reading section (the fourth point) Unlike class inheritance, where each class inherits from just one super class, a class can mix in any number of traits. A trait can have abstract as well as concrete members. Here is a simplified example of the Ordered trait from the Scala standard library:

```
trait Ordered[T] {
  // compares receiver (this) with argument of the same type
  def compare(that: T): Int
  def <(that: T): Boolean = (this compare that) < 0
  def >(that: T): Boolean = (this compare that) > 0
  def <=(that: T): Boolean = (this compare that) <= 0
  def >=(that: T): Boolean = (this compare that) >= 0
}
```

Example 1.16

The Ordered trait takes a type parameter, T, and has an abstract method, compare. All of the other methods are defined in terms of that method. A class can add the functionalities defined by <, >, and so on, just by defining the compare method. The compare method should return a negative integer if the receiver is less than the argument, positive if the receiver is greater than the argument, and 0 if both objects are the same.

Going back to our Point example, we can define a rule to say that a point, p1, is greater than p2 if the distance of p1 from the origin is greater than that of p2:

```
case class Point(x: Int, y: Int) extends Ordered[Point] {

  def add(that: Point): Point = new Point(x + that.x, y + that.y)
  def compare(that: Point) = (x ^ 2 + y ^ 2) ^ 1 / 2 - (that.x ^ 2 +
that.y ^ 2) ^ 1 / 2


}
```

Example 1.17

With the definition of `compare` now in place, we can perform a comparison between two arbitrary points, as follows:

```scala
scala> val p1 = Point(1,1)
p1: Point = Point(1,1)

scala> val p2 = Point(2,2)
p2: Point = Point(2,2)

scala> println(s"p1 is greater than p2: ${p1 > p2}")
p1 is greater than p2: false
example 1.18
```

In this section, we looked at objects, classes, and traits. In the next section, we are going to look at HOFs.

Working with higher-order functions (HOFs)

In Scala, functions are first-class citizens, which means function values can be assigned to variables, passed to functions as arguments, or returned by a function as a value. HOFs take one or more functions as arguments or return a function as a value.

A method can also be passed as an argument to an HOF because the Scala compiler will coerce a method into a function of the required type. For example, let's define a function literal and a method, both of which take a pair of integers, perform an operation, and then return an integer:

```scala
//function literal

val add: (Int, Int) => Int = (x, y) => x + y

//a method

def multiply(x: Int, y: Int): Int = x * y
```

Example 1.19

Let's now define a method that takes two integer arguments and performs an operation, op, on them:

```scala
def op(x: Int, y: Int) (f: (Int, Int) => Int): Int = f(x,y)
```

Example 1.20

We can pass any function (or method) of type (Int, Int) => Int to op, as the following example illustrates:

```
scala> op(1,2)(add)
res15: Int = 3

scala> op(2,3)(multiply)
res16: Int = 6
```

Example 1.21

This ability to pass functions as parameters is extremely powerful as it allows us to write generic code that can execute arbitrary user-supplied functions. In fact, many of the methods defined in the Scala collection library require functions as arguments, as we will see in the next section.

Examples of HOFs from the Scala collection library

Scala collections provide transformers that take a base collection, run some transformations over each of the collection's elements, and return a new collection. For example, we can transform a list of integers by doubling each of its elements using the map method, which we will cover in a bit:

```
scala> List(1,2,3,4).map(_ * 2)
res17: List[Int] = List(2, 4, 6, 8)
```

Example 1.22

A traversable trait, which is a base trait for all kinds of Scala collections, implements behaviors common to all collections, in terms of a foreach method, with the following signature:

```
def foreach[U](f: A => U): Unit
```

Example 1.23

The argument f is a function of type A => U, which is shorthand for Function1[A,U], and thus foreach is an HOF. This is an abstract method that needs to be implemented by all classes that mix in Traversable. The return type is Unit, which means this method does not return any meaningful value and is primarily used for side effects.

Here is an example that prints the elements of a List:

```
scala> /** let's start with a foreach call that prints the numbers in
a list
     |    * List(1,2,3,4).foreach((i: Int) => println(i))
     |    * we can skip the type argument and let Scala infer it
     |    * List(1,2,3,4).foreach( i => println(i))
     |    * Scala provides a shorthand to replace arguments using _
     |    * if the arguments are used only once on the right side
```

```
      |   * List(1,2,3,4).foreach(println(_))
      |   * finally Scala allows to leave the argument altogether
      |   * if there is only one argument used on the right side
      |   */
      | List(1,2,3,4).foreach(println)
1
2
3
4
```

Example 1.24

For the rest of the examples, we will continue to use the List collection type, but they are available for other types of collections, such as Array, Map, and Set.

map is similar to foreach, but instead of returning a unit, it returns a collection by applying the function f to each element of the base collection. Here is the signature for List [A]:

```
final def map[B] (f: (A) ⇒ B): List[B]
```

Example 1.25

Using the list from the previous example, if we want to double each of the elements in the list, but return a list of Doubles instead of Ints, it can be achieved by using the following:

```
scala> List(1,2,3,4).map(_ * 2.0)
res22: List[Double] = List(2.0, 4.0, 6.0, 8.0)
```

Example 1.26

The preceding expression returns a list of Double and can be chained with foreach to print the values contained in the list:

```
scala> List(1,2,3,4).map(_ * 2.0).foreach(println)
2.0
4.0
6.0
8.0
```

Example 1.27

A close cousin of map is flatMap, which comprises of two parts—map and flatten. Before looking into flatMap, let's look at flatten:

```
//converts a list of traversable collections into a list
//formed by the elements of the traversable collections
def flatten[B]: List[B]
```

Example 1.28

As the name suggests, it flattens the inner collections:

```
scala> List(Set(1,2,3), Set(4,5,6)).flatten
res24: List[Int] = List(1, 2, 3, 4, 5, 6)
```

Example 1.29

Now that we have seen what flatten does, let's go back to flatMap.

Let's say that for each element of List(1,2,3,4), we want to create List of elements from 0 to that number (both inclusive) and then combine all of those individual lists into a single list. Our first pass at it would look like the following:

```
scala> List(1,2,3,4).map(0 to _).flatten
res25: List[Int] = List(0, 1, 0, 1, 2, 0, 1, 2, 3, 0, 1, 2, 3, 4)
```

Example 1.30

With flatMap, we can achieve the same result in one step:

```
scala> List(1,2,3,4).flatMap(0 to _)
res26: List[Int] = List(0, 1, 0, 1, 2, 0, 1, 2, 3, 0, 1, 2, 3, 4)
```

Example 1.31

Scala collections also provide filter, which accepts a function that returns a Boolean as an argument, which is then used to filter elements of a given collection:

```
def filter(p: (A) ⇒ Boolean): List[A]
```

Example 1.32

For example, to filter all of the even integers from List of numbers from 1 to 100, try the following:

```
scala> List.tabulate(100)(_ + 1).filter(_ % 2 == 0)
res27: List[Int] = List(2, 4, 6, 8, 10, 12, 14, 16, 18, 20, 22, 24,
26, 28, 30, 32, 34, 36, 38, 40, 42, 44, 46, 48, 50, 52, 54, 56, 58,
60, 62, 64, 66, 68, 70, 72, 74, 76, 78, 80, 82, 84, 86, 88, 90, 92,
94, 96, 98, 100)
```

Example 1.33

There is also `withFilter`, which provides performance benefits over `filter` through the lazy evaluation of intermediate collections. It is part of the `TraversableLike` trait, with the `FilterMonadic` trait providing the abstract definition:

```
trait FilterMonadic[+A, +Repr] extends Any {
  //includes map, flatMap and foreach but are skipped here
  def withFilter(p: A => Boolean): FilterMonadic[A, Repr]
}
```

Example 1.34

`TraversableLike` defines the `withFilter` method through a member class, `WithFilter`, that extends `FilterMonadic`:

```
def withFilter(p: A => Boolean): FilterMonadic[A, Repr] = new
WithFilter(p)

class WithFilter(p: A => Boolean) extends FilterMonadic[A, Repr] {

  // implementation of map, flatMap and foreach skipped here
  def withFilter(q: A => Boolean): WithFilter = new WithFilter(x =>
  p(x) && q(x)
  )
}
```

Example 1.35

Please note that `withFilter` returns an object of type `FilterMonadic`, which only has map, `flatMap`, `foreach`, and `withFilter`. These are the only methods that can be chained after a call to `withFilter`. For example, the following will not compile:

```
List.tabulate(50)(_ + 1).withFilter(_ % 2 == 0).forall(_ % 2 == 0)
```

Example 1.36

It is quite common to have a sequence of `flatMap`, `filter`, and map chained together and Scala provides syntactic sugar to support that through **for comprehensions**. To see it in action, let's consider the following `Person` class and its instances:

```
case class Person(firstName: String, isFemale: Boolean, children:
Person*)

val bob = Person("Bob", false)
val jennette = Person("Jennette", true)
val laura = Person("Laura", true)
val jean = Person("Jean", true, bob, laura)
val persons = List(bob, jennette, laura, jean)
```

Example 1.37

`Person*` represents a variable argument of type `Person`. A variable argument of type T needs to be the last argument in a class definition or method signature and accepts zero, one, or more instances of type T.

Now say we want to get pairs of mother and child, which would be (Jean, Bob) and (Jean, Laura). Using `flatMap`, `filter`, and map we can write it as follows:

```
scala> persons.filter(_.isFemale).flatMap(p => p.children.map(c =>
(p.firstName, c.firstName)))
res32: List[(String, String)] = List((Jean,Bob), (Jean,Laura))
```

Example 1.38

The preceding expression does its job, but it is not quite easy to understand what is happening. This is where `for` comprehension comes to the rescue:

```
scala> for {
     |    p <- persons
     |    if p.isFemale
     |    c <- p.children
     |  } yield (p.firstName, c.firstName)
res33: List[(String, String)] = List((Jean,Bob), (Jean,Laura))
```

Example 1.39

It is much easier to understand what this snippet of code does. Behind the scenes, the Scala compiler will convert this expression into the first one (the only difference being `filter` will be replaced with `withFilter`).

Scala also provides methods to combine the elements of a collection using the `fold` and `reduce` families of functions. The primary difference between the two can be understood by comparing the signatures of `foldLeft` and `reduceLeft`:

```
def foldLeft[B](z: B)(op: (B, A) ⇒ B): B
```

```
def reduceLeft[A1 >: A](op: (A1, A1) ⇒ A1): A1
```

Example 1.40

Both of these methods take a binary operator to combine the elements from left to right. However, `foldLeft` takes a zero-argument, z, of type B (this value is returned if `List` is empty), and the output type can differ from the types of the elements in `List`. On the other hand, `reduceLeft` requires A1 to be a supertype of A (`>:` signifies a lower bound). So, we can sum up `List[Int]` and return the value as `Double` using `foldLeft`, as follows:

```
scala> List(1,2,3,4).foldLeft[Double](0) ( _ + _ )
res34: Double = 10.0
```

Example 1.41

We cannot do the same with reduceLeft (since Double is not a supertype of Int). Trying to do so will raise a compile-time error of type arguments [Double] do not conform to method reduce's type parameter bounds [A1 >: Int]:

```
scala> List(1,2,3,4).reduce[Double] ( _ + _ )
<console>:12: error: type arguments [Double] do not conform to method
reduce's type parameter bounds [A1 >: Int]
       List(1,2,3,4).reduce[Double] ( _ + _ )
                    ^
```

Example 1.42

foldRight and reduceRight combine the elements of a collection from right to left. There is also fold and reduce, and for both, the order in which the elements are combined is unspecified and may be nondeterministic.

In this section, we have seen several examples of HOFs from the Scala collection library. By now, you should have noticed that each of these functions uses type parameters. These are called polymorphic functions, which is what we will cover next.

Understanding polymorphic functions

A function that works with multiple types of input arguments or can return a value of different types is called a **polymorphic function**. While writing a polymorphic function, we provide a comma-separated list of type parameters surrounded by square brackets after the name of the function. For example, we can write a function that returns the index of the first occurrence of an element within List:

```
scala> def findFirstIn[A](as: List[A], p: A => Boolean): Option[Int] =
     |     as.zipWithIndex.collect { case (e, i) if p(e) => i
}.headOption
findFirstIn: [A](as: List[A], p: A => Boolean)Option[Int]
example 1.43
```

This function will work for any type of list: List[Int], List[String], and so on. For example, we can search for the index of element 5 in a list of integers from 1 to 20:

```
scala> import scala.util.Random
import scala.util.Random

scala> val ints = Random.shuffle((1 to 20).toList)
ints: List[Int] = List(7, 9, 3, 8, 6, 13, 12, 18, 14, 15, 1, 11, 10,
16, 2, 5, 20, 17, 4, 19)

scala> findFirstIn[Int](ints, _ == 5)
res38: Option[Int] = Some(15)
```

Example 1.44

In the next section, we are going to look at another property of type parameters, called variance, which defines subtyping relationships between objects, as we will see in the following section.

Variance

As mentioned earlier, functions are first-class objects in Scala. Scala automatically converts function literals into objects of the `FunctionN type` (N = 0 to 22). For example, consider the following anonymous function:

```
val f: Int => Any = (x: Int) => x
```

Example 1.45

This function will be converted automatically to the following:

```
val f = new Function1[Int, Any] {def apply(x: Int) = x}
```

Example 1.46

Please note that the preceding syntax represents an object of an anonymous class that extends `Function1[Int, Any]` and implements its abstract `apply` method. In other words, it is equivalent to the following:

```
class AnonymousClass extends Function1[Int, Any] {
   def apply(x: Int): Any = x
}

val f = new AnonymousClass
```

Example 1.47

If we refer to the type signature of the `Function1` trait, we would see the following:

```
Function1[-T1, +T2]
```

Example 1.48

T1 represents the argument type and T2 represents the return type. The type variance of T1 is contravariant and that of T2 is covariant. In general, covariance designed by + means if a class or trait is covariant in its type parameter T, that is, `C[+T]`, then `C[T1]` and `C[T2]` will adhere to the subtyping relationship between T1 and T2. For example, since Any is a supertype of Int, `C[Any]` will be a supertype of `C[Int]`.

The order is reversed for contravariance. So, if we have C[-T], then C[Int] will be a supertype of C[Any].

Since we have Function1[-T1, +R], that would then mean type Function1[Int, Any] will be a supertype of, say, Function1[Any, String].

To see it in action, let's define a method that takes a function of type Int => Any and returns Unit:

```
def caller(op: Int => Any): Unit = List
  .tabulate(5)(i => i + 1)
  .foreach(i => print(s"$i "))
```

Example 1.49

Let's now define two functions:

```
scala> val f1: Int => Any = (x: Int) => x
f1: Int => Any = $Lambda$9151/1234201645@34f561c8

scala> val f2 : Any => String = (x: Any) => x.toString
f2: Any => String = $Lambda$9152/1734317897@699fe6f6
```

Example 1.50

A function (or method) with a parameter of type T can be invoked with an argument that is either of type T or its subtype. And since Int => Any is a supertype of Any => String, we should be able to pass both of these functions as arguments. As can be seen, both of them indeed work:

```
scala> caller(f1)
1 2 3 4 5
scala> caller(f2)
1 2 3 4 5
```

Example 1.51

Option type

Scala's option type represents optional values. These values can be of two forms: Some(x), where x is the actual value, or None, which represents a missing value. Many of the Scala collection library methods return a value of the Option[T] type. The following are a few examples:

```
scala> List(1, 2, 3, 4).headOption
res45: Option[Int] = Some(1)

scala> List(1, 2, 3, 4).lastOption
res46: Option[Int] = Some(4)
```

```
scala> List("hello,", "world").find(_ == "world")
res47: Option[String] = Some(world)

scala> Map(1 -> "a", 2 -> "b").get(3)
res48: Option[String] = None
```

Example 1.52

Option also has a rich API and provides many of the functions from the collection library API through an implicit conversion function, option2Iterable, in the companion object. The following are a few examples of methods supported by the Option type:

```
scala> Some("hello, world!").headOption
res49: Option[String] = Some(hello, world!)

scala> None.getOrElse("Empty")
res50: String = Empty

scala> Some("hello, world!").map(_.replace("!", ".."))
res51: Option[String] = Some(hello, world..)

scala> Some(List.tabulate(5)(_ + 1)).flatMap(_.headOption)
res52: Option[Int] = Some(1)
```

Example 1.53

Collections

Scala comes with a powerful collection library. Collections are classified into mutable and immutable collections. A mutable collection can be updated in place, whereas an immutable collection never changes. When we add, remove, or update elements of an immutable collection, a new collection is created and returned, keeping the old collection unchanged.

All collection classes are found in the scala.collection package or one of its subpackages: mutable, immutable, and generic. However, for most of our programming needs, we refer to collections in either the mutable or immutable package.

A collection in the scala.collection.immutable package is guaranteed to be immutable and will never change after it is created. So, we will not have to make any defensive copies of an immutable collection, since accessing a collection multiple times will always yield the same set of elements.

On the other hand, collections in the `scala.collection.mutable` package provide methods that can update a collection in place. Since these collections are mutable, we need to defend against any inadvertent update, p, by other parts of the code base.

By default, Scala picks immutable collections. This easy access is provided through the `Predef` object, which is implicitly imported into every Scala source file. Refer to the following example:

```
object Predef {
  type Set[A] = immutable.Set[A]
  type Map[A, +B] = immutable.Map[A, B]
  val Map = immutable.Map
  val Set = immutable.Set
  // ...
}
```

Example 1.54

The `Traversable` trait is the base trait for all of the collection types. This is followed by `Iterable`, which is divided into three subtypes: `Seq`, `Set`, and `Map`. Both `Set` and `Map` provide sorted and unsorted variants. `Seq`, on the other hand, has `IndexedSeq` and `LinearSeq`. There is quite a bit of similarity among all these classes. For instance, an instance of any collection can be created by the same uniform syntax, writing the collection class name followed by its elements:

```
Traversable(1, 2, 3)
Map("x" -> 24, "y" -> 25, "z" -> 26)
Set("red", "green", "blue")
SortedSet("hello", "world")
IndexedSeq(1.0, 2.0)
LinearSeq(a, b, c)
```

Example 1.55

The following is the hierarchy for `scala.collection.immutable` collections taken from the `docs.scala-lang.org` website.

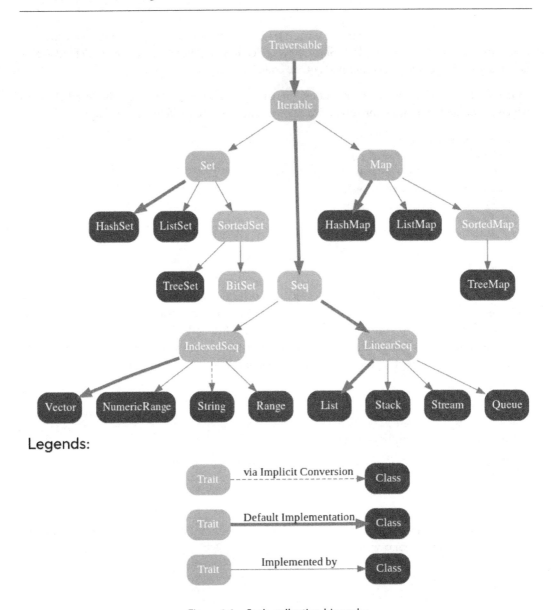

Figure 1.1 – Scala collection hierarchy

The Scala collection library is very rich and has various collection types suited to specific programming needs. If you want to delve deep into the Scala collection library, please refer to the *Further reading* section (the fifth point).

In this section, we looked at the Scala collection hierarchy. In the next section, we will gain a high-level understanding of pattern matching.

Understanding pattern matching

Scala has excellent support for pattern matching. The most prominent use is the `match` expression, which takes the following form:

```
selector match { alternatives }
```

`selector` is the expression that the alternatives will be tried against. Each alternative starts with the `case` keyword and includes a pattern, an arrow symbol =>, and one or more expressions, which will be evaluated if the pattern matches. The patterns can be of various types, such as the following:

- Wildcard patterns
- Constant patterns
- Variable patterns
- Constructor patterns
- Sequence patterns
- Tuple patterns
- Typed patterns

Before going through each of these pattern types, let's define our own custom `List`:

```
trait List[+A]

case class Cons[+A](head: A, tail: List[A]) extends List[A]

case object Nil extends List[Nothing]

object List {
   def apply[A](as: A*): List[A] = if (as.isEmpty) Nil else Cons(as.
head, apply(as.tail: _*))
}
```

Example 1.56

Wildcard patterns

The wildcard pattern (_) matches any object and is used as a default, catch-all alternative. Consider the following example:

```
scala> def emptyList[A](l: List[A]): Boolean = l match {
     |    case Nil => true
     |    case _   => false
```

```
     | }
emptyList: [A](l: List[A])Boolean

scala> emptyList(List(1, 2))
res8: Boolean = false
```

Example 1.57

A wildcard can also be used to ignore parts of an object that we do not care about. Refer to the following code:

```
scala> def threeElements[A](l: List[A]): Boolean = l match {
     |    case Cons(_, Cons(_, Cons(_, Nil))) => true
     |    case _                              => false
     | }
threeElements: [A](l: List[A])Boolean

scala> threeElements(List(true, false))
res11: Boolean = false

scala> threeElements(Nil)
res12: Boolean = false

scala> threeElements(List(1, 2, 3))
res13: Boolean = true

scala> threeElements(List("a", "b", "c", "d"))
res14: Boolean = false
```

Example 1.58

In the preceding example, the `threeElements` method checks whether a given list has exactly three elements. The values themselves are not needed and are thus discarded in the pattern match.

Constant patterns

A constant pattern matches only itself. Any literal can be used as a constant – 1, `true`, and hi are all constant patterns. Any `val` or singleton object can also be used as a constant. The `emptyList` method from the previous example uses `Nil` to check whether the list is empty.

Variable patterns

Like a wildcard, a variable pattern matches any object and is bound to it. We can then use this variable to refer to the object:

```scala
scala> val ints = List(1, 2, 3, 4)
ints: List[Int] = Cons(1,Cons(2,Cons(3,Cons(4,Nil))))

scala> ints match {
     |    case Cons(_, Cons(_, Cons(_, Nil))) => println("A three
element list")
     |    case l => println(s"$l is not a three element list")
     | }
Cons(1,Cons(2,Cons(3,Cons(4,Nil)))) is not a three element list
```

Example 1.59

In the preceding example, l is bound to the entire list, which then is printed to the console.

Constructor patterns

A constructor pattern looks like Cons(_, Cons(_, Cons(_, Nil))). It consists of the name of a case class (Cons), followed by a number of patterns in parentheses. These extra patterns can themselves be constructor patterns, and we can use them to check arbitrarily deep into an object. In this case, checks are performed at four levels.

Sequence patterns

Scala allows us to match against sequence types such as Seq, List, and Array among others. It looks similar to a constructor pattern. Refer to the following:

```scala
scala> def thirdElement[A](s: Seq[A]): Option[A] = s match {
     |    case Seq(_, _, a, _*) => Some(a)
     |    case _                => None
     | }
thirdElement: [A](s: Seq[A])Option[A]

scala> val intSeq = Seq(1, 2, 3, 4)
intSeq: Seq[Int] = List(1, 2, 3, 4)

scala> thirdElement(intSeq)
res16: Option[Int] = Some(3)

scala> thirdElement(Seq.empty[String])
res17: Option[String] = None
```

Example 1.60

As the example illustrates, `thirdElement` returns a value of type `Option[A]`. If a sequence has three or more elements, it will return the third element, whereas for any sequence with less than three elements, it will return `None`. `Seq(_, _, a, _*)` binds a to the third element if present. The `_*` pattern matches any number of elements.

Tuple patterns

We can pattern match against tuples too:

```scala
scala> val tuple3 = (1, 2, 3)
tuple3: (Int, Int, Int) = (1,2,3)

scala> def printTuple(a: Any): Unit = a match {
     |     case (a, b, c) => println(s"Tuple has $a, $b, $c")
     |     case _         =>
     | }
printTuple: (a: Any)Unit

scala> printTuple(tuple3)
Tuple has 1, 2, 3
```

Example 1.61

Running the preceding program will print `Tuple has 1, 2, 3` to the console.

Typed patterns

A typed pattern allows us to check types in the pattern match and can be used for type tests and type casts:

```scala
scala> def getLength(a: Any): Int =
     |    a match {
     |       case s: String    => s.length
     |       case l: List[_]   => l.length //this is List from Scala
collection library
     |       case m: Map[_, _] => m.size
     |       case _            => -1
     |    }
getLength: (a: Any)Int

scala> getLength("hello, world")
res3: Int = 12
```

```
scala> getLength(List(1, 2, 3, 4))
res4: Int = 4

scala> getLength(Map.empty[Int, String])
res5: Int = 0
```

Example 1.62

Please note that the argument a of type Any does not support methods such as length or size in the result expression. Scala automatically applies a type test and a type cast to match the target type. For example, case s: String => s.length is equivalent to the following snippet:

```
if (s.isInstanceOf[String]) {
  val x = s.asInstanceOf[String]
  x.length
}
```

Example 1.63

One important thing to note, though, is that Scala does not maintain type arguments during runtime. So, there is no way to check whether list has all integer elements or not. For example, the following will print A list of String to the console. The compiler will emit a warning to alert about the runtime behavior. Arrays are the only exception because the element type is stored with the array value:

```
scala> List.fill(5)(0) match {
     |     case _: List[String] => println("A list of String")
     |     case _               =>
     | }
<console>:13: warning: fruitless type test: a value of type List[Int]
cannot also be a List[String] (the underlying of List[String]) (but
still might match its erasure)
        case _: List[String] => println("A list of String")
                ^
A list of String
```

Example 1.64

Implicits in Scala

Scala provides implicit conversions and parameters. Implicit conversion to an expected type is the first place the compiler uses implicits. For example, the following works:

```
scala> val d: Double = 2
d: Double = 2.0
```

Example 1.65

This works because of the following implicit method definition in the `Int` companion object (it was part of `Predef` prior to 2.10.x):

```
implicit def int2double(x: Int): Double = x.toDouble
```

Example 1.66

Another application of implicit conversion is the receiver of a method call. For example, let's define a `Rational` class:

```
scala> class Rational(n: Int, d: Int) extends Ordered[Rational] {
     |
     |     require(d != 0)
     |     private val g = gcd(n.abs, d.abs)
     |     private def gcd(a: Int, b: Int): Int = if (b == 0) a else
gcd(b, a % b)
     |     val numer = n / g
     |     val denom = d / g
     |     def this(n: Int) = this(n, 1)
     |     def +(that: Rational) = new Rational(
     |     this.numer * that.numer + this.denom * that.denom,
     |     this.denom * that.denom
     |     )
     |     def compare(that: Rational) = (this.numer * that.numer -
this.denom * that.denom)
     |     override def toString = if (denom == 1) numer.toString else
s"$numer/$denom"
     | }
defined class Rational
```

Example 1.67

Then declare a variable of the `Rational` type:

```
scala> val r1 = new Rational(1)
r1: Rational = 1

scala> 1 + r1
<console>:14: error: overloaded method value + with alternatives:
   (x: Double)Double <and>
   (x: Float)Float <and>
   (x: Long)Long <and>
   (x: Int)Int <and>
```

```
        (x: Char)Int <and>
        (x: Short)Int <and>
        (x: Byte)Int <and>
        (x: String)String
  cannot be applied to (Rational)
          1 + r1
          ^
```

Example 1.68

If we try to add `r1` to 1, we will get a compile-time error. The reason is the + method in `Int` does not support an argument of type `Rational`. In order to make it work, we can create an implicit conversion from `Int` to `Rational`:

```
scala> implicit def intToRational(n: Int): Rational = new Rational(n)
intToRational: (n: Int)Rational

scala> val r1 = new Rational(1)
r1: Rational = 1

scala> 1 + r1
res11: Rational = 2
```

Example 1.69

Summary

This was a long chapter and we covered a lot of topics. We started this chapter with a brief introduction to functional programming, looked at why it is useful, and reviewed examples of RT. We then looked at various language features and constructs, starting with classes, objects, and traits. We looked at HOFs, which are one of the fundamental building blocks of functional programming. We looked at polymorphic functions and saw how they enable us to write reusable code. Then, we looked at variance, which defines subtyping relationships between objects, took a detailed tour of pattern matching, and finally, ended with implicit conversion, which is a powerful language feature used in design patterns such as type classes.

In the next chapter, we are going to focus on setting up the environment, which will allow you to follow along with the rest of the chapters.

Further reading

- *Programming in Scala, Fourth Edition*, Martin Odersky, Lex Spoon, and Bill Venners
- If you are interested in learning more about functional programming, please refer to *Functional Programming in Scala* by Paul Chiusano and Rúnar Bjarnaso

- A nice explanation of how app traits actually work
- `https://stackoverflow.com/questions/53468358/how-Scala-app-trait-and-main-works-internally`
- Scala's stackable trait pattern by Bill Venners: `https://www.artima.com/articles/Scalas-stackable-trait-pattern`
- Please refer to the Scala docs for more details on the collection library: `https://docs.scala-lang.org/overviews/collections/overview.html`

2

Environment Setup

In this chapter, we will outline two different environments for developing data engineering pipelines.

The first environment will use cloud-based tooling and services and will require no local environment setup. This is beneficial for multiple reasons. First, this type of environment is highly portable because you will be able to access it from any machine and any location as long as you have an internet connection and a browser. Second, it requires the least amount of setup to get started. The downside to this type of environment is that there are costs associated with another organization maintaining the systems you will be using for development.

The second environment will utilize your local machine to develop your pipeline code. This moves all the work of setting up environments to you but avoids the cloud costs mentioned earlier.

We will be covering the following topics in this chapter:

- Setting up a cloud environment
- Local environment setup

Technical requirements

In order to follow along, you need to have a working internet connection.

Setting up a cloud environment

An easy and fast way to start writing data engineering code in Scala is to use cloud-based services. This route bypasses the need to do extensive setup on local machines and eliminates the need to manage dependencies between software libraries.

In this book, we will be using Microsoft Azure as our cloud provider. There are generally costs associated with running services in the cloud. Please take that into consideration while deciding on setting up a cloud development environment. All code and examples used in this book can be done on the cloud or in your local development environment.

Leveraging cloud object storage

Cloud object storage has become the cheapest way to store large volumes of data. These storage services have become the foundation for data lakes and lakehouses, which are used for data engineering, data science, and data analysis workloads.

Each cloud service offers its own storage, and you can pick whichever works best for you, but on Azure, the storage service dedicated to big data analytics is called **Azure Data Lake Storage Gen2 (ADLS Gen2)**.

You can follow the directions in the following link to create an ADLS storage account to use throughout this book: `https://learn.microsoft.com/en-us/azure/storage/blobs/create-data-lake-storage-account`.

Using Databricks

Databricks is a platform that simplifies the experience of data engineers, data scientists, and data analysts by combining the capabilities of those personas required into a managed service. As a managed service, you will not have to install components of your environment separately. While Databricks has many features for data science and data warehousing, we will primarily utilize Databricks notebooks and compute for our data engineering needs.

Databricks offers a free community edition that allows you to use Databricks without setting up a cloud account for free. For the most up-to-date instructions on enrolling in the Community Edition, please see the following URL: `https://docs.databricks.com/getting-started/community-edition.html`.

After following the setup instructions, you should receive a welcome email that allows you to create a password for your Databricks account:

Welcome to Databricks Community Edition!

Databricks Community Edition provides you with access to a free micro-cluster as well as a cluster manager and a notebook environment - ideal for developers, data scientists, data engineers and other IT professionals to get started with Spark.

We need you to verify your email address by clicking on this link. You will then be redirected to Databricks Community Edition!

Figure 2.1 – Email upon successful setup

You will then be able to log in to Databricks and see the following:

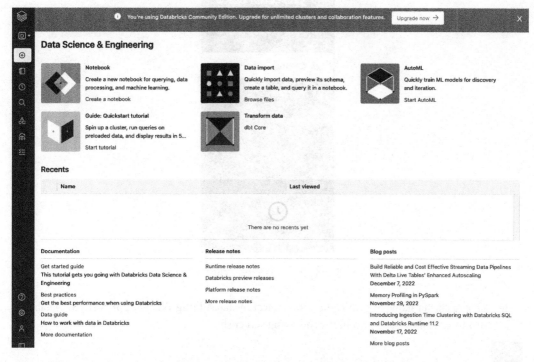

Figure 2.2 – Databricks landing page

Let us begin.

Setting up a compute cluster

In order to use Scala on Databricks, you have to first set up a cluster where you can run your code. Here are the steps to do this:

1. In the left navigation pane, while in the **Data Science & Engineering** view, select Compute as shown in the following screenshot:

Figure 2.3 – Creating a cluster

2.   Enter a cluster name of your choice, then select the latest **Long Term Support (LTS)** Databricks runtime version, as shown in the following screenshot:

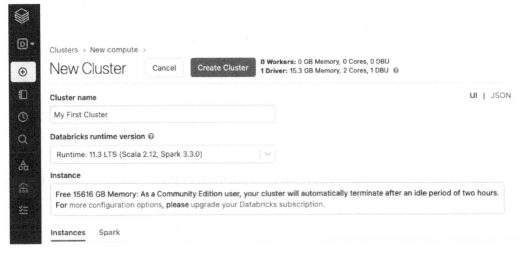

Figure 2.4 – Cluster configuration

3.   After clicking on **Create Cluster**, your cluster should immediately begin the startup process.

By default, it will terminate after a 2-hour idle period. If you need to restart your cluster, you can do so on this same page. You can also terminate, clone, or delete the cluster by clicking on the **More …** button.

Setting up a notebook

Now that our compute is set up, let's create a notebook where we can execute some Scala code:

1. In the left navigation pane, click on **Workspace** and then on the **Home** button:

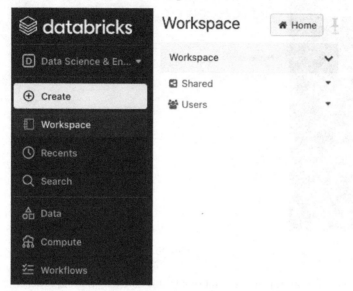

Figure 2.5 – Workspace

2. Next, right-click on the white space below your email, and select **Create | Notebook**:

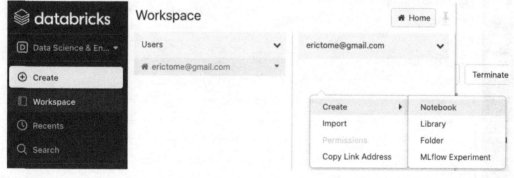

Figure 2.6 – Navigating to Notebook

The notebook creation dialog will allow you to create your notebook, specify **Scala** as your language, and select the cluster you just created:

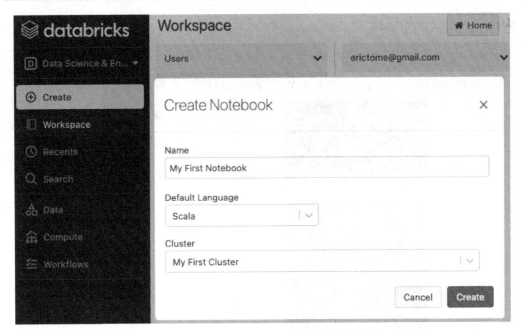

Figure 2.7 – Creating a notebook

3.   At this point, you should have a notebook that is able to run Scala code.

To verify this, create two command cells with the following code, and select **Run all** at the top of the notebook:

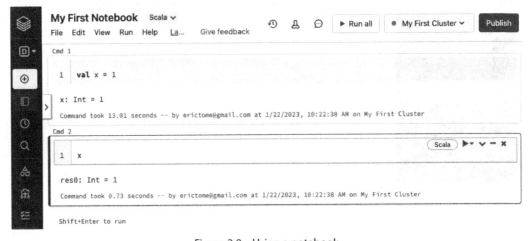

Figure 2.8 – Using a notebook

Now that we looked at how to set up your environment in the cloud, we will now turn to setting up your environment locally.

Local environment setup

In this chapter, we are going to look at some of the tools that the rest of the book will use.

The build tool

We will be using sbt as the build tool. It was the first build tool that was specifically created for Scala. sbt uses a standard project directory structure underneath the main project directory, also called the **base directory** in sbt parlance. For example, if we created a project named hello in the /tmp/ foo directory, then /tmp/foo is the base directory of the project. Here is what a typical directory structure will look like under the base directory:

```
build.sbt
project/
src/
-- main/
    |-- java/
    |-- resources/
    |-- scala/
|-- test/
    |-- java/
    |-- resources/
    |-- scala/
target/
```

The build definition is described in the build.sbt file in the project's base directory. In addition to build.sbt, the project directory can contain .scala files that define helper objects and one-off plugins.

We recommend you install sbt on your machine by following the steps described in the sbt reference manual. For ease of reference, we have included links to setup steps by operating systems:

- For Windows: https://www.scala-sbt.org/1.x/docs/Installing-sbt-on-Windows.html

- For macOS: https://www.scala-sbt.org/1.x/docs/Installing-sbt-on-Mac.html

- For Linux: https://www.scala-sbt.org/1.x/docs/Installing-sbt-on-Linux.html

JDK

Whether or not you choose to install standalone sbt on your machine, you need to install JDK as sbt runs on jvm. We recommend installing JDK 8, and the steps to install it can be found in the instructions for installing sbt listed earlier.

Installing an IDE

In this section, we are going to look at two of the popular IDEs, **Visual Studio Code** (**VS Code**) and IntelliJ IDEA, and outline the steps to install both of them on Windows, Mac, and Linux.

IntelliJ IDEA

Irrespective of the operating system you are using, you can go to the *IntelliJ IDEA – the leading Java and Kotlin IDE* web page (`https://www.jetbrains.com/idea/`) and click on **Download**. It should automatically recognize your operating system and take you to the right tab. If it does not, please select your operating system and refer to the following sections.

Windows

Download the `.exe` file and install IntelliJ by following the prompts. Upon installation, start IntelliJ by clicking on the **Desktop** icon and, if prompted, accept the terms of the user agreement:

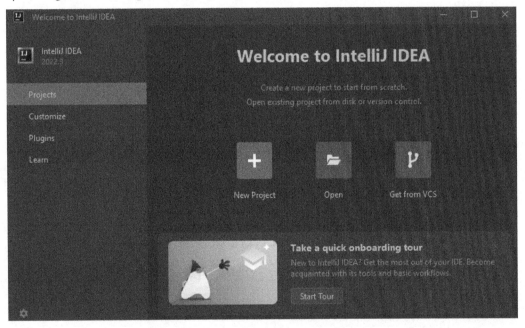

Figure 2.9 – IntelliJ IDEA landing page

If you are new to IntelliJ, we recommend you go through the onboarding tour by clicking on **Start Tour**. To make sure that IntelliJ is able to automatically recognize JDK installed on your machine, click on **New Project** and make sure the **JDK** drop-down list is pre-populated:

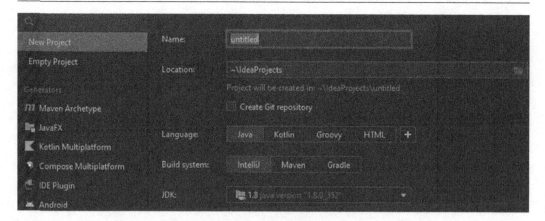

Figure 2.10 – Creating a new project

Mac

You can download the `.dmg` Intellij IDEA Community Edition file from the download pages listed earlier. Once downloaded, mount the `.dmg` file and drag the IntelliJ IDEA app to the `applications` folder. You can now launch the IntelliJ application from your `applications` folder!

Linux

You can click on the **Download** button and download the `.tar` file. It should download the latest Community Edition. At the time of this writing, it was `ideaIC-2022.3.tar.gz`. You can check the SHA-256 digest of the file through *Download and verify the file SHA-256 checksum* (`https://download.jetbrains.com/idea/ideaIC-2022.3.tar.gz.sha256?_gl=1*1y8i897*_ga*MjQyODcyODUyLjE2NTEyMzA5MzU.*_ga_9J976DJZ68*MTY3MTE3NDkxNS4xLjEuMTY3MTE3NzEwMS4wLjAuMA..&_ga=2.168089699.353063352.1671174916-242872852.1651230935`) It is advisable to compare the checksum with this output to ensure the integrity of the downloaded file:

```
sha256sum ideaIC-2022.3.tar.gz
a3f53de8293b55739d916868d732bde521e33e59a5181e758d6f1691d-
479da9e  ideaIC-2022.3.tar.gz
```

Once you have verified the hash, you can install it by following the next steps:

1. Extract `intellij` to `/opt` directory: `sudo tar -xvf <intellij.tar> -C /opt/`.

2. Create a `Desktop Entry` file called `idea.desktop` in your home directory. `.desktop` files are a combination of meta information and a shortcut of an application:

```
[Desktop Entry]

Encoding=UTF-8

Name=IntelliJ IDEA

Comment=IntelliJ IDEA

Exec=/opt/idea-IC-223.7571.182/bin/idea.sh

Icon=/opt/idea-IC-223.7571.182/bin/idea.svg

Terminal=false

StartupNotify=true

Type=Application
```

3. Move `idea.desktop` from your home directory to `/usr/share/applications`: `sudo mv ~/idea.desktop /usr/share/applications/`. The IDE can then be launched by clicking on the icon.

4. It is also useful to create a soft link in `/usr/local/bin`: `ln -s /opt/idea-IC-223.7571.182/bin/idea.sh /usr/local/bin/idea`. This will allow launching the application from the terminal, as long as `/usr/local/bin` is in the search path.

IntelliJ IDEA is also available as a Snap package. If you do not have Snap installed, please refer here to install `snapd`: `https://snapcraft.io/docs/installing-snapd`. Once you have snapd installed, you can install IntelliJ by running the following code:

```
sudo snap install intellij-idea-community --classic
```

Scala plugin

To work with Scala in IntelliJ IDEA, we need to install the Scala plugin. When starting IntelliJ for the first time, we can install the plugin by going to the **Plugins** tab and installing Scala. Otherwise, you can use the **Settings | Plugins** page for the installation. Once the plugin has been installed, restart it for the update to take effect:

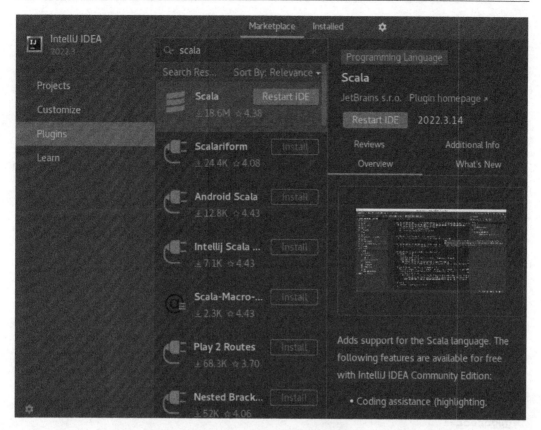

Figure 2.11 – Scala plugin in IntelliJ

If you run into any issues while installing the plugin, please refer to the *Discover Intellij IDEA for Scala* web page (https://www.jetbrains.com/help/idea/discover-intellij-idea-for-scala.html). The Scala plugin also includes support for the sbt console.

In the next section, we are going to look at VS Code, another popular editor, and go through the installation steps.

VS Code

Go to the *Download Visual Studio Code* web page (https://code.visualstudio.com/Download), and you will find options to download VS Code for Windows, Mac, and Linux. Depending on your operating system, please refer to the steps outlined next.

Windows

Download the .exe file and install VS Code by following the prompts. Once installation is complete, proceed to the *Metals extension* section ahead.

Mac

Download the `.zip` file from the VS Code download page and unzip the file. This will extract the `Visual Studio Code.app` file from the `.zip` file. Now, drag this file to your `applications` folder and launch it as any with other Mac application.

Linux

Depending on your distribution, you can download either the `.deb` or `.rpm` package and use your native package manager to install VS Code. If you choose to download the `.tar` file, you can install VS Code by referring to the steps covered for IntelliJ IDEA. The only difference will be the executable, which is `VSCode-linux-x64/bin/code`.

You can also install the package from the command line. For example, you can install VS Code on **Red Hat Enterprise Linux (RHEL)** 8 by running the following commands:

```
#import GPG public key
sudo rpm --import https://packages.microsoft.com/keys/microsoft.asc


#add VS Code repo
sudo tee /etc/yum.repos.d/vscode.repo <<ADDREPO
[code]
name=Visual Studio Code
baseurl=https://packages.microsoft.com/yumrepos/vscode
enabled=1
gpgcheck=1
gpgkey=https://packages.microsoft.com/keys/microsoft.asc
ADDREPO


#install code
sudo dnf install code
```

If you are on Debian 10, you can run the following commands to install VS Code:

```
#install the dependencies
sudo apt install gnupg2 software-properties-common apt-transport-https
curl


#import GPG key
curl -sSL https://packages.microsoft.com/keys/microsoft.asc | sudo
apt-key add -


#add repo
sudo add-apt-repository "deb [arch=amd64] https://packages.microsoft.
com/repos/vscode stable main"
```

```
#install code
sudo apt install code
```

Finally, VS Code is also available as a Snap package. If you do not have Snap installed, please refer to the *Installing the daemon* web page at `https://snapcraft.io/docs/installing-snapd`. Once you have Snap installed, you can install VS Code by running `sudo snap install code -classic`.

Metals extension

To work with Scala in VS Code, you need to install the Metals extension. To do that, open VS Code, press *Ctrl + P*, paste the following command in the search bar, and hit *Enter*:

```
ext install scalameta.metals
```

Docker

Docker is an open source containerization technology for building and containerizing applications. We recommend you install **Docker Community Edition** (**Docker CE**) on your machine. Please note that the Docker engine was renamed Docker CE. Based on your operating system, please follow the steps outlined in *Docker Docs* to install Docker CE:

- For Windows: `https://docs.docker.com/desktop/install/windows-install/`
- For macOS: `https://docs.docker.com/desktop/install/mac-install/`
- For Linux: `https://docs.docker.com/engine/install/#server`

In the next section, we are going to look at the steps to configure a local Spark instance for downloading the binaries, but you also have the option to create a Spark cluster using Docker containers.

Spark

You may want to install Spark locally. Spark runs on JVM. If your machine does not have Java installed, you may want to check the steps outlined in The *build tool* section. We will be using Apache Spark 3.3.1 pre-built for Hadoop 3.3 for installation instructions. The binary packages are available in `spark-3.3.1` (`https://spark.apache.org/news/spark-3-3-1-released.html`

Windows

In order to configure Spark on a Windows machine, follow the steps outlined here:

1. Go to Download Apache Spark at `https://spark.apache.org/downloads.html` and select Spark 3.3.1 pre-built for Hadoop. It will automatically populate the link under option *3* after making a selection in option *2* of the link. Click on the link:

Download Apache Spark™

1. Choose a Spark release: | 3.3.1 (Oct 25 2022) ⌄ |

2. Choose a package type: | Pre-built for Apache Hadoop 3.3 and later ⌄ |

3. Download Spark: spark-3.3.1-bin-hadoop3.tgz

Figure 2.12 – Spark download

2. Click on any of the links provided for downloading spark 3.3.1, and a file named spark-3.3.1-bin-hadoop3.tgz should automatically get downloaded.

3. Compare the hashes to check the integrity of the file:

```
>cd %HOMEDRIVE%%HOMEPATH%\Downloads


>curl --output spark-3.3.1-bin-hadoop3.tgz.sha512 --url https://
downloads.apache.org/spark/spark-3.3.1/spark-3.3.1-bin-hadoop3.
tgz.sha512


>type spark-3.3.1-bin-hadoop3.tgz.sha512
769db39a560a95fd88b58ed3e9e7d1e92fb68ee406689fb4d30c033cb-
5911e05c1942dcc70e5ec4585df84e80aabbc272b9386a208debda89522efff-
1335c8ff   spark-3.3.1-bin-hadoop3.tgz


>certutil -hashfile spark-3.3.1-bin-hadoop3.tgz SHA512
SHA512 hash of spark-3.3.1-bin-hadoop3.tgz:
769db39a560a95fd88b58ed3e9e7d1e92fb68ee406689fb4d30c033cb-
5911e05c1942dcc70e5ec4585df84e80aabbc272b9386a208debda89522efff-
1335c8ff
CertUtil: -hashfile command completed successfully.
```

4. Create a Spark directory in your C: drive:

```
C:\>mkdir Spark


C:\>cd Spark
```

5. Extract the .tar file to the Spark folder using a file archiver such as 7-Zip.

6. Configure the environment variable by going to the Control Panel and following the next steps in sequence:

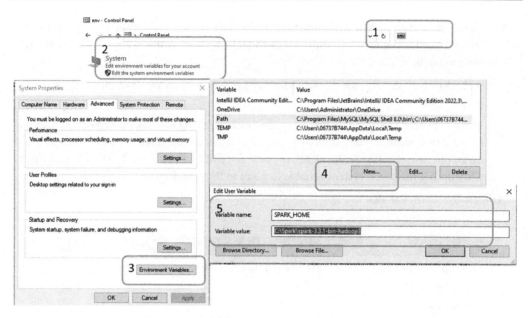

Figure 2.13 – Adding system environment variable

7. Update the `Path` user variable to add `%SPARK_HOME%\bin` by following the next steps in sequence:

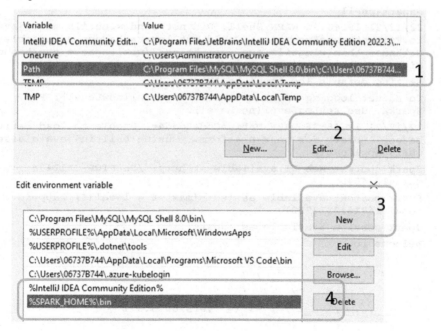

Figure 2.14 – Adding user environment variable

8. Ensure the JAVA_HOME environment variable does not contain any spaces. If you installed JDK 8 by following the steps outlined in the *JDK* section, you will see JAVA_HOME set to something like:

    ```
    C:\Program Files (x86)\Eclipse Adoptium\jdk-8.0.352.8-
    hotspot.
    ```

    These embedded spaces in the directory name are likely going to break spark-shell. In order to avoid that, please create a directory named Java in the C: directory and move jdk to the Java directory. Update JAVA_HOME to point to C:\Java\jdk-8.0.352.8-hotspot\. Also, update the path system variable to point to the new directory, as shown here:

Edit environment variable   ✕

C:\Java\jdk-8.0.352.8-hotspot\bin	New
C:\Program Files (x86)\Microsoft SDKs\Azure\CLI2\wbin	
%SystemRoot%\system32	Edit
%SystemRoot%	

Figure 2.15 – Updating JAVA_HOME

9. Run spark-shell to make sure it works. This shows it running successfully:

    ```
    >spark-shell
    22/12/21 19:48:30 WARN Shell: Did not find winutils.exe: java.
    io.FileNotFoundException: Could not locate Hadoop executable:
    C:\hadoop\bin\winutils.exe -see https://wiki.apache.org/hadoop/
    WindowsProblems
    Setting default log level to "WARN".
    To adjust logging level use sc.setLogLevel(newLevel). For
    SparkR, use setLogLevel(newLevel).
    22/12/21 19:48:36 WARN NativeCodeLoader: Unable to load native-
    hadoop library for your platform... using builtin-java classes
    where applicable
    Spark context Web UI available at http://DESKTOP-IA1I494.
    default:4040
    Spark context available as 'sc' (master = local[*], app id =
    local-1671632317752).
    Spark session available as 'spark'.
    Welcome to
    ```

    ```
          ____              __
         / __/__  ___ _____/ /__
        _\ \/ _ \/ _ `/ __/  '_/
       /___/ .__/\_,_/_/ /_/\_\   version 3.3.1
          /_/
    ```

```
Using Scala version 2.12.15 (OpenJDK Client VM, Java 1.8.0_352)
Type in expressions to have them evaluated.
Type :help for more information.

scala>
```

In order to run `spark-submit`, you need to create a `C:\hadoop\bin` directory, download `winutils.exe`, and put it in that directory. Finally, create a HADOOP_HOME environment variable and set it to `C:\hadoop`:

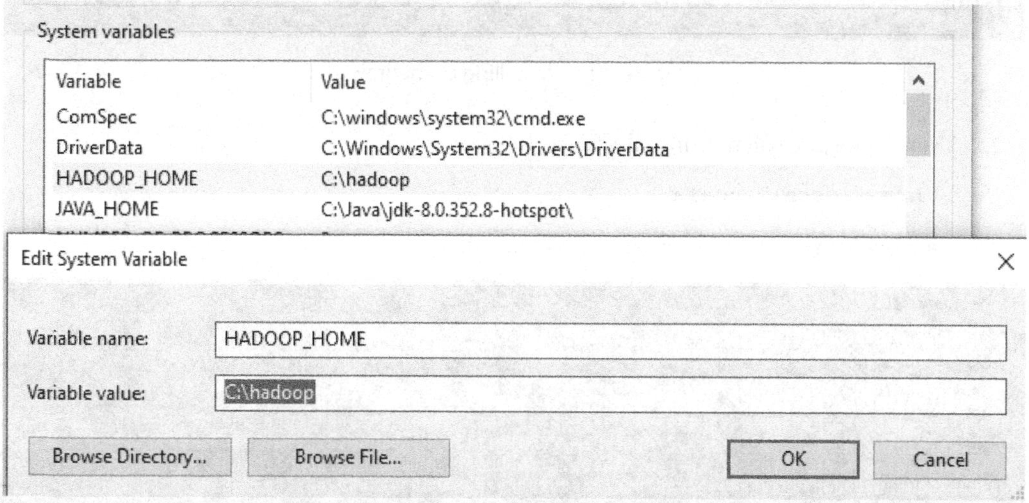

Figure 2.16 – Setting HADOOP_HOME

You can now launch `spark-submit` to make sure it is working, as follows:

```
>spark-submit ^
  --class org.apache.spark.examples.SparkPi ^
  --master local[*] ^
  %SPARK_HOME%\examples\jars\spark-examples_2.12-3.3.1.jar ^
  100
```

You should see `Pi` is roughly `3.1412963141296313` in the output.

Mac

The installation steps for macOS are outlined as follows:

1. Install Homebrew by running this command in your terminal:

   ```
   /bin/bash -c "$(curl -fsSL https://raw.githubusercontent.com/
   Homebrew/install/HEAD/install.sh)"
   ```

This is how the command outputs:

```
> /bin/bash -c "$(curl -fsSL https://raw.githubusercontent.com/Homebrew/install/HEAD/install.sh)"
==> Checking for `sudo` access (which may request your password)...
Password:
==> This script will install:
/opt/homebrew/bin/brew
/opt/homebrew/share/doc/homebrew
/opt/homebrew/share/man/man1/brew.1
/opt/homebrew/share/zsh/site-functions/_brew
/opt/homebrew/etc/bash_completion.d/brew
/opt/homebrew

Press RETURN/ENTER to continue or any other key to abort:
```

Figure 2.17 – Installing Homebrew

2. Using `brew`, we will now install Scala as follows:

    ```
    brew install scala
    ```

    Here is what we get when we run the command:

```
> brew install scala
Running `brew update --auto-update`...
==> Fetching dependencies for scala: giflib, libpng, freetype, fontconfig, pcre2, gettext, glib,
bxext, libxrender, lzo, pixman, cairo, graphite2, icu4c, harfbuzz, jpeg-turbo, lz4, xz, zstd, lib
==> Fetching giflib
    Downloading https://ghcr.io/v2/homebrew/core/giflib/manifests/5.2.1
################################################################### 100.0%
    Downloading https://ghcr.io/v2/homebrew/core/giflib/blobs/sha256:6a1194d7b2d991583e3b5d46782a
    Downloading from https://pkg-containers.githubusercontent.com/ghcr1/blobs/sha256:6a1194d7b2d9
################################################################### 100.0%
==> Fetching libpng
    Downloading https://ghcr.io/v2/homebrew/core/libpng/manifests/1.6.39
################################################################### 100.0%
    Downloading https://ghcr.io/v2/homebrew/core/libpng/blobs/sha256:c437aaaf373f369e948259378543
    Downloading from https://pkg-containers.githubusercontent.com/ghcr1/blobs/sha256:c437aaaf373f
################################################################### 100.0%
```

Figure 2.18 – Installing Scala

3. Next, we will install Apache Spark:

    ```
    brew install apache-spark
    ```

    Here is the output:

```
Homebrew's installation does not include `sbtn`.
> brew install apache-spark
==> Fetching apache-spark
    Downloading https://ghcr.io/v2/homebrew/core/apache-spark/manifests/3.3.1
################################################################### 100.0%
    Downloading https://ghcr.io/v2/homebrew/core/apache-spark/blobs/sha256:71f9e3e760180ae4621e27
    Downloading from https://pkg-containers.githubusercontent.com/ghcr1/blobs/sha256:71f9e3e76018
####################                                                26.4%
```

Figure 2.19 – Installing Spark

Linux

There is a great article at https://linuxconfig.org/how-to-install-spark-on-redhat-8 that covers the steps to install a Spark cluster on RHEL8 in detail. For brevity, we are not going to repeat the steps here and would recommend you look it up. If you are using any other flavor of Linux, the steps should be very similar if not identical.

Once the installation is complete, check to make sure both spark-submit and spark-shell are working:

```
# uses the standalone cluster we just setup
# replace <hostname> with your hostname
# you should see Pi is roughly 3.1399691139969113 in the output
spark-submit \
  --class org.apache.spark.examples.SparkPi \
  --master spark://<hostname>:7077 \
  /opt/spark/examples/jars/spark-examples_2.12-3.2.1.jar \
  100

# uses the standalone cluster we just setup
# replace <hostname> with your hostname
spark-shell --master spark://<hostname>:7077
```

If you open http://localhost:8080/ on your browser, you should see the following:

▾ Running Applications (1)

Application ID	Name	Cores	Memory per Executor	Resources Per Executor	Submitted Time
app-20221220181501-0001 (kill)	Spark shell	8	1024.0 MiB		2022/12/20 18:15:01

▾ Completed Applications (1)

Application ID	Name	Cores	Memory per Executor	Resources Per Executor	Submitted Time
app-20221220181252-0000	Spark Pi	8	1024.0 MiB		2022/12/20 18:12:52

Figure 2.20 – Spark UI

In this section, we covered the steps to install Spark locally. You also have the option to choose to create a Spark cluster using Docker containers. If you choose to do so, please refer to https://hub.docker.com/r/apache/spark.

MySQL

We will be using MySQL as the database instance in the upcoming chapters. We suggest you install the same on your machine if you do not have it already.

Windows

The simplest and recommended method is to download MySQL Installer (for Windows) and let it install and configure a specific version of MySQL Server. Perform the following steps to install MySQL on your machine:

1. You can download the installer from `https://dev.mysql.com/downloads/installer/`:

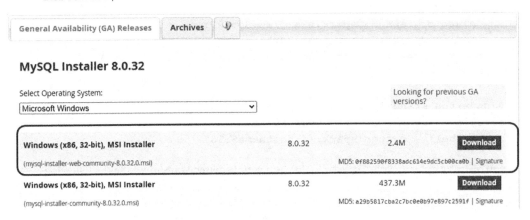

Figure 2.21 – MySQL Installer download

2. Run the installer, which will prompt you to select **Server only**, and follow the prompts. We suggest you keep the defaults:

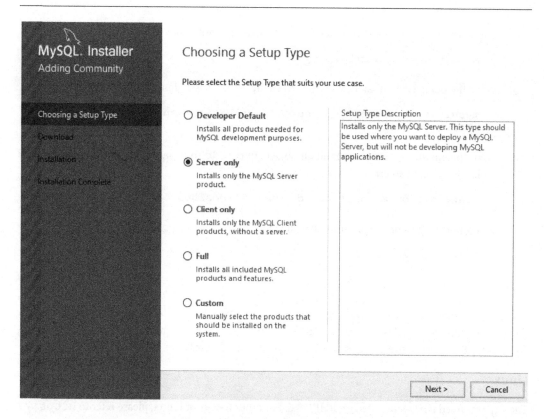

Figure 2.22 – MySQL installation wizard

3. After you have MySQL Server installed, type `mysql 8.0 command line client` in the Windows search bar and launch the command-line tool. It will ask for the root password you created in the setup step:

```
Enter password: ********************
Welcome to the MySQL monitor.  Commands end with ; or \g.
Your MySQL connection id is 11
Server version: 8.0.32 MySQL Community Server - GPL

Copyright (c) 2000, 2023, Oracle and/or its affiliates.

Oracle is a registered trademark of Oracle Corporation and/or
its
affiliates. Other names may be trademarks of their respective
owners.
```

4. Once you log in, you can create a my_db database as shown next:

```
mysql> create database my_db;
```

5. Once the database is created, you need to create a db_user database user as shown next:

```
mysql> create user 'db_user'@'localhost' identified by
'A1Im1zIW54cF1^';
```

6. Grant permission to db_user on all objects in my_db in order for them to be able to read tables, views, and so on:

```
grant all on my_db.* to 'db_user'@'localhost';
```

7. Reload privileges for the grant to take effect:

```
mysql> flush privileges;
```

Mac

There are various options for installing MySQL on macOS. Please follow the instructions here for the latest installation guides: https://dev.mysql.com/doc/mysql-installation-excerpt/8.0/en/macos-installation-notes.html.

Linux

The steps outlined next were tested on RHEL 8.6. For other flavors of Linux, please refer to https://dev.mysql.com/doc/refman/8.0/en/linux-installation.html.

Follow these steps to install MySQL on your machine:

1. To start the installation, we need to add the MySQL yum repository to our local yum repository list. The first step is to add the MySQL **GNU Privacy Guard** (**GPG**) key to our system:

```
sudo rpm --import https://repo.mysql.com/RPM-GPG-KEY-mysql-2022
```

2. Next, we add the yum repository:

```
sudo yum localinstall https://dev.mysql.com/get/mysql80-
community-release-el8-4.noarch.rpm
```

3. Once done, we can check to make sure the yum repository has been successfully added:

```
yum repolist enabled | grep "mysql.*-community.*"
mysql-connectors-community MySQL Connectors Community
mysql-tools-community MySQL Tools Community
mysql80-community MySQL 8.0 Community Server
```

4. After verifying that the yum repository has been updated, we can proceed to install MySQL Community Edition:

    ```
    sudo yum install mysql-community-server
    ```

5. During installation, a temporary password is created. To find the password, start the MySQL community server, which logs the password in a log file:

    ```
    sudo systemctl start mysqld
    sudo grep 'A temporary password' /var/log/mysqld.log | tail -1
    2023-01-19T09:48:40.087823Z 6 [Note] [MY-010454] [Server] A
    temporary password is generated for root@localhost: %w%yXL1Uq7MZ
    ```

6. Run a secure installation script that ships with MySQL, which helps to improve the security of the MySQL installation:

    ```
    /usr/bin/mysql_secure_installation
    ```

    And provide the **one-time password (OTP)** generated during installation. It will prompt you to change the root user password. We suggest you set a strong password. For the rest of the options, we recommend you press *Y* for better security.

7. Next, we will log in to MySQL using root:

    ```
    mysql -u root -p
    Enter password:
    Welcome to the MySQL monitor.  Commands end with ; or \g.
    Your MySQL connection id is 14
    Server version: 8.0.32 MySQL Community Server - GPL

    Copyright (c) 2000, 2023, Oracle and/or its affiliates.

    Oracle is a registered trademark of Oracle Corporation and/or
    its
    affiliates. Other names may be trademarks of their respective
    owners.

    Type 'help;' or '\h' for help. Type '\c' to clear the current
    input statement.
    ```

8. Create a my_db database:

    ```
    mysql> create database my_db;
    ```

9. Create a db_user database user:

    ```
    mysql> create user 'db_user'@'localhost' identified by
    'uAbjdNiuL01^';
    ```

10. Grant permission to db_user on all objects in my_db:

```
mysql> grant all on my_db.* to 'db_user'@'localhost';
```

11. Finally, reload privileges for the grants to take effect:

```
mysql> flush privileges;
```

Now that we have seen how to install MySQL by downloading the package, let's take a look at how we can set it up as a Docker container. Before you proceed, please ensure that you have Docker installed on your machine. If you do not have Docker, please refer to the steps outlined earlier in this chapter. To do that, pull the latest MySQL server image:

```
docker pull mysql
```

Start a container named mysql_server in detached mode:

```
docker run --name mysql_server --restart on-failure -e MYSQL_ROOT_
PASSWORD='n1288TQ2jJ0YN' -d mysql:latest
```

Execute the mysql command to start the shell:

```
docker exec -it mysql_server mysql -uroot -p
Enter password:
Welcome to the MySQL monitor.  Commands end with ; or \g.
Your MySQL connection id is 9
Server version: 8.0.32 MySQL Community Server - GPL

Copyright (c) 2000, 2023, Oracle and/or its affiliates.

Oracle is a registered trademark of Oracle Corporation and/or its
affiliates. Other names may be trademarks of their respective
owners.

Type 'help;' or '\h' for help. Type '\c' to clear the current input
statement.

mysql>
```

You can now create a database and a user, grant privileges, and so on by following the steps already covered in this section.

Object storage

For local development, we will be using MinIO for object storage.

Windows

Here are the steps to install it in Windows:

1. **Install the MinIO server**: Download the MinIO executable (`https://dl.min.io/ server/minio/release/windows-amd64/minio.exe`). You call the executable to launch the server.

2. **Launch the MinIO server**: In PowerShell or Command Prompt, navigate to the location of the executable or add the path of the `minio.exe` file to the `$PATH` system variable:

   ```
   minio.exe server C:\minio --console-address :9090
   ```

3. **Connect your browser to the MinIO server**: Access the MinIO console by opening `https://127.0.0.1:9000` or one of the console addresses specified in the MinIO server command's output. Use the user ID and password that is printed on your screen. It is `minioadmin` by default.

   You can use the MinIO console for general administration tasks such as **identity and access management (IAM)**, metrics and log monitoring, or server configuration. Each MinIO server includes its own embedded MinIO console:

Figure 2.23 – MinIO UI

4. **Install the MinIO client**: The MinIO client allows you to work with your MinIO volume from the command line.

Download the standalone client from `https://dl.min.io/client/mc/release/windows-amd64/mc.exe`.

5.   Double-click on the file to run it. Or, run the following in Command Prompt or PowerShell:

```
\path\to\mc.exe --help
```

6.   Use `mc.exe alias set` to quickly authenticate and connect to the MinIO deployment:

```
mc.exe alias set local http://127.0.0.1:9000 minioadmin
minioadmin
mc.exe admin info local
```

Mac

Here are the steps to install MinIO on a Mac:

1.   **Install the MinIO server**:

```
brew install minio/stable/minio
```

2.   **Launch the MinIO server**: From the terminal, use the MinIO server to start a local MinIO instance in the `~/data` folder. Any other folder that you have read, write, and delete access to can be used as well:

```
export MINIO_CONFIG_ENV_FILE=/etc/default/minio
minio server --console-address :9090
```

3.   **Connect your browser to the MinIO server**: Access the MinIO console by going to a browser (such as Safari) and going to `https://127.0.0.1:9000` or one of the console addresses specified in the `minio server` command's output. For example, `http://192.0.2.10:9090` `http://127.0.0.1:9090` in the output indicates two possible addresses to use for connecting to the console. Use the user ID and password that is printed on your screen. It is `minioadmin` by default.

You can use the MinIO console for general administration tasks such as IAM, metrics and log monitoring, or server configuration. Each MinIO server includes its own embedded MinIO console:

Figure 2.24 – MinIO UI

4. **Install the MinIO client**: The MinIO client allows you to work with your MinIO server from the command line. Here's how to install it:

```
brew install minio/stable/mc
```

Use mc alias set to quickly authenticate and connect to the MinIO deployment:

```
mc alias set local http://127.0.0.1:9000 minioadmin minioadmin
mc admin info local
```

Linux

The steps outlined ahead are for RHEL 8.6. For other Linux distributions, please refer to the installation guide (https://min.io/docs/minio/linux/index.html#procedure):

1. Install the MinIO server:

```
wget https://dl.min.io/server/minio/release/linux-amd64/archive/
minio-20230125001954.0.0.x86_64.rpm -O minio.rpm
sudo dnf install minio.rpm
```

2. Launch the MinIO server:

```
mkdir ~/minio
minio server ~/minio --console-address :9090
```

3. **Connect your browser to the MinIO server**: Use any of the URLs displayed in the output of the previous command under the console. For example, on our machine, we have `http://192.168.0.106:9090`. While the `9000` port is used for connecting to the API, MinIO automatically redirects browser access to the MinIO console. Use the user ID and password that is printed on your screen. It is `minioadmin` by default.

    You can use the MinIO console for general administration tasks such as IAM, metrics and log monitoring, or server configuration. Each MinIO server includes its own embedded MinIO console:

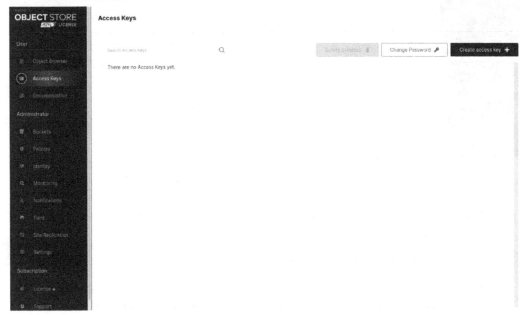

Figure 2.25 – MinIO UI

4. **Install the MinIO client**: The MinIO client allows you to work with your MinIO server from the command line. Download the `mc` client and install it to a location on your `PATH` system variable, such as `/usr/local/bin`:

```
wget https://dl.min.io/client/mc/release/linux-amd64/mc

chmod +x mc

sudo mv mc /usr/local/bin/mc
```

Use mc alias set to create a new alias associated with your local deployment. You can run mc commands against this alias:

```
mc alias set local  http://9.43.25.136:9000  minioadmin minioadmin
```

You can use any of the URLs from the API section of the console output of the minio server ~/ minio --console-address :9090 command from the previous section.

Please note that if you stop and restart the MinIO server, the API URLs are likely to change. That would require running mc alias set to use the new API endpoint.

Summary

In this chapter, we looked at various tools and technologies that we will need in subsequent chapters. We started with how to create a development environment in the cloud and then went through the steps to install the necessary software locally. We looked at how to install sbt, as well as how to configure IDEs such as VS Code and IntelliJ IDEA to work with Scala. We briefly looked at Docker, which is one of the most popular container engines; if you do not have it installed locally, we highly recommend you do so. We covered configuring Spark in detail, but you also have the option of setting up a Spark cluster using Docker containers. We covered the steps to install MySQL, which we will use in our chapter on working with databases. We also covered MinIO, which is a high-performance, **Simple Storage Service (S3)**-compatible object storage solution.

This chapter's purpose was to prepare the tooling required for the subsequent chapters. In the next chapter, we will look at Spark and some of its most commonly used APIs for data engineering.

Further reading

- Please refer to how-to-install-intellij-idea-on-ubuntu
- For additional details, please refer to how-to-install-visual-studio-code-on-centos-8-rhel-8
- For detailed steps, please refer to how-to-install-visual-studio-code-on-debian-10

Part 2 – Data Ingestion, Transformation, Cleansing, and Profiling Using Scala and Spark

In this part, *Chapter 3* introduces Apache Spark as a scalable data processing framework, covering its basics, Scala application development, and the Dataset/DataFrame APIs. *Chapter 4* explores relational databases in data pipelines, highlighting Spark's JDBC API. *Chapter 5* discusses the rise of data lakes and lake houses, while *Chapter 6* delves into advanced Spark data transformation. *Chapter 7* focuses on data quality with the Deequ library for checks and metrics.

This part has the following chapters:

- *Chapter 3, An Introduction to Apache Spark and Its APIs – DataFrame, Dataset, and Spark SQL*

- *Chapter 4, Working with Databases*

- *Chapter 5, Object Stores and Data Lakes*

- *Chapter 6, Understanding Data Transformation*

- *Chapter 7, Data Profiling and Data Quality*

3

An Introduction to Apache Spark and Its APIs – DataFrame, Dataset, and Spark SQL

Apache Spark is written in Scala and has become the dominant distributed data processing framework due to its ability to ingest, enrich, and prepare at-scale data for analytical use cases. As a data engineer, you will eventually have to work with data volumes that won't be processable on a single machine. This chapter will teach you how to leverage Spark and its various APIs to do that processing on a cluster of machines.

In this chapter, we're going to cover the following main topics:

- Working with Apache Spark
- Creating a Spark application using Scala
- Understanding the Spark Dataset API
- Understanding the Spark DataFrame API

Technical requirements

Please refer to our GitHub repository for all the code used in this chapter. The repository is located at the following URL: https://github.com/PacktPublishing/Data-Engineering-with-Scala.

Working with Apache Spark

According to spark.apache.org, Spark is described as "*a unified analytics engine for large-scale data processing. It provides high-level APIs in Java, Scala, Python, R, and an optimized engine.*" Spark can be used for data engineering, **machine learning** (**ML**), and data science. Our focus will be on how it can be used for data engineering in Scala.

Spark is built and designed to process vast amounts of data, which is accomplished by making the compute used by Spark easily scalable and distributable. A Spark application is written by leveraging one of the Spark APIs that we will cover later in the chapter. For now, let's take a look at how Spark applications work.

How do Spark applications work?

A Spark application runs on a Spark cluster, which is a connected group of nodes. These nodes can be **virtual machines** (**VMs**) or bare-metal servers. In terms of Spark architecture, there is one driver node and one to *n* executors that run on your Spark cluster. The driver will control the executors and provide instructions (defined in your Spark application) to the executors. Generally, the driver never actually touches the data you are processing. The executors are where data is manipulated, given instructions from the driver. This is depicted in the following diagram:

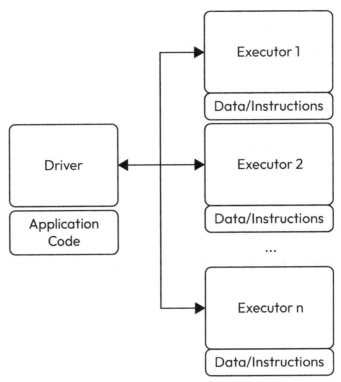

Figure 3.1 – Spark driver and executor architecture

Note that the following calculations assume linear scalability, which is not always the case. The actual gain from distributing the work across many nodes depends on the nature of the data and the transformations applied to the data.

On open source Spark, you can configure the number of executors and memory to precisely what you need to process your data. On platforms such as Databricks, you can provision compute and auto-scale as required. Regardless of where you run Spark, you can scale your processing power as needed, either up or down.

But what does this really mean? Imagine we have 6,000,000 records to process, and it takes 1 server 1 second to process 60 records How long would it take to process all the records? Let's break this down:

6,000,000 records / 60 records per second = 100,000 seconds

= 1,666.66 minutes

= 27.77 hours

Now, what if we had a Spark cluster with 100 executors? This is how long it would take:

6,000,000 records / (60 records per second * 100 executors) = 1,000 seconds

= 16.67 minutes

What if we had a Spark cluster with 1,000 executors? It would take the following amount of time:

6,000,000 records / (60 records per second * 1000 executors) = 100 seconds

= 1.67 minutes

Running Spark on a cloud platform allows you to configure just the amount of compute you need for your workload. You may be happy with a 16.67-minute processing time. In that case, create a job with 100 executors to process your data. Or, you may want your processing to be completed in under 2 minutes, so create a job with 1,000 executors. Now, let's explore what actually happens on executors.

What happens on executors?

As we stated previously, executors can be thought of as a subset of your total compute power where a subset of your data, called a **partition**, is processed as a task of a job. A *task* is a given set of instructions provided by your job that is defined in your Spark application. A Spark application can have one or more jobs, with one or more stages, with one or more tasks. This is depicted in the following diagram:

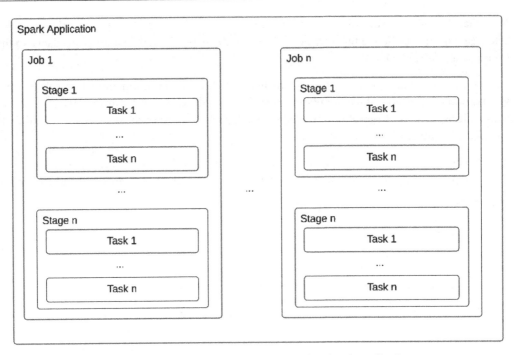

Figure 3.2 – This shows what happens inside a Spark application

Each task runs on an executor grouped inside a stage, and there is a one-to-one map between partitions and executors while a partition is processed. If there are more partitions than executors, the $(n+1)^{th}$ partition will wait until any of the $1...n$ executors finish processing their partition before picking it up.

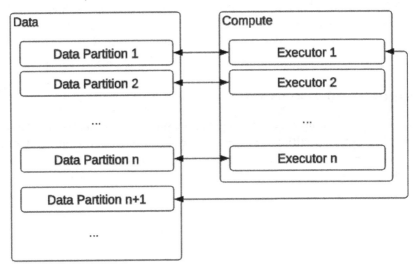

Figure 3.3 – This shows how data partitions relate to Spark executors

You do not need to understand Spark's architecture in order to build and run Spark applications, but you do need an understanding of this to tune your applications for performance. Later, in *Chapter 10*, we will dive deeper into the Spark architecture and how to leverage the knowledge of your data and application to do that performance tuning.

We have learned the basics of Apache Spark, its architecture, and how it is used to process distributed data at scale. We've introduced Spark applications and how they run on Spark clusters. We'll now move on to building your first Spark application in Scala.

Creating a Spark application using Scala

To create data engineering pipelines in Scala, we need to leverage the Spark framework and create a Spark application. Spark provides various types of APIs to work with data, each with pros and cons. Regardless of which API we use, we need to encapsulate them in a Spark application. Let's create one now.

Each Spark application written in Scala needs a SparkSession. The SparkSession is an object that provides the entry point to the Spark APIs.

In order to use the SparkSession, we need to create a Scala object. The object is an implementation of the singleton pattern. We use objects because each Spark application needs a single instance of Spark, which we can guarantee with an object. Let's create a Scala object with some commonly used imports for our first Spark application:

```
package com.packt.descala.scalaplayground
import org.apache.spark.sql.{
DataFrame,
Dataset,
Row,
SparkSession
}
import org.apache.spark.sql.functions.{avg, sum}
object FirstSparkApplication extends App {
```

Now, inside the `FirstSparkApplication` object, instantiate a SparkSession with the following code:

```
val spark: SparkSession = SparkSession
.builder()
.master("local[1]")
.appName("SparkPlayground")
.getOrCreate()
import spark.implicits._
```

We now have a starting point for exploring Spark's architecture and APIs in the next few sections. We'll start by exploring Spark stages and how they work when executing code on our Spark cluster.

Spark stages

Let's dive into Spark stages and how they work by writing and running some Spark code. Understanding how stages work helps you to understand how Spark processes data on the Spark cluster and will be vital to understand how to performance-tune your application.

Consider the following code:

```
val source_storage_location = "my location"
val df: DataFrame = spark
.read
.format("parquet")
.load(source_storage_location)
```

We defined df as an instance of Spark DataFrame using our SparkSession to read some Parquet files from a source location. When this code is run, one job is created with one stage. Using the Spark UI (more on this in our performance tuning section), we can visualize what this looks like:

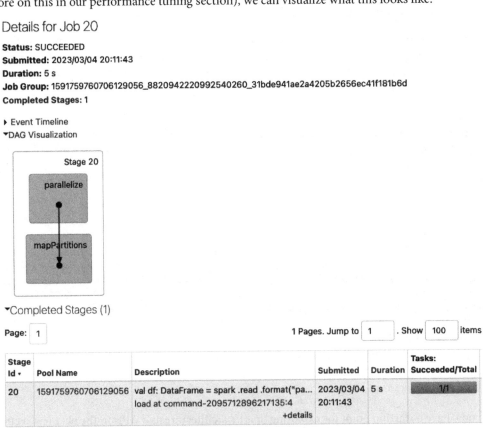

Figure 3.4 – Spark UI showing our stage being processed

Our one Scala command created this bounded stage whose only job is to read our Parquet files into our DataFrame. This isn't very useful at the moment because we aren't doing anything with our data, so let's add another Scala command:

```
println(df.count)
```

The count function on the DataFrame object will count all the records in the DataFrame and return a Long data type. The println function will display the value in stdout.

When we run this command, we can see this **directed acyclic graph (DAG)** from the Spark UI:

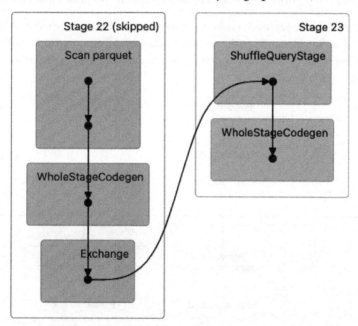

Figure 3.5 – Details of the stages in our DAG

A lot is happening here for just one simple count function. *Stage 22* is doing a local count of the records on individual executors. If you recall, the data is moved to executors as data partitions. If *Stage 22* has completed its counting on all of the local executors, then *Stage 23* will generate a shuffle query, which will designate one executor to read the local counts in a global count to generate a total count of records in our dataset. There is a logical boundary between all Spark stages, and they will not run processes until the previous stages are complete. A stage needs all of its tasks to complete before being marked as complete. Spark has robust fault tolerance and will retry tasks but may eventually fail some tasks. If one or more tasks fail, the stage fails its processing.

Let's take a closer look at shuffles and what they mean for Spark applications.

Shuffling

Certain operations are considered *expensive* in Spark. An operation that causes data movement between executors is called a **shuffle** and is a *wide* transformation that operates across executors. There are times when you want and need to use these wide transformations. For example, our `count` function is useful during development when you want to verify record counts, but a `count` function should be avoided in production processes because it adds additional computation time, which slows down your pipelines.

A valid use case for causing a shuffle is to repartition the data based on values within a column. By default, Spark uses 200 partitions, so it will create 200 separate partitions from the data it ingests.

Let's take an example where you have a column called `Groups` that has the values A, B, C, X, Y, and Z. Spark would read in data files and put those records into 200 different partitions without any thought to the values in the `Groups` column. You may want to decrease the number of partitions based on the values of the `Groups` column:

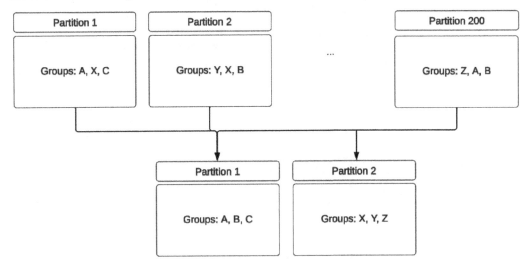

Figure 3.6 – Example showing how shuffling works

This repartitioning would cause a wide transformation and a shuffling of data across executors. This is an expensive operation but may be required for your particular use case and therefore be a cost you are willing to pay. Other types of operations that trigger a shuffle are `groupBy`, joins, and aggregations. We will cover these topics in later chapters.

Understanding the Spark Dataset API

Spark provides various APIs for interacting with data. They are powerful tools for building data engineering pipelines in Scala because you can use the functionality they provide without having to write those functions yourself. The first API we will work with is the Dataset API.

A Dataset is a type of object that is a collection of other objects called **Rows**. These Row objects have a structure and data types that hold the data we process. The Dataset rows can be processed in parallel on our Spark cluster, as explained previously. Explicitly defining a structure and data types of objects is called **strong typing**. Being strongly typed means that each column in your row data is associated with a specified data type for that column. Because Datasets are strongly typed, at compile time, they are checked for errors, which is better than finding out you have a data type problem at runtime! Strong typing means you have to put in a little work ahead of time to define the data structure of the Dataset. The easiest way to do this is to create a Scala case class and type your Datasets at the time of creation using the case class.

Let's create a case class called `Person` with some fields:

```
case class Person(
personId: Int,
firstName: String,
lastName: String
  )
```

Using the `person` data files, we can load this data from Parquet and type them with our `Person` class, as follows:

```
val personDataLocation: String = "dbfs:/tmp/erictome/person/"
val personDs: Dataset[Person] = spark
.read
.format("parquet")
.load(personDataLocation)
.as[Person]
```

Notice that when we define our `val personDf instance`, we specify the `Dataset` class with a type of `Person`. We also need to type `spark.read` with `.as[Person]`. Having done so, Spark will create the following object:

```
personDs: org.apache.spark.sql.Dataset[Person] = [personId: int, firstName: string ... 1 more field]
```

Figure 3.7 – Dataset[Person] in the Spark console

Spark Datasets are also immutable, which means that each time you modify a Dataset, Spark actually creates a new Dataset as the source Dataset cannot be changed. Now, let's take a look at the DataFrame API.

Understanding the Spark DataFrame API

DataFrames are the most commonly used Spark API. They are a special type of Dataset with a type of Row (that is, `Dataset [Row]`). The major difference between DataFrames and Datasets is that DataFrames are not strongly typed, hence, data types are not checked at compile time. Because of this, they are arguably easier to work with as they do not require you to provide any structure while defining them.

We do this by creating a DataFrame similar to how we created a Dataset:

```
val personDf: DataFrame = spark
.read
.format("parquet")
.load(personDataLocation)
```

This is the output in the Spark console:

```
personDf: org.apache.spark.sql.DataFrame = [personId: int, firstName: string ... 1 more field]
```

Figure 3.8 – DataFrame with our person data in the Spark console

The main difference is that we are not required to specify a type while instantiating the `DataFrame` object or on `spark.read`. Now, let's take a look at the Spark SQL module.

Spark SQL

Spark SQL is another way to interact with data in Apache Spark. Spark SQL is considered a module of Spark and uses Datasets and DataFrames as the source of a SQL table. There are various ways to interact with the data. Let's use the `select` function of the DataFrame API to select our data.

The select function

Here is the `select` function:

```
personDf.select($"personId").show(10)
```

The preceding command uses the `personDf` DataFrame and calls the `select` function on the DataFrame. We then specify the `personId` column and call the `show` function, passing two parameters. The first parameter is the number of records to return. The second parameter is to specify whether the data in the columns will be truncated on display or not. The default value is `1` or `true`, which will truncate the values. We will set the first parameter to `10` to show the number of records, and `0` (or `false`) to not truncate the column values. The results will look something like this:

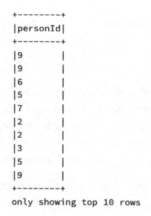

```
+--------+
|personId|
+--------+
|9       |
|9       |
|6       |
|5       |
|7       |
|2       |
|2       |
|3       |
|5       |
|9       |
+--------+
only showing top 10 rows
```

Figure 3.9 – Results of our select and show operation

This same method works with Datasets. For example, `personDs.select($"personId").show(10,0)` returns the same results. We've shown that you can access Spark SQL by using the `select` function on the DataFrame or Dataset API, but you can also write SQL as a string and pass it to the SQL function of the APIs. To do this, we need to create temporary views of our data.

Creating temporary views

Another method to run SQL on Spark objects is to create a temporary view from your Dataset or DataFrame object. Here is how to do that:

```
personDs.createOrReplaceTempView("personDsView")
spark.sql("select * from personDsView").show(10,0)
```

In the preceding example, we use the `createOrReplaceTempView` function to define a temporary view called `personDs`. In the next line, we use the SparkSession object, and the `sql` function passes a SQL query to the Dataset. These are the results:

```
+--------+---------+---------+
|personId|firstName|lastName |
+--------+---------+---------+
|9       |gbeujn97 |buhgcq11 |
|9       |tswjqj174|vleoep80 |
|6       |vaigau185|zbucri136|
|5       |yszunc154|cbxvsm46 |
|7       |ooqyzh38 |iyytjl237|
|2       |amqigg84 |jwixba185|
|2       |wujokp70 |qzfqos137|
|3       |uuaxow228|lxpjsy168|
|5       |lqwrax131|slmunc154|
|9       |hbvega125|wotzet169|
+--------+---------+---------+
only showing top 10 rows
```

Figure 3.10 – Returned data from our select statement

Both preceding methods are using Scala objects to act as SQL queryable data sources!

Summary

In this chapter, we learned how distributed data processing works on Spark. You now understand how Spark uses Scala code encapsulated in a Spark application to break down datasets into pieces that are run on executors on a Spark cluster. You have created a simple Spark application that uses a SparkSession to interact with the Spark APIs to manipulate data. You now have the basics to move on to more challenging topics such as data ingestion, transforming data, and loading that data into target sources.

In the next chapter, we are going to look at various database operations starting with Spark JDBC API and work our way through building a small Database API of our own.

4

Working with Databases

In this chapter, we are going to look at how to work with relational databases. Databases remain one of the most common sources that the data pipeline reads data from and writes to, so it is important that we understand how to work with them efficiently. We will start off by looking at the Spark API and then create a simple database library that provides a simple interface to work with databases.

Specifically, we will look at the following topics

- Understanding the Spark JDBC API

- Working with the Spark JDBC API

- Loading the database configuration

- Creating a database interface

- Performing various database operations

Technical requirements

We are going to use a `mysql` database for the examples in this chapter. If you have not set it up, please refer to *Chapter 2* for the steps to set up a local `mysql` instance. The source code for all of the examples covered in this chapter is available in the official GitHub repository for this book at `https://github.com/PacktPublishing/Data-Engineering-with-Scala`.

Understanding the Spark JDBC API

JDBC is a specification for an **application programming interface** (**API**) that allows Java applications to access databases. A JDBC driver is an actual implementation of the specification for a given database.

In order to work with databases, we need to understand the JDBC API offered by Spark. This section will explore the Spark JDBC API in detail by going through several examples.

To begin with, let's take a look at the interface provided by Spark. The following example is inspired by the Spark documentation and shows a basic template for creating a DataFrame using a database table:

```
val jdbcDF = spark.read
    .format("jdbc")
    .option("url", "jdbc:postgresql:dbserver")
    .option("dbtable", "schema.tablename")
    .option("user", "username")
    .option("password", "password")
    .load()
```

Example 4.1

Here is a similar example for database write operations:

```
jdbcDF.write
    .format("jdbc")
    .option("url", "jdbc:postgresql:dbserver")
    .option("dbtable", "schema.tablename")
    .option("user", "username")
    .option("password", "password")
    .save()
```

Example 4.2

The `format` method takes various values such as `.json`, `.csv`, `.parquet`, and so on. The `option` method is used to specify extra options. *Examples 4.1* and *4.2* cover the minimum options we must specify while reading from or writing to a database. For a comprehensive set of options, please refer to the Spark documentation: `https://spark.apache.org/docs/3.3.1/sql-data-sources-jdbc.html`.

It should be noted that user credentials should never be provided as plain text. They should instead be managed by the configuration manager and supplied through environment variables or secrets at runtime. Refer to the *Loading the database configuration* section for more details.

In this section, we introduced the JDBC API provided by Spark and looked at the minimal set of options that we need to provide values for in order to work with databases. In the next section, we will look at examples of using the JDBC API to work with databases.

Working with the Spark JDBC API

In the previous section, we introduced the Spark JDBC API and some of its most commonly used options. In order to understand them better, we need to see them in action, which is going to be the focus of this section. It is now time to start working with the `mysql` community server that we installed in *Chapter 2*.

Follow the steps outlined ahead to create a few tables needed for the examples covered in this chapter:

1. Log in to the `mysql` service using the following command:

```
mysql --local-infile=1 -u root -p
Enter password:
Welcome to the MySQL monitor.    Commands end with ; or \g.
Your MySQL connection id is 11
Server version: 8.0.32 MySQL Community Server - GPL
Copyright (c) 2000, 2023, Oracle and/or its affiliates.
Oracle is a registered trademark of Oracle Corporation and/or
its
affiliates. Other names may be trademarks of their respective
owners.
Type 'help;' or '\h' for help. Type '\c' to clear the current
input statement.

mysql> use my_db
Reading table information for completion of table and column
names
You can turn off this feature to get a quicker startup with -A

Database changed
```

Example 4.3

2. Create airlines, airports and flights tables as follows:

This is for airlines:

```
mysql> create table airlines(
    ->      iata_code          varchar(50),
    ->      airline            varchar(500)
    -> );
Query OK, 0 rows affected (0.02 sec)
```

Example 4.4

This is for airports:

```
mysql> create table airports(
    ->      iata_code          varchar(50),
    ->      airport            varchar(500),
    ->      city                  varchar(100),
    ->      state                varchar(100),
    ->      country              varchar(100),
    ->      latitude           double,
```

```
    ->      longitude           double
    -> );
Query OK, 0 rows affected (0.01 sec)
```

Example 4.5

This is for flights:

```
mysql> create table flights(
    ->      year                    smallint,
    ->      month                   smallint,
    ->      day                     smallint,
    ->      day_of_week         smallint,
    ->      airline                 varchar(50),
    ->      flight_number       smallint,
    ->      tail_number         varchar(50),
    ->      origin_airport      varchar(50),
    ->      destination_airport  varchar(50),
    ->      scheduled_departure  varchar(15),
    ->      departure_time      varchar(15),
    ->      departure_delay     smallint,
    ->      taxi_out                smallint,
    ->      wheels_off          varchar(15),
    ->      scheduled_time      smallint,
    ->      elapsed_time        smallint,
    ->      air_time                smallint,
    ->      distance                smallint,
    ->      wheels_on           varchar(15),
    ->      taxi_in                 smallint,
    ->      scheduled_arrival   varchar(15),
    ->      arrival_time        varchar(15),
    ->      arrival_delay       smallint,
    ->      diverted                smallint,
    ->      cancelled               smallint,
    ->      cancellation_reason  varchar(500),
    ->      air_system_delay    smallint,
    ->      security_delay      smallint,
    ->      airline_delay       smallint,
    ->      late_aircraft_delay  smallint,
    ->      weather_delay       smallint
            -> );
Query OK, 0 rows affected (0.01 sec)/
```

Example 4.3

3. Then, download the data files (`https://www.kaggle.com/code/smiller933/basic-info-flights-csv-airports-csv-airlines-csv/data`) and move them to your home directory. Load the files into the tables:

```
mysql> LOAD DATA LOCAL INFILE 'airlines.csv' INTO TABLE airlines
    -> FIELDS TERMINATED BY ','
    -> ENCLOSED BY '"'
    -> LINES TERMINATED BY '\n'
    -> IGNORE 1 LINES;
Query OK, 14 rows affected (0.02 sec)
Records: 14    Deleted: 0    Skipped: 0    Warnings: 0
mysql> LOAD DATA LOCAL INFILE 'airports.csv' INTO TABLE airports
    -> FIELDS TERMINATED BY ','
    -> ENCLOSED BY '"'
    -> LINES TERMINATED BY '\n'
    -> IGNORE 1 LINES;
Query OK, 322 rows affected, 6 warnings (0.00 sec)
Records: 322    Deleted: 0    Skipped: 0    Warnings: 6

mysql> LOAD DATA LOCAL INFILE 'flights.csv' INTO TABLE flights
    -> FIELDS TERMINATED BY ','
    -> LINES TERMINATED BY '\n'
    -> IGNORE 1 LINES;
Query OK, 5819079 rows affected, 65535 warnings (42.91 sec)
Records: 5819079    Deleted: 0    Skipped: 0    Warnings:
24361132
```

Example 4.7

The preceding warnings are caused by mysql treating empty fields as empty strings and trying to load them into integer fields. You can see the warnings by using the following command:

```
mysql> show warnings limit 10;
```

Example 4.8

For our purposes, you can ignore these warnings. You may want to check the record counts to make sure all three tables have been loaded. Here's how you can do that:

```
mysql> select count(1) from airlines; select count(1) from
airports; select count(1) from flights;
+----------+
| count(1) |
+----------+
|    14    |
+----------+
1 row in set (0.00 sec)
+----------+
```

```
|  count(1)  |
+-----------+
|    322    |
+-----------+
1 row in set  (0.00 sec)
+-----------+
|  count(1)  |
+-----------+
|  5819079  |
+-----------+
1 row in set  (0.64 sec)
```

Example 4.9

Spark does not come bundled with the mysql JDBC driver. Before we can establish a connection, we need to download the JDBC driver from https://dev.mysql.com/downloads/connector/j/ and add the .jar file to the classpath. The GitHub repository for this book already has the driver included and should be automatically included in the classpath once the project compiles on your machine.

Here is a simple application to read records from the airports table:

```
package com.packt.dewithscala.chapter4

import org.apache.spark.sql.SparkSession

object ReadTable extends App {
  private[chapter4] val session = SparkSession
    .builder()
    .appName("de-with-scala")
    .master("local[*]")
    .getOrCreate()

  private[chapter4] val airportsDF = session.read
    .format("jdbc")
    .option("url", "jdbc:mysql://localhost:3306/my_db")
    .option("user", "root")
    .option("password", "****") // replace the password
    .option("dbtable", "airports")
    .load()

  airportsDF.show()
}
```

Example 4.10

The following screenshot shows the output printed to our console:

```
+---------+-----------------+------------+-----+-------+--------+----------+
|iata_code|          airport|        city|state|country|latitude| longitude|
+---------+-----------------+------------+-----+-------+--------+----------+
|      ABE|Lehigh Valley Int...|   Allentown|   PA|    USA|40.65236|  -75.4404|
|      ABI|Abilene Regional ...|     Abilene|   TX|    USA|32.41132|  -99.6819|
|      ABQ|Albuquerque Inter...| Albuquerque|   NM|    USA|35.04022|-106.60919|
|      ABR|Aberdeen Regional...|    Aberdeen|   SD|    USA|45.44906| -98.42183|
|      ABY|Southwest Georgia...|      Albany|   GA|    USA|31.53552| -84.19447|
|      ACK|Nantucket Memoria...|   Nantucket|   MA|    USA|41.25305| -70.06018|
|      ACT|Waco Regional Air...|        Waco|   TX|    USA|31.61129| -97.23052|
|      ACV|    Arcata Airport|Arcata/Eureka|   CA|    USA|40.97812|-124.10862|
|      ACY|Atlantic City Int...|Atlantic City|   NJ|    USA|39.45758| -74.57717|
|      ADK|     Adak Airport|        Adak|   AK|    USA|51.87796|-176.64603|
|      ADQ|   Kodiak Airport|      Kodiak|   AK|    USA|57.74997|-152.49386|
|      AEX|Alexandria Intern...|  Alexandria|   LA|    USA|31.32737| -92.54856|
|      AGS|Augusta Regional ...|     Augusta|   GA|    USA|33.36996|  -81.9645|
|      AKN|King Salmon Airport| King Salmon|   AK|    USA| 58.6768|-156.64922|
|      ALB|Albany Internatio...|      Albany|   NY|    USA|42.74812| -73.80298|
|      ALO|Waterloo Regional...|    Waterloo|   IA|    USA|42.55708| -92.40034|
|      AMA|Rick Husband Amar...|    Amarillo|   TX|    USA|35.21937|-101.70593|
|      ANC|Ted Stevens Ancho...|   Anchorage|   AK|    USA|61.17432|-149.99619|
|      APN|Alpena County Reg...|      Alpena|   MI|    USA|45.07807| -83.56029|
|      ASE|Aspen-Pitkin Coun...|       Aspen|   CO|    USA|39.22316|-106.86885|
+---------+-----------------+------------+-----+-------+--------+----------+
```

Figure 4.1 – Airports: loading the airports table and printing to the console

By default, the `show` method outputs 20 records and truncates the fields. You can change that behavior by supplying the number of records to display and setting the flag to turn off truncation, like so:

```
airportsDF.show(5,false)
```

Example 4.11

The following screenshot shows just five records from the `airports` table without truncation:

```
+---------+-----------------------------------+------------+-----+-------+--------+----------+
|iata_code|airport                            |city        |state|country|latitude|longitude |
+---------+-----------------------------------+------------+-----+-------+--------+----------+
|ABE      |Lehigh Valley International Airport|Allentown   |PA   |USA    |40.65236|-75.4404  |
|ABI      |Abilene Regional Airport           |Abilene     |TX   |USA    |32.41132|-99.6819  |
|ABQ      |Albuquerque International Sunport   |Albuquerque |NM   |USA    |35.04022|-106.60919|
|ABR      |Aberdeen Regional Airport          |Aberdeen    |SD   |USA    |45.44906|-98.42183 |
|ABY      |Southwest Georgia Regional Airport |Albany      |GA   |USA    |31.53552|-84.19447 |
+---------+-----------------------------------+------------+-----+-------+--------+----------+
```

Figure 4.2 – airports without truncation: printing five records to the console without column truncation

The `dbtable` option accepts SQL queries as well. For example, if you want to list all of the airports in North Carolina, you can get a list using the following code:

```
val texasAirportsDF = session.read
    .format("jdbc")
    .option("url", "jdbc:mysql://localhost:3306/my_db")
    .option("user", "root")
    .option("password", "****") // replace the password
    .option(
        "dbtable",
        "(select airport, city from airports where state = 'NC') qry"
    )
    .load()
texasAirportsDF.show(numRows = 100, truncate = 200, vertical = true)
```

Example 4.12

The following screenshot shows airports and cities in a vertically stacked table:

```
-RECORD 0------------------------------------------------------------
 airport | Asheville Regional Airport
 city    | Asheville
-RECORD 1------------------------------------------------------------
 airport | Charlotte Douglas International Airport
 city    | Charlotte
-RECORD 2------------------------------------------------------------
 airport | Coastal Carolina Regional Airport (Craven County Regional)
 city    | New Bern
-RECORD 3------------------------------------------------------------
 airport | Fayetteville Regional Airport
 city    | Fayetteville
-RECORD 4------------------------------------------------------------
 airport | Piedmont Triad International Airport
 city    | Greensboro
-RECORD 5------------------------------------------------------------
 airport | Wilmington International Airport
 city    | Wilmington
-RECORD 6------------------------------------------------------------
 airport | Albert J. Ellis Airport
 city    | Jacksonville
-RECORD 7------------------------------------------------------------
 airport | Raleigh-Durham International Airport
 city    | Raleigh
```

Figure 4.3 – Stacked output printing DataFrame as a stacked table instead of a flat table

In this section, we looked at examples of how using the JDBC API we can read tables from a database. However, you might have noticed that we are passing database credentials in clear text, which must be avoided under all circumstances.

Before leaving this section, we would encourage you to try the following:

- Print a schema of the airport dataset to your console

- Determine how many airports there are in Texas

In the next section, we are going to look at how we can manage the configuration using an open source library that allows you to read various parameters from environment variables.

Loading the database configuration

Before proceeding further, let's address one of the issues with code that you might have noticed already—we are passing the credentials as clear text, which is not only a bad practice but also poses a major security risk. In production code, secrets are supplied as environment variables and loaded at runtime by a configuration loader.

For this book, we are going to use `PureConfig` to load the configuration: `https://pureconfig.github.io/docs/index.html`.

In order to add `PureConfig` to your project, you need to add the following dependency in your `build.sbt` file:

```
libraryDependencies += "com.github.pureconfig" %% "pureconfig" %
"0.17.2"
```

Example 4.13

For this section, we are interested in loading the database configuration at runtime. For that, we can create a `Config` file with the following case classes and a helper object:

```
package com.packt.dewithscala

import pureconfig._
import pureconfig.generic.auto._

final case class Opaque(value: String) extends AnyVal {
  override def toString = "****"
}
case class Database(
    name: String,
    scheme: String,
    host: String,
    port: String,
    username: Opaque,
    password: Opaque
)
```

```
case class ProjectConfig(db: List[Database])
object Config {
 val cfg = ConfigSource.default.loadOrThrow[ProjectConfig]
 def getDB(name: String): Option[Database] = cfg.db.filter(_.name ==
name).headOption
}
```

Example 4.14

Then, we create an `application.conf` file with the following content:

```
db = [
    {
            name = "my_db"
            scheme = "jdbc:mysql"
            host = "localhost"
            port = "3306"
            username = ${?MYSQL_USER}
            password = ${?MYSQL_PASS}
    }
]
```

Example 4.15

You must have noticed that both `username` and `password` are now loaded from environment variables. Also, notice that the `getDB` method in *Example 4.14* returns an object of type `Option[Database]` and thus delegates the handling of errors on the application side if a matching database is not found.

We can now rewrite *Example 4.10* as follows:

```
package com.packt.dewithscala.chapter4

import org.apache.spark.sql.SparkSession

import com.packt.dewithscala.Config
import com.packt.dewithscala._

@SuppressWarnings(Array("org.wartremover.warts.OptionPartial"))
object ReadTableUsingConfig extends App {

  private val session = SparkSession
    .builder()
    .appName("de-with-scala")
    .master("local[*]")
    .getOrCreate()
```

```
    private val mysqlDB = Config.getDB("my_db")

    def getDBParams(param: String): Option[String] = param match {
      case "scheme"    => mysqlDB.map(_.scheme)
      case "host"      => mysqlDB.map(_.host)
      case "port"      => mysqlDB.map(_.port)
      case "name"      => mysqlDB.map(_.name)
      case "username"  => mysqlDB.map(_.username.value)
      case "password"  => mysqlDB.map(_.password.value)
      case _           => None
    }

    private val scheme   = getDBParams("scheme").get
    private val host     = getDBParams("host").get
    private val port     = getDBParams("port").get
    private val name     = getDBParams("name").get
    private val username = getDBParams("username").get
    private val password = getDBParams("password").get
    private val airportsDF = session.read
      .format("jdbc")
      .option("url", s"$scheme://$host:$port/$name")
      .option("user", username)
      .option("password", password)
      .option("dbtable", "airports")
      .load()

    airportsDF.show()

}
```

Example 4.16

In the preceding example, we loaded the database configuration by using the getDB method and then read individual parameters using getDBParams. We then passed those variables to the JBDC API to read the table.

In this section, we looked at how we can use the PureConfig library to load configuration parameters at runtime. Though this is a good start, it has several pitfalls. For example, the getDBParams method takes a string as its argument, and it will not throw any warning if instead of passing scheme, we pass schema. This will go undetected till it manifests itself only at runtime. This can be overcome with a trait, singleton objects that inherit that trait, and using the trait as the argument type for the getDBParams method. Also, getDBParams needs to be defined each time we want to read database parameters in different applications and it is cumbersome to use getDBParams("parameter"). get repeatedly to read various parameters.

In the next section, we are going to refine our code and come up with an interface that will alleviate some of the pitfalls outlined previously.

Creating a database interface

In the previous section, we looked at how we can use a configuration manager library such as PureConfig to read environment variables. However, the getDBParams function is not very useful as this needs to be repeated each time we need to access the host, port, and so on for a given database. One possible option would be to update getDBParams by passing a Database object instead, as shown here:

```scala
package com.packt.dewithscala.chapter4

import org.apache.spark.sql.SparkSession

import com.packt.dewithscala.Config
import com.packt.dewithscala._

@SuppressWarnings(Array("org.wartremover.warts.OptionPartial"))
object UpdatedDBParamMethod extends App {

  private val session = SparkSession
    .builder()
    .appName("de-with-scala")
    .master("local[*]")
    .getOrCreate()

  private val mysqlDB = Config.getDB("my_db").get

  def getDBParams(db: Database): String => Option[String] = param =>
    param match {
      case "scheme"   => Some(db.scheme)
      case "host"     => Some(db.host)
      case "port"     => Some(db.port)
      case "name"     => Some(db.name)
      case "username" => Some(db.username.value)
      case "password" => Some(db.password.value)
      case _          => None
    }
}
```

```
private val scheme   = getDBParams(mysqlDB)("scheme").get
private val host     = getDBParams(mysqlDB)("host").get
private val port     = getDBParams(mysqlDB)("port").get
private val name     = getDBParams(mysqlDB)("name").get
private val username = getDBParams(mysqlDB)("username").get
private val password = getDBParams(mysqlDB)("password").get

private val airportsDF = session.read
  .format("jdbc")
  .option("url", s"$scheme://$host:$port/$name")
  .option("user", username)
  .option("password", password)
  .option("dbtable", "airports")
  .load()

airportsDF.show()

}
```

Example 4.17

This will certainly make getDBParams a bit more generic, but it is still cumbersome to write this on the application side. It would have been nice if we could write the following instead:

```
val db = Database("my_db")
val host = db.host
val port = db.port
//and so on
```

Example 4.18

It is quite easy to provide that functionality. We can create a Database trait that provides that API and then implement it through a private class. Finally, the companion object defines a factory method to create a Database instance, as the following example shows:

```
package com.packt.dewithscala.utils

import com.packt.dewithscala.Config._
import com.packt.dewithscala.Opaque

trait Database {
 def scheme: String
 def host: String
 def port: String
 def name: String
```

```
  def jbdcURL: String
  def username: Opaque
  def password: Opaque
}
object Database {
  def apply(name: String): Database = new DatabaseImplementation(name)

  private class DatabaseImplementation(dbname: String)
  extends Database {
      private val db = getDB(dbname).get
      def scheme = db.scheme
      def host = db.host
      def port = db.port
      def name = db.name
      def jbdcURL = s"$scheme://$host:$port/$name"
      def username = db.username
      def password = db.password
  }
}
```

Example 4.19

With the interface now defined, we can simplify *Example 4.17* as follows:

```
package com.packt.dewithscala.chapter4

import org.apache.spark.sql.SparkSession

import com.packt.dewithscala.utils.Database

object WithSimlifiedConfig extends App {

  private val session = SparkSession
    .builder()
    .appName("de-with-scala")
    .master("local[*]")
    .getOrCreate()

  private val mysqlDB = Database("my_db")

  private val url      = mysqlDB.jbdcURL
  private val username = mysqlDB.username.value
  private val password = mysqlDB.password.value
```

```
  private val airportsDF = session.read
    .format("jdbc")
    .option("url", url)
    .option("user", username)
    .option("password", password)
    .option("dbtable", "airports")
    .load()

  airportsDF.show()

}
```

Example 4.20

In this section, we went through the steps to create a Database interface that makes it easier to work with database objects. In the next section, we are going to create a factory method for SparkSession.

Creating a factory method for SparkSession

So far, we have been creating a SparkSession object for each of the applications. It would be better to provide a simple interface through which each of the application files in our examples can create a Spark session. For example, we can create a Spark object with an initSparkSession method as follows:

```
package com.packt.dewithscala.utils
import org.apache.spark.sql.SparkSession

object Spark {
  def initSparkSession(appName: String) = SparkSession
    .builder()
    .appName(appName)
    .master("local[*]")
    .getOrCreate()
}
```

Example 4.21

Any application file can now create a SparkSession object by importing a Spark object and calling the initSparkSession method as follows:

```
val session = initSparkSession("app-name")
```

Example 4.22

This simple factory method provides an easy way to create a `SparkSession` object, and we are going to use it from now on.

So far, we've looked at how to read records from a table. However, it is not uncommon to be able to drop and create tables, perform grants, update database statistics, and so on. For example, in order to avoid impact to downstream applications—for example, a **business intelligence** (**BI**) dashboard—you may wish to create a set of temporary fact and dimension tables, load them (after running checks to make sure the data is accurate), update database statistics to improve query runtime, drop existing fact and dimension tables, and then rename these temporary tables.

In the next section, we are going to look at how we can use `doobie`—an open source, purely functional JDBC library—to provide those functionalities through our database interface.

Performing various database operations

In this section, we are going to extend our Database API to provide additional capabilities such as creating tables, dropping tables, returning query results as collections, and so on. But before we proceed, we need to update our dependencies by adding `doobie`:

```
object Version {
  val spark = "3.3.1"
  val deequ = "2.0.4-spark-3.3"
  val pureconfig = "0.17.2"
  val doobie = "1.0.0-RC1"
}
val mainDeps: Seq[ModuleID] = spark ++ Seq(deequ, pureconfig, doobie)
```

Example 4.23

`doobie` is a functional JDBC layer for Scala and is based on design patterns such as functional I/O, monadic effects, and so on. We are not going to do a deep dive to understand how the library works or all of the functionalities it offers. We will instead focus on aspects of the library that allow us to write a database API with desired functionalities.

In this section, we updated our dependencies in order to work with `doobie`. In the next section, we will look at `doobie` in action.

Working with databases

In order to work with databases, we need to establish a connection first. To do this in `doobie`, we create an object of type `ConnectionIO[A]`, which specifies computations that take place in a context where `java.sql.Connection` is available and produces a value of type A. Given an object of type `ConnectionIO[A]`, we need a connection to work with. There are multiple ways to do it in `doobie`, but the easiest option is through a `Transactor` object. A `Transactor` object knows how to connect to a database, handle connections, and so on. You can read more about Transactor objects at https://tpolecat.github.io/doobie/docs/14-Managing-Connections.html.

In the following code snippet, we query the mysql database to retrieve a literal and current timestamp:

```scala
package com.packt.dewithscala.chapter4

import doobie._
import doobie.implicits._

import cats.effect.IO
import cats.effect.unsafe.implicits.global

import com.packt.dewithscala.utils.Database

import cats.syntax.all._

object WorkingWithDoobie extends App {

  private val db = Database("my_db")

  private val constant: ConnectionIO[String] =
    sql"select 'hello'".query[String].unique

  private val random: ConnectionIO[Double] =
    sql"select rand();".query[Double].unique

  // create a transactor object
  private val transactor = Transactor.fromDriverManager[IO](
    db.driver,
    db.jbdcURL,
    db.username.value,
    db.password.value
  )

  private val run = for {
    c <- constant
    r <- random
  } yield (println(s"($c,$r)"))

  run.transact(transactor).unsafeRunSync()

  final case class Airports(
      iata_code: String,
```

```
        airport: String,
        city: String,
        state: String,
        country: String,
        latitude: Double,
        longitude: Double
    )

    private val airports: List[Airports] =
      sql"select * from my_db.airports"
        .query[Airports]        // Query0[Airports]
        .to[List]               // ConnectionIO[List[Airports]]
        .transact(transactor)   // IO[List[Airports]]
        .unsafeRunSync()        // List[Airports]

    // print the cities with airports in North Carolina
    airports
      .collect { case a if a.state === "NC" => a.city }
      .foreach(a => println(a))

    private val airports2: List[Airports] =
      db.records[Airports]("select * from my_db.airports")

    airports2
      .collect { case a if a.state === "NC" => a.city }
      .foreach(a => println(a))

    private val airports3 =
      db.records[(String, String, String, String, String, Double,
Double)](
        "select * from my_db.airports"
      )

    airports3.collect { case a if a._5 === "NC" => a._3 }.foreach(a =>
println(a))


}
```

Example 4.24

The `sql` interpolator is supplied by `doobie.implicits` and is used to create `sql` fragments. We also need to import `cats` to bring types such as `IO` in scope. `unsafeRunSync` comes from the `cats.effect` library and performs side effects (in this case, connecting to the `mysql` database).

In fact, there is a whole family of `unsafe` functions available in `cats.effect` for side-effecting operations. Such a function should be called at the end of the application and is sometimes referred to as **end of the world.**

As you might have noticed already, there is no `SparkContext` at play. The other thing you might have noticed is in order to create a database connection, we need to provide driver details. Before we proceed any further, let's update our config so that driver information is available as a part of a `Database` object. To do that, we need to perform the following steps:

1. We need to update the `Database` case class in the `config` object by adding a `driver` field, shown as follows:

```
case class Database(
      driver: String,
      name: String,
      scheme: String,
      host: String,
      port: String,
      username: Opaque,
      password: Opaque
  )
```

Example 4.25

2. Then, we update the `Database` trait by adding an abstract `driver` method:

```
sealed trait Database {
  def driver: String
  def scheme: String
  def host: String
  def port: String
  def name: String
  def jbdcURL: String
  def username: Opaque
  def password: Opaque
}
```

Example 4.26

3. Then, we provide a concrete implementation of the `driver` method in a private class:

```
object Database {
  def apply(name: String): Database = new
DatabaseImplementation(name)

  private class DatabaseImplementation(dbname: String)
```

```
        extends Database {
        private val db = getDB(dbname).get
        def driver = db.driver
        def scheme = db.scheme
        def host = db.host
        def port = db.port
        def name = db.name
        def jbdcURL = s"$scheme://$host:$port/$name"
        def username = db.username
        def password = db.password
    }
}
```

Example 4.27

4. Then, we add a driver to `application.conf`:

```
db = [
    {
            driver = "com.mysql.cj.jdbc.Driver"
            name = "my_db"
            scheme = "jdbc:mysql"
            host = "localhost"
            port = "3306"
            username = ${?MYSQL_USER}
            password = ${?MYSQL_PASS}
    }
]
```

Example 4.28

With these changes, we can define the `Transactor` object from *Example 4.24* as follows:

```
val transactor = Transactor.fromDriverManager[IO](
    db.driver,
    db.jbdcURL,
    db.username.value,
    db.password.value
)
```

Example 4.29

Earlier in this chapter, we created a `my_db.airports` table and loaded some records into that table. Here is the schema of that table:

```
mysql> describe my_db.airports;
+-------------+--------------+------+-----+---------+-------+
| Field       | Type         | Null | Key | Default | Extra |
+-------------+--------------+------+-----+---------+-------+
| iata_code   | varchar(50)  | YES  |     | NULL    |       |
| airport     | varchar(500) | YES  |     | NULL    |       |
| city        | varchar(100) | YES  |     | NULL    |       |
| state       | varchar(100) | YES  |     | NULL    |       |
| country     | varchar(100) | YES  |     | NULL    |       |
| latitude    | double       | YES  |     | NULL    |       |
| longitude   | double       | YES  |     | NULL    |       |
+-------------+--------------+------+-----+---------+-------+
```

Example 4.30

We can read the records from this table by using a case class as follows:

```
case class Airports(
        iata_code: String,
        airport: String,
        city: String,
        state: String,
        country: String,
        latitude: Double,
        longitude: Double
)
val airports: List[Airports] =
    sql"select * from my_db.airports"
        .query[Airports] // Query0[Airports]
        .to[List] // ConnectionIO[List[Airports]]
        .transact(transactor) // IO[List[Airports]]
        .unsafeRunSync() // List[Airports]

// print the cities with airports in North Carolina
airports.collect { case a if a.state == "NC" => a.city
}.foreach(println)

// Asheville
// Charlotte
// New Bern
// Fayetteville
```

```
// Greensboro
// Wilmington
// Jacksonville
// Raleigh
```

Example 4.31

Based on this example, we can think of a `records` method that can be added to the database interface, with the following signature:

```
def records[T: Read](selectStatement: String): List[T]
```

Example 4.32

The actual implementation is pretty similar to the preceding example. The only difference is that instead of the `sql` interpolator, we are using a `Fragment` statement. The reason is that the `sql` interpolator will substitute any variable with `?` and return a `Fragment` statement; in other words, the `"$selectStatement"` SQL will not work:

```
def records[T: Read](selectStatement: String): List[T] = {
        Fragment.const(selectStatement)
            .query[T]
            .to[List]
            .transact(transactor)
            .unsafeRunSync()
    }
```

Example 4.33

With the `records` method added, we can rewrite *Example 4.31* as follows:

```
val airports2: List[Airports] =
    db.records[Airports]("select * from my_db.airports")
 airports2.collect { case a if a.state == "NC" => a.city
}.foreach(println)
```

Example 4.34

The `T: Read` type parameter syntax is known as context-bound, and it automatically introduces an implicit argument of type `Read[T]`. `doobie` can automatically derive a type class instance of type `Read[T]` for T types such as `Int`, `String`, and `Tuple`, case classes, and so on. We could have used a `Tuple` type instead of a case class. Refer to the following code snippet:

```
val airports3 =
        db.records[(String, String, String, String, String, Double,
    Double)](
            "select * from my_db.airports"
```

```
        )
    airports3.collect { case a if a._5 == "NC" => a._3 }.foreach(println)
```

Example 4.35

doobie also allows running **data definition language** (DDL) statements such as `create`, `drop` `tables` and `views`, and so on. To do that, we will use `update` instead of `query`. For example, let's create a `flight_count` table that captures the total number of flights between origin and destination airports:

```
create table my_db.flight_count(
    origin_state                varchar(100),
    origin_city                  varchar(100),
    origin_airport              varchar(500),
    destination_state        varchar(100),
    destination_city          varchar(100),
    destination_airport    varchar(500),
    number_of_flights        int
)
```

Example 4.36

The syntax for creating tables is very similar to a query. However, instead of `query`, we will use `update`:

```
Fragment
    .const("""|
        |create table my_db.flight_count(
        |      origin_state                varchar(100),
        |      origin_city                  varchar(100),
        |      origin_airport              varchar(500),
        |      destination_state        varchar(100),
        |      destination_city          varchar(100),
        |      destination_airport    varchar(500),
        |      number_of_flights        int
        |);""".stripMargin)
    .update // Update0
    .run // ConnectionIO[Int]
    .transact(transactor) // IO[Int]
    .unsafeRunSync()
```

Example 4.37

The return type of the preceding expression is `Int`, and in this particular case, it returns 0. Let's create a `runDDL` method that will run any arbitrary DDL statement against the database. Here is its signature:

```
def runDDL(statement: String): Database
```

Example 4.38

The return type of `Database` is going to enable chaining such method calls together:

```
def runDDL(statement: String): Database = {
    Fragment
        .const(statement)
        .update
        .run
        .transact(transactor)
        .unsafeRunSync()
    this
}
```

Example 4.39

Running DML statements such as `insert`, `update`, and `delete` is identical to running DDL statements. However, in order to segregate DDL and DML statements, it may be useful to create a separate method for DML statements:

```
def runDML(statement: String): Database = runDDL(statement)
```

Example 4.40

We do not need to provide a separate implementation as both are identical. With these in place, let's see how they play together.

In the following example, we drop the `flight_count` table if it exists, create a table, insert records, query the table and load the result in a list. Finally, we print out all of the flights within a given state:

```
val createTable =
        """|
            |create table my_db.flight_count(
            |    origin_state        varchar(100),
            |    origin_city         varchar(100),
            |    origin_airport      varchar(500),
            |    destination_state   varchar(100),
            |    destination_city    varchar(100),
            |    destination_airport varchar(500),
            |    number_of_flights   int
            |);""".stripMargin
val insert =
        """|
            |insert into my_db.flight_count
            |select
            |    oa.state    o_state
```

```
              |, oa.city         o_city
              |, oa.airport o_airport
              |, da.state        d_state
              |, da.city         d_city
              |, da.airport d_airport
              |, count(1)
              |from my_db.airlines
              |inner join my_db.flights on airlines.iata_code =
flights.airline
              |inner join my_db.airports oa on flights.origin_
airport = oa.iata_code
              |inner join my_db.airports da on flights.destination_
airport = da.iata_code
              |group by
              |   oa.state
              |, oa.city
              |, oa.airport
              |, da.state
              |, da.city
              |, da.airport
              |""".stripMargin

case class FlightCount(
        origin_state: String,
        origin_city: String,
        origin_airport: String,
        destination_state: String,
        destination_city: String,
        destination_airport: String,
        number_of_flights: Int
)

val flightCount: List[FlightCount] = db
    .runDDL("drop table if exists my_db.flight_count;")
    .runDDL(createTable)
    .runDML(insert)
    .records[FlightCount]("select * from my_db.flight_count;")
flightCount
    .collect { case fc if fc.origin_state == fc.destination_state =>
fc }
    .foreach(println)
```

Example 4.41

In this section, we looked at adding functionalities to our database interface in order to enable table creation, deletion, running queries, and so on. At this point, our interface lacks the ability to perform read and write operations using the Spark JDBC API, which is what we are going to look at in the next section.

Updating the Database API with Spark read and write

With the changes discussed in the previous section, here is what our updated Database API looks like:

```
package com.packt.dewithscala.utils
import com.packt.dewithscala.Config._
import com.packt.dewithscala.Opaque
import doobie._
import doobie.implicits._
import cats.effect.IO
import cats.effect.unsafe.implicits.global
sealed trait Database {
 def driver: String
 def scheme: String
 def host: String
 def port: String
 def name: String
 def jbdcURL: String
 def username: Opaque
 def password: Opaque
 def records[T: Read](selectStatement: String): List[T]
 def runDDL(statement: String): Database
 def runDML(statement: String): Database = runDDL(statement)
}
```

Example 4.42

This is a good start but it lacks any interface for working with Spark. It would be nice if we could perform Spark read/write operations through a database object. In order to do that, let's add the following methods to the interface:

```
def singlePartitionRead(session: SparkSession, dbTable: String):
DataFrame

 def multiPartitionRead(
         session: SparkSession,
         dbTable: String,
         partitionCol: String,
         upperBound: String,
         lowerBound: String,
         numPartitions: Int
```

```
): DataFrame

    def singlePartitionWrite(
        session: SparkSession,
        dbTable: String,
        df: DataFrame,
        saveMode: SaveMode
): Database

def multiPartitionWrite(
        session: SparkSession,
        dbTable: String,
        df: DataFrame,
        numPartitions: Int,
        saveMode: SaveMode
): Database
```

Example 4.43

The implementation is straightforward, as can be seen here:

```
def singlePartitionRead(session: SparkSession, dbTable: String):
DataFrame =
        session.read
            .format("jdbc")
            .option("url", jbdcURL)
            .option("user", username.value)
            .option("password", password.value)
            .option("dbtable", dbTable)
            .load()
    def multiPartitionRead(
            session: SparkSession,
            dbTable: String,
            partitionCol: String,
            upperBound: String,
            lowerBound: String,
            numPartitions: Int
    ) = session.read
        .format("jdbc")
        .option("url", jbdcURL)
        .option("user", username.value)
        .option("password", password.value)
        .option("dbtable", dbTable)
        .option("partitionColumn", partitionCol)
```

```
        .option("numPartitions", numPartitions)
        .option("upperBound", upperBound)
        .option("lowerBound", lowerBound)
        .load()

def singlePartitionWrite(
        session: SparkSession,
        dbTable: String,
        df: DataFrame,
        saveMode: SaveMod
) = {
    df.write
        .format("jdbc")
        .option("url", jbdcURL)
        .option("user", username.value)
        .option("password", password.value)
        .option("dbtable", dbTable)
        .mode(saveMode)
        .save()
    this
}

def multiPartitionWrite(
        session: SparkSession,
        dbTable: String,
        df: DataFrame,
        numPartitions: Int,
        saveMode: SaveMode
) = {
    df.write
        .format("jdbc")
        .option("url", jbdcURL)
        .option("user", username.value)
        .option("password", password.value)
        .option("dbtable", dbTable)
        .option("numPartitions", numPartitions)
        .mode(saveMode)
        .save()
        this
}
```

Example 4.44

With these updates, we will be able to perform both single- and multi-partition reads, save data in tables, and so on, as the following example illustrates:

```
// single partition read
db.singlePartitionRead(
    session,
    "(select * from my_db.flight_count order by number_of_flights
desc limit 5) qry"
).show()
// to store upper and lower bounds
case class MaxMin(max: Int, min: Int)
// upper and lower bounds
val bounds = db
    .records[MaxMin](
        "select max(number_of_flights) max, min(number_of_flights)
min from my_db.flight_count"
    )
    .head
// multiple partition read
val df = db.multiPartitionRead(
    session = session,
    dbTable = "my_db.flight_count",
    partitionCol = "number_of_flights",
    upperBound = bounds.max.toString,
    lowerBound = bounds.min.toString,
    10
)
// write df to two new tables
// one with single partition write
// another with multi partition write
db
    .singlePartitionWrite(
        session,
        "my_db.flight_count_2",
        df,
        SaveMode.Overwrite
    )
    .multiPartitionWrite(
        session,
        "my_db.flight_count_3",
        df,
        10,
        SaveMode.Overwrite
    )
```

Example 4.45

Summary

We started this chapter with a brief overview of the Spark JDBC API and some of its most commonly used options. We then looked at examples of how to read and write to a database using the `mysql` database installed in *Chapter 2*. We covered configuration loading through the `PureConfig` library and finally created an interface that makes it easy to work with databases.

In the next chapter, we are going to look at cloud object storage as well as streaming.

5
Object Stores and Data Lakes

Enterprises have leaned heavily on databases and data warehouses for many decades. Around the turn of the millennium, the internet age was beginning to take hold. The proliferation of connected devices began to present a volume and variety of data that traditional databases and warehouses could no longer keep up with.

While developing a web indexing solution using this large influx of data, Google published a paper in 2003 titled the *Google File System* (*GFS*) that would shape industry solutions for the next two decades. This solution allowed for the development of data lakes, which led to lakehouses. Data lakes are a distributed file system that provide a cost-efficient method to store structured, unstructured, and semi-structured data. Lakehouses are a combination of data warehouses and data lake capabilities. We're going to learn how to work with object stores, which are the foundational technology and storage for both data lakes and lakehouses.

In this chapter, we will cover the following topics:

- Understanding distributed file systems
- Deep diving into lakehouses
- Understanding streaming data
- Working with streaming sources

Understanding distributed file systems

The GFS paper outlined to the technology world how to successfully store and access data on a massive (for the time) scale. At the time, hundreds of terabytes were spread across thousands of commodity servers. Not only could they store and access vast amounts of data but they also provided the ability to store non-traditional types of data.

However, the rise of the internet brought with it video files, images, audio, email, and HTML. Data warehouses did not have the capability to store and use these types of data, so the new **distributed file system** was a perfect solution. This solution very quickly took hold in the industry through Apache Hadoop, in 2005, as the first widely adopted distributed file system, called **Hadoop Distributed File System** (**HDFS**), and processing framework (MapReduce). The newly found scalability in storage and compute at commodity prices brought on the rise of **data lakes**.

Now, let's dive into data lakes and explore how they work and why they are important for data engineers.

Data lakes

Distributed storage and compute allowed companies to store and analyze large amounts of data that could be of any variety, such as images, unstructured text, sound files, and so on. This was a complete paradigm shift from database systems and the limited scalability that was present pre-internet. In addition to this large shift in architecture, the pricing model made it possible for companies of all sizes to get started. Hadoop was open source and could be installed on commodity hardware with a scale-as-needed mentality. As datasets grew, the underlying clusters' compute could expand to grow with them. Combining this cheap, scalable infrastructure with the ability to deliver advanced analytical capabilities came to be known as a data lake.

With data lakes, teams could bring in any kind of data, and as much of it as they chose. There was no need to specify a schema, so decisions about data modeling were a thing of the past. A great benefit of this was data sources did not have to be scrutinized before capturing them. Business units did not have to make a strong case to store raw data in perpetuity because storage was cheap and developer involvement could be minimal. That allowed data to be captured before a specific use for it was determined. The ability to do that ensured that all data was captured and minimized data loss. However, each immense technology shift comes with its own set of growing pains. Business units were allowed to store just about anything they chose without much scrutiny. This could easily turn into full-time staff dedicated to infrastructure maintenance and scaling out the solution. Hadoop systems also suffered from a single point of failure and bottleneck called the **NameNode**. This functioned as the coordinator between all of the other nodes in the cluster and was responsible for knowing where all of the blocks were stored, replication of those blocks for redundancy, fault tolerance between the worker nodes, and coordinating all of the requests for information. Amazon saw a market opportunity with these shortcomings and launched its first generally available service on **Amazon Web Services** (**AWS**) called **Simple Storage Service** (**S3** for short).

Object stores

S3 (https://aws.amazon.com/s3/) was launched in 2006 as the first widely used, hosted, object storage service. Object stores revolutionized the storage industry by providing instantly scalable storage that was durable (eleven nines of durability) and extraordinarily cheap at only $0.023 per gigabyte.

The access to this data was scalable, in part due to the shift from hierarchical namespaces that existed in traditional file systems to key-value lookups. Take, for example, the organization of a filing cabinet. This cabinet could be organized into folders, sub-folders, and nested sub-folders. On the other hand, object stores would organize this cabinet into a flat structure where each file was in its own folder with the full path labeled on it.

Hierarchical namespaces allow for quick point lookups while object stores allow for higher throughput at scale. Traditionally, in order to scale storage on your system, one would also need to scale compute. The easiest way to add storage to a Hadoop cluster was to add more nodes to it. This is another area where object stores changed the dynamic.

S3 was accessible at the lowest levels through the REST API, which helped in two areas:

- It allowed programmers to think about storage and compute as two completely different entities and cost models. The need for more storage no longer required more nodes in a cluster.

- The REST API took away the bottleneck of the NameNode.

It was Amazon's responsibility to be able to handle the throughput requirements demanded by programmers interfacing with it.

Hadoop began supporting S3 as a data source upon its launch in 2006, giving credit to S3's almost immediate prominence. Nearly a decade later, other cloud providers released their own object stores to compete with Amazon. Microsoft Azure went through a few iterations and eventually landed on an interesting solution called **Azure Data Lake Storage Gen2** (**ADLS Gen2**). Its goal was to combine hierarchical storage with features of an object store to give it the big data throughput capabilities and low cost with the benefits that hierarchical storage provided. This solved a nagging issue that S3 introduced with object stores, which was *atomic metadata interactions*. This meant that renaming a file or deleting a file would immediately be seen by all other applications.

Currently, S3 is more scalable than ADLS Gen2 by providing requests per second at the object level (5,500 GET requests per second), while Azure limits throughput at the storage account level (20,000 GET requests per second). S3 has become the gold standard for object storage implementations with many smaller vendors implementing their own object stores with S3-compatible APIs. These include providers such as MinIO, Wasabi, and Dell's Enterprise Object Storage.

While there are many S3-compatible APIs, for the sake of brevity, this book will briefly introduce lower-level S3 interaction using the AWS Java SDK (S3 SDK) with Scala. Then, the majority of the book will abstract this lower-level interaction through the Apache Spark APIs and Scala. For the S3 SDK, all that is required is an S3 bucket and a key for the object. With these two pieces of information, Scala can add an object with some text, shown as follows:

```
import com.amazonaws.regions.Regions
import com.amazonaws.services.s3.AmazonS3ClientBuilder

val BUCKET_NAME = "scala-data-engineering"
```

```
val OBJECT_PATH = "my/first/object.csv"

val s3Client = AmazonS3ClientBuilder.standard().withRegion(Regions.
US_EAST_1).build()
s3Client.putObject(BUCKET_NAME, OBJECT_PATH, "id,name\n1,john")
```

From the preceding code, we see that a client is built first for interacting with S3 with default credentials. Credentials can be user access keys saved in the AWS profile locally. Another option is to use **Amazon Elastic Compute Cloud (EC2)** and an instance profile for more integrated security. By utilizing the same S3 client and variables, you can read the object that was recently written using the following syntax:

```
val s3Object = s3Client.getObject(new GetObjectRequest(BUCKET_NAME,
OBJECT_PATH))
val myData = Source.fromInputStream(s3Object.getObjectContent()).
getLines()
for (line <- myData){
  print(line)
}
```

Finally, if desired, the object can be deleted by issuing the following command:

```
s3Client.deleteObject(BUCKET_NAME, OBJECT_PATH)
```

Now that we've shown how to manipulate objects in S3 with the S3 SDK, we are going to move on to working with Spark to manage large amounts of data. Let's see how to work with S3 in Spark by first building a local `SparkSession` with default AWS credentials:

```
val spark = SparkSession
  .builder()
  .appName("Spark SQL basic example")
  .config("fs.s3a.aws.credentials.provider","com.amazonaws.auth.
profile.ProfileCredentialsProvider")
  .master("local[*]")
  .getOrCreate()
```

The Spark Session can then be used to read from object storage and perform operations such as displaying the contents of the DataFrame, as follows:

```
spark.read.option("header","true").csv("s3a://scala-data-engineering/
my/first/").show()
```

Instead of specifying the object key specifically, Spark can take in the prefix location and process all objects within that location. The preceding simple example uses a CSV reader, but Spark provides many abstractions for different object types, including binary, csv, text, avro, parquet, and ORC.

Now that we've shown how to read data from S3, we also need to write data in data engineering pipelines. In order to write data back to object storage, Spark uses the `write` method and can put files back into storage in one of the supported formats. Let's do this using the following code:

```
val DF = spark.read.option("header","true").csv("s3a://scala-data-
engineering/my/first/")
DF.write.csv("s3a://scala-data-engineering/my/first_write")
```

By default, this code will create the prefix if it does not exist and append data as one or multiple objects to the prefix. The number of objects created will depend on the number of partitions that the Spark processing produced up until `write`. In this simple example, it will produce a single output object, but if the source object was large then Spark would have split `read` into multiple partitions for parallelization. In order to truncate the prefix and overwrite all of the data, the `mode` method can be used:

```
DF.write.mode(SaveMode.Overwrite).csv("s3a://scala-data-engineering/
my/first_write")
```

Now that we've shown how to read and write data to S3, let's talk about object store resiliency.

Object store resiliency

Object stores are the next evolution in distributed big data storage. They provide rich APIs for manipulation with extremely durable storage guarantees. These durable guarantees are made possible by transparently replicating data across multiple data centers in a region, so even if a single storage array goes down, others are there to serve up requests completely transparently to the users.

Additional global replication can be configured to redundantly copy data across regions for disaster recovery scenarios. These are simple configurations done at the bucket or container level with the cloud providers taking care of the physical copying of data. Besides having nearly unlimited storage available in a durable manner, object stores use economies of scale to provide these services at an extremely low cost. For AWS S3, this costs around $23 per terabyte of storage.

Object stores solved many of the problems of the early Hadoop days, but as companies adopted them at scale, cracks soon formed in their abilities. These cracks have led companies to look at new ways of utilizing object stores, namely lakehouses.

Deep diving into lakehouses

Data lake usage was really able to scale because of the introduction of object stores. Without cloud provider object stores, data lakes would have faced a scalability problem with storage on-premise (on-prem). The introduction of Apache Spark made big data processing attainable through easy-to-use APIs and DataFrame abstractions. These technologies did not come without their own set of faults, however.

Limitations of data lakes

In order to read for a prefix, Spark would first have to list all of the objects in that location. This was a single-node operation and would become a large bottleneck in jobs that required reading from a prefix that had millions of files. In some instances, this would even cause the driver node to crash because it could not hold all of the metadata in memory. This was called a **metadata scaling problem**. The simple listing could produce almost as much of a memory footprint as the actual data itself.

There was no schema enforcement for data objects. A writer was allowed to put any data it wanted to in a prefix, unchecked, causing consumers of that data to fail if breaking schema changes were introduced. One writer could be writing a column as an integer while another was adding data as a decimal. This would cause production pipelines to fail and be extremely tedious for on-call engineers to be able to figure out exactly which object or objects were causing the issue, clean them up, and restart pipelines.

Standard data manipulation was a struggle. Because objects could only be created or overwritten, there was no easy way to do things such as deletes, updates, or merges. In order to change records, the entire set of records would need to be read, updated in memory, and then fully replaced again. This caused other issues with consistency while a writer was appending, overwriting, or trying to manipulate data with an overwrite. Readers would not be isolated from these manipulations and would get partial or dirty reads. This also meant that small objects could not be combined safely to produce larger objects that were needed for read efficiency and contributed to the metadata scaling issue.

Object stores also could not provide traditional enhancements such as indexing, time travel, rollback, and change feeds. All of the preceding issues, combined with the lack of enhanced capabilities, created a requirement for engineers to create robust processing pipelines that could scale cheaply, only to copy the final results into secondary infrastructure to be able to serve data out to business users for consumption. Reporting required data that could not be accidentally changed, was consistent, and was performant. This was not a possibility with traditional data lake formats.

In order to overcome these challenges, new formats beyond `parquet`, `orc`, and `avro` would be needed. Organizations began developing what became known as **lakehouse formats** to solve these issues.

What do we get with a lakehouse?

Lakehouses are an emerging technology paradigm that aims to unify the data landscape across data engineering, data science and machine learning, and business intelligence.

Three main abstractions were developed to be able to close the gaps between object stores and data lakes. In 2016, Uber developed its own in-house storage format called **Hudi** to solve its internal struggles with managing data lakes. In 2020, it became a top-level Apache project. Another lakehouse format was Apache Iceberg. Iceberg was first developed internally at Netflix, in 2017, to solve internal struggles highlighted in the previous paragraphs. It was donated to the Apache Software Foundation and became a top-level project in 2020. However, the first commercially developed lakehouse format, called **Delta Lake (Delta)**, was developed by Databricks and initially released in 2019 for their customers. This format went through battle testing with a wide variety of commercial customers of Databricks before it was open sourced through the Linux Foundation later, in 2019. Delta Lake received the widest use among many organizations because it was not developed initially as an internal company project. This gave Delta the opportunity to develop a wide array of functionality that was generalized to a large population of issues to solve.

Delta changed the way big data processing could happen on cheap, durable object stores. Delta uses Parquet files as its underlying storage mechanism on object stores but adds a metadata transaction log on top that is stored alongside the Parquet files. The transaction log acts as a scalable interface for readers and writers to interact with before ever needing to open the Parquet files. This metadata layer will tell applications information about the underlying Parquet files such as which files are in the current version of the table, statistics about the columns in the data, the schema of the table, and information about the different versions in the table. This transaction log is JSON files describing all of this information. It is periodically checkpointed into Parquet for faster metadata retrieval. Writes to the Delta tables either fully commit or fail without a new transaction entry being committed.

See *Figure 5.1* for an example of what this looks like on object storage.

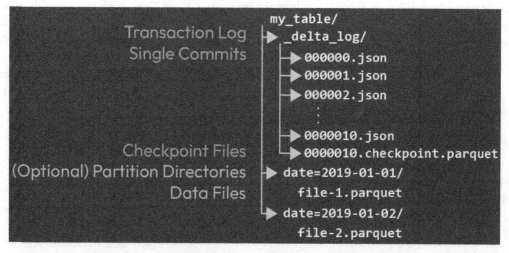

Figure 5.1 – Example of a Delta Lake transaction log file structure

By interacting with the transaction log first, applications can get all of the objects included in that version. The default behavior is to read the current transaction, which is nothing more than the current data of the table. This solves two earlier issues:

- Readers will get a consistent isolated read of the table where no other writers can modify that version again. Even if writers are continually writing to the table, the readers will be pinned to the current version they are reading from at the time they issue their read.

- This solves the metadata scaling problem. Readers will get a list of the objects needed and be able to skip the file listing step completely in a transparent way. This allows the reader to start in a distributed manner and side-step the driver bottleneck completely.

With the schema being stored as part of the transaction log, it can now be enforced at the Delta location. This means that writers can no longer blindly push data into locations that do not conform to the current schema. Readers are safe from reading data that they do not understand. Of course, some situations require a safe way to evolve the schema as data changes. Delta allows for the option to alter the table and add columns. Or, by turning on schema evolution, writers can automatically evolve the schema as new columns are added.

The transaction log allows readers to be isolated from the writers of a table. This allows writers to have more robust manipulation capabilities. Delta tables can accept traditional statements such as DELETE, UPDATE, and MERGE without causing inconsistent behavior. Transactions will either fully succeed or fail and roll back. Additionally, compaction can be issued against a table with small files to reduce the read latency of many small files. This compaction can also be coupled with adding clustered indexes on the table, providing another layer of read enhancement beyond simple partitioning. Pipelines can then cluster on columns with high cardinality to co-located data and provide a faster data-skipping mechanism that can go beyond traditional date column partitioning.

Additional edge features are made possible by the transaction log in Delta. Each version of the table is saved, which allows for queries against older snapshot views of the table and rolling back the table to an older version in case of issues in the processing pipelines such as bugs. Each change to the table can also be optionally made available for processing incremental changes beyond simple appends. Capturing all changes in the table as a feed is called a **Change Data Feed**. If this is turned on, then each update, delete, and insert operation is recorded for finer-grained downstream processing, often useful in streaming applications. See the following code for how to enable this on an existing Delta table:

```
ALTER TABLE myDeltaTable SET TBLPROPERTIES (delta.enableChangeDataFeed
= true)
```

Let's take a look at some Spark processing commands to see some Delta examples. In order to write to a Delta table, the write command simply specifies the format as Delta:

```
val spark = SparkSession
 .builder()
 .appName("Spark SQL basic example")
 .config("fs.s3a.aws.credentials.provider","com.amazonaws.auth.
profile.ProfileCredentialsProvider")
 .config("spark.sql.extensions", "io.delta.sql.
DeltaSparkSessionExtension")
 .config("spark.sql.catalog.spark_catalog", "org.apache.spark.sql.
delta.catalog.DeltaCatalog")
 .master("local[*]")
 .getOrCreate()
val DF = spark.read.option("header","true").csv("s3a://scala-data-
engineering/my/first/")
DF.write.format("delta").mode(SaveMode.Overwrite).save("s3a://scala-
data-engineering/my/first_delta")
```

To update entries in the table, an `update` command can be used:

```
val deltaTable= DeltaTable.forPath(spark, "s3a://scala-data-
engineering/my/first_delta")
deltaTable.update(
 col("id") ===1,
 Map("name" -> lit("jane"))
)
spark.read.format("delta").load("s3a://scala-data-engineering/my/
first_delta").show()
```

An insert or update is called an upsert and can be done from a source DataFrame using the `merge` command. This `update` DataFrame could be from any source, but for this simplistic example, we have created a static one:

```
val rowData = Seq(Row(1,"john"),
 Row(2,"jane"))
val schema = StructType( Array(
 StructField("id", IntegerType,true),
 StructField("name", StringType,true)
))

val updatesDF = spark.createDataFrame(rowData,schema)
val deltaTable= DeltaTable.forPath(spark, "s3a://scala-data-
engineering/my/first_delta").as("target")
deltaTable.merge(
 updatesDF.as("updates"),
 "target.id = updates.id")
.whenMatched
.updateExpr(
  Map("name" -> "updates.name"))
.whenNotMatched
.insertExpr(
  Map(
    "id" -> "updates.id",
    "name" -> "updates.name"))
.execute()
spark.read.format("delta").load("s3a://scala-data-engineering/my/
first_delta").show()
```

Finally, data can be selectively deleted or fully deleted when removing the predicate conditions:

```
deltaTable.delete(col("id") === "1")
```

Beyond simple data manipulation commands, Delta also offers more advanced features such as time travel, restore, cluster indexes, and compaction, to name a few. In order to look at time travel and restore commands, it is helpful to first understand the history mechanism of the Delta table. Let's use the following code to look at the history of our Delta table:

```
deltaTable.history().
select("version","timestamp","operation","operationParameters","
operationMetrics")
        .show(false)
```

This command will display all of the operations that have taken place on the table and metadata about those operations such as how many rows were added, updated, or deleted.

Figure 5.2 – Output of the operations

With the history information, a delta table can be restored to a previous version either by version number or by a timestamp using the following command:

```
deltaTable.restoreToVersion(0)
```

The combination of the aforementioned features brings together the scalability, reliability, and cost-effectiveness of object stores, while also providing the capability to execute robust manipulation commands against them in a consistent and dependable manner. This allows data engineering pipelines to move away from traditional database processing mechanisms, which can be expensive and hard to scale. Instead, pipelines that require things such as slowly changing dimensions, deletes, and updates can scale out on commodity storage mediums.

A lakehouse needs to go beyond being able to do robust data engineering on a variety of data. Delta alone will only be able to provide consistency and mechanisms that surface database features. After data is transformed, it needs to be able to be used for **business intelligence** (**BI**) and **machine learning** (**ML**) use cases without the need to copy data to different systems. By not moving data to purpose-built systems, organizations can eliminate data duplication, consolidate governance models, decrease complexity, and decrease cost.

Let's move on to streaming data and how to use it with our object storage.

Streaming data

Streaming data is often a misunderstood topic as streaming is often thought of as being required for real-time data processing. This level of processing needs some type of compute resource to be running continuously to keep the data as close to up to date as possible and is thought of as being very expensive. Some engineering teams will avoid this architecture because of budgetary constraints, and because the use case only requires data to be fresh at some type of frequency, such as daily, hourly, twice a day, and so on. While this is true for many scenarios, it misses the main purpose of streaming architecture, which is incremental processing. This type of processing is the holy grail of data engineering because the less data that is processed typically means less cost is associated with a pipeline.

This section will show how to stream from different sources and process these streams into different destinations or sinks.

There are many different ways to set up a streaming architecture in today's data landscape. In order to ingest streaming data, three things are needed: a source that can be read from incrementally, a processing engine reading from this source, and finally, some place to put the results after processing.

The first piece is a source – usually, a message service such as Kafka, Kinesis, Azure Event Hubs, or AWS SQS. It can also come in the form of object stores or a lakehouse format on top of object stores. All of the sources have in common the fact that what has been processed can be tracked so that each message or object is only processed once. The second piece that is needed is some type of compute component that can read from these sources, do some type of processing, track what it has processed, and be able to write the results to a sink for consumption.

Processing engines can take the form of serverless functions on cloud providers, Apache Flink, and Apache Spark. However, we will focus on using Spark as our processing engine. Spark operates using a concept called a **micro-batch**, which means that, every time code is executed it will read data from the source that it has not processed already, process it according to the code specified, and place it into a sink micro-batch The key here is the idea of when it is executed. This execution can be as soon as the last micro-batch is completed, every second, every five minutes, every hour, once a day, and so on. The benefits of a streaming architecture are that only new data is processed. How fast this data is processed is completely up to the use case at hand. If a streaming pipeline is serving an analytical use case for fresh dashboards, then the pipeline might be run every hour. Each time the pipeline runs, it will process new data and then stop processing. This is beneficial because it balances fresh data with cost. The pipeline does not need to be running continuously and creates costs for a use case that only requires fresh data every hour. At the opposite end of the spectrum, a use case around fraud detection would require this pipeline to be processing data continuously, computing the probability that a transaction is fraudulent, and pushing these inferences to a sink for immediate alerting and action.

We have learned what streaming is, now let's explore how to use streaming sources with Spark.

Working with streaming sources

Apache Spark uses the structured streaming API to read from a large variety of streaming sources. This API is easy for developers to use because it is very interoperable with Spark's batch API, so developers can reuse their knowledge across both use cases. The following are some examples of using Spark to read from Kafka and Kinesis and show the results in the console. The `writeStream` portion will be covered in more detail later in this section:

```
//KINESIS

val spark = SparkSession
 .builder()
 .appName("Spark SQL basic example")
 .master("local[*]")
 .getOrCreate()

var df = spark.readStream.format("kinesis")
 .option("streamName","scala-book")
 .option("region","us-east-1")
 .option("initialPosition","TRIM_HORIZON")
 .option("awsAccessKeyId",sys.env.getOrElse("AWS_ACCESS_KEY_ID",""))
 .option("awsSecretKey",sys.env.getOrElse("AWS_SECRET_ACCESS_KEY",""))
 .load()
df = df.withColumn("data",col("data").cast("string"))
 .selectExpr("from_json(data,'id int, name string') as data")
 .select("data.*")
val query = df.writeStream.trigger(Trigger.ProcessingTime("10
seconds")).format("console").start()
query.awaitTermination()


// KAFKA
var df = spark.readStream.format("kafka")
 .option("subscribe", "scala-book")
 .option("kafka.bootstrap.servers", sys.env.getOrElse("BOOTSTRAP_
SERVERS",""))
 .option("kafka.sasl.mechanism", "PLAIN")
 .option("kafka.security.protocol", "SASL_SSL")
 .option("kafka.sasl.jaas.config", sys.env.getOrElse("JAAS_
CONFIG",""))
 .option("kafka.request.timeout.ms", "10000")
 .option("kafka.session.timeout.ms", "10000")
 .option("failOnDataLoss", "true")
 .load()
```

For each message, the consumer follows the same basic structure, starting with `readStream` and a `format` setting to tell the consumer which type of streaming source to consume from. The REST of the options are source-specific. Both of these sources will have `base64` encoded data that needs to be cast to a string first, and then a typical pattern is to decode JSON from the payload to be able to work on a simple DataFrame of columns coming out of the source. The ultimate result looks like the following screenshot:

Figure 5.3 – Console output of our process

Object stores are another common place to stream data from. This is a very typical pattern when data is being placed from source systems into a staging area for a data lake or lakehouse to process, enrich, and save for analytical processing to take place. Staging locations can come in the forms of CSV, JSON, Parquet, or lakehouse formats such as Delta Lake. Here are two examples – the first is an S3 location that is reading CSV data; the second is a Delta table as a source:

```
//CSV
val df = spark.readStream.format("csv").option("header","true").
schema("id int, name string").load("s3a://scala-data-engineering/my/
first/")
val query = df.writeStream.trigger(Trigger.ProcessingTime("10
seconds")).format("console").start()
query.awaitTermination()


//DELTA
val df = spark.readStream.format("delta").load("s3a://scala-data-
engineering/my/first_delta")
val query = df.writeStream.trigger(Trigger.ProcessingTime("10
seconds")).format("console").start()
query.awaitTermination()
```

As with the message services, object streaming follows the same API pattern. Simply specify the format (in this case, CSV or Delta) and provide the options specific to that format. These formats could be switched out for JSON, ORC, or Parquet. Notice that there is a slight difference between CSV and Delta (or `json/parquet/orc`) in that a schema is not specified when reading from it. This is because the Delta format houses the schema within the object location and the reader will be able to know the schema upon scanning the Delta log first. We will understand the details of this in the next section.

Processing and sinks

A streaming source is only the first part of a streaming architecture. Nothing valuable can be obtained from simply reading from one of the preceding sources. To gain value, data needs to be processed in some way and then saved to some type of destination. Processing in Spark can take on many forms depending on the use case at hand. Sometimes a simple conversion from a raw form such as CSV or JSON needs to be transformed into Parquet or Delta for better read performance without any changes to the data structure itself. Other times, joins for enrichment or aggregations for summarization are needed for richer data analysis.

The following examples will walk us through some very common data processing needs in a streaming architecture. Each of these examples will use the console sink for simplicity, leaving the details of sinks for later in this section.

The simplest processing example of just reading from a raw file location without any transformations and writing to the console sink was covered in the previous section. The first type of transformations that will be discussed here are **unions** and **joins**. Unions are typically used when two different streaming sources need to be brought together and written to a sink. The syntax for union will be very familiar to someone familiar with the Dataframe API.

Any streaming source can be substituted in the following example and multiple DataFrames can be used:

```
val df_a = spark.readStream.format("csv").option("header","true").
schema("id int, name string").load("s3a://scala-data-engineering/my/
first/")
val df_b = spark.readStream.format("csv").option("header","true").
schema("id int, name string").load("s3a://scala-data-engineering/my/
first/")
val df_c = df_a.union(df_b)
```

Joins are another common engineering task that is used to enrich data and can be handled in a few different ways depending on the scenario.

Joining a stream to static data

One of the more common use cases involves a streaming source that needs to be enriched from a static dataset. This is relevant when a streaming source needs to be enriched but the enriching dataset changes sporadically. In this example, one Dataframe is a streaming source and the other is a batch source. There could be one to many batch joins in this scenario:

```
val df_a = spark.readStream.format("csv").option("header","true").
schema("id int, name string").load("s3a://scala-data-engineering/my/
first/")
val df_b = spark.read.format("csv").option("header","true").schema("id
int, name string").load("s3a://scala-data-engineering/my/first/")
```

This next line of code will join both of the previous datasets together on `id`:

```
val df_c = df_a.join(df_b,"id")
```

Joining a stream to another stream

The second type of streaming join is a stream-to-stream join. This type of pattern is common when the context of two streams is time bound and will introduce the concept of watermarking and the state store. An illustrative scenario that highlights the necessity of a stream-to-stream join is within the realm of ad analytics. In this context, streaming data pertaining to a presented ad and the subsequent user interaction with that ad are both in motion. By combining these two streams, prompt actions can be taken to capitalize on sales opportunities or enhance user engagement. As time progresses, the correlation between these streams gradually diminishes. To address this, a time window, represented by a watermark, is implemented. The watermark serves as a control mechanism, dictating how long Spark retains the join state. Thus, even if clicks arrive in different micro-batches, successful joins can still be achieved based on the watermark's defined threshold. It is crucial to strike a balance between the duration for which state is preserved and the associated costs while considering the relevance of the information at hand. In the following example, a watermark is set for 10 seconds:

```
val adsDF = Seq(
  (10,5, Timestamp.valueOf("2022-03-08 17:02:03")) ,
  (10,6, Timestamp.valueOf("2022-03-08 17:02:03"))
).toDF("p_ad_id","p_user_id","present_time")

val clickDF = Seq(
  (10,5,Timestamp.valueOf("2022-03-08 17:02:05")),
  (10,6,Timestamp.valueOf("2022-03-08 17:03:15"))
).toDF("c_ad_id","c_user_id","click_time")

adsDF.write.mode(SaveMode.Append).format("delta").save("s3a://scala-
data-engineering/ads/input/presented")
clickDF.write.mode(SaveMode.Append).format("delta").save("s3a://scala-
data-engineering/ads/input/clicked")

val presentStream = spark.readStream.format("delta").load("s3a://
scala-data-engineering/ads/input/presented").withWatermark("present_
time","10 seconds")
val clickStream = spark.readStream.format("delta").load("s3a://scala-
data-engineering/ads/input/clicked").withWatermark("click_time","10
seconds")

val resultDF = presentStream.join(clickStream, expr("""
 p_ad_id = c_ad_id AND
 p_user_id = c_user_id AND
```

```
click_time >= present_time AND
click_time < present_time + interval 10 seconds""")
,"left" )
```

The next processing concept that will be covered is streaming aggregations.

Aggregating streams

In the preceding example, ad presentation and ad clicks were joined together to help understand the correlation between the two events. A secondary use case would involve making sure that ads are not being presented too often to users within a certain amount of time. If a user were to see the same ad multiple times in a short period of time, they may get ad fatigue and leave the website. In order to do this, a windowed aggregation is needed to encompass a certain timeframe, which looks at the number of ads for each user. Similar to the join example, a watermark is also needed to make sure late-arriving data is not missed. Let's take a look at how this is done. First, we need to create a dataset to work with:

```
import spark.implicits._
val adsDF = Seq(
  (10,5, Timestamp.valueOf("2022-03-08 17:02:03")) ,
  (10,6, Timestamp.valueOf("2022-03-08 17:02:03")),
  (10,5, Timestamp.valueOf("2022-03-08 17:05:06")),
  (10,6, Timestamp.valueOf("2022-03-08 17:10:03")),
  (10,6, Timestamp.valueOf("2022-03-08 17:10:13")),
  (10,5, Timestamp.valueOf("2022-03-08 17:12:16")),
  (10,6, Timestamp.valueOf("2022-03-08 18:02:03")),
  (10,6, Timestamp.valueOf("2022-03-08 19:09:03"))
).toDF("p_ad_id","p_user_id","present_time")

adsDF.write.format("delta").mode(SaveMode.Append).save("s3a://scala-
data-engineering/ads/input/presented")
val presentStream = spark.readStream.format("delta").load("s3a://
scala-data-engineering/ads/input/presented")
```

Next, we need to use a watermark and a window to get a count of our data:

```
val resultDF = presentStream
  .withWatermark("present_time","10 minutes")
  .groupBy(
    window($"present_time", windowDuration = "10 minutes",
slideDuration = "5 minutes"),
    $"p_user_id"
  ).count()
```

The following results show that user 5 had 3 ad presentations within one of the 10-minute windows, that then slide into 5-minute increments:

```
+-----------------------------------------------------+----------+-----+
|window                                               |p_user_id|count|
+-----------------------------------------------------+----------+-----+
|{2022-03-08 17:05:00, 2022-03-08 17:15:00}|5          |2     |
|{2022-03-08 17:10:00, 2022-03-08 17:20:00}|6          |2     |
|{2022-03-08 17:55:00, 2022-03-08 18:05:00}|6          |1     |
|{2022-03-08 16:55:00, 2022-03-08 17:05:00}|6          |2     |
|{2022-03-08 17:00:00, 2022-03-08 17:10:00}|5          |3     |
|{2022-03-08 18:00:00, 2022-03-08 18:10:00}|6          |1     |
|{2022-03-08 17:05:00, 2022-03-08 17:15:00}|6          |2     |
|{2022-03-08 17:00:00, 2022-03-08 17:10:00}|6          |2     |
|{2022-03-08 17:10:00, 2022-03-08 17:20:00}|5          |1     |
|{2022-03-08 16:55:00, 2022-03-08 17:05:00}|5          |2     |
+-----------------------------------------------------+----------+-----+
```

Figure 5.4 – Results of our streaming aggregation

Duplicate records are a prevalent problem in data engineering. Data may be sent more than once from source systems due to accidents, bugs in the code, or data backfills and refreshes. Regardless of the cause of duplicates, the pipeline needs to be able to consistently handle these and potentially remove them depending on the use case. Take the following example of data input:

```
val adsDF = Seq(
  (10,5, Timestamp.valueOf("2022-03-08 17:02:03")) ,
  (10,6, Timestamp.valueOf("2022-03-08 17:02:03")),
  (10,5, Timestamp.valueOf("2022-03-08 17:05:06")),
  (10,6, Timestamp.valueOf("2022-03-08 17:10:03")),
  (10,6, Timestamp.valueOf("2022-03-08 17:10:03")),
  (10,5, Timestamp.valueOf("2022-03-08 17:12:16")),
  (10,6, Timestamp.valueOf("2022-03-08 18:02:03")),
  (10,6, Timestamp.valueOf("2022-03-08 19:09:03"))
).toDF("p_ad_id","p_user_id","present_time")
```

p_user_id 6 had two records come in with the same timestamp. If the pipeline aggregates these without taking duplicates into account, then the results will look like the following:

```
+-----------------------------------------------------+----------+-----+
|window                                               |p_user_id|count|
+-----------------------------------------------------+----------+-----+
|{2022-03-08 17:05:00, 2022-03-08 17:15:00}|5          |2    |
|{2022-03-08 17:10:00, 2022-03-08 17:20:00}|6          |2    |
|{2022-03-08 17:55:00, 2022-03-08 18:05:00}|6          |1    |
|{2022-03-08 16:55:00, 2022-03-08 17:05:00}|6          |1    |
|{2022-03-08 17:00:00, 2022-03-08 17:10:00}|5          |2    |
|{2022-03-08 18:00:00, 2022-03-08 18:10:00}|6          |1    |
|{2022-03-08 17:05:00, 2022-03-08 17:15:00}|6          |2    |
|{2022-03-08 17:00:00, 2022-03-08 17:10:00}|6          |1    |
|{2022-03-08 17:10:00, 2022-03-08 17:20:00}|5          |1    |
|{2022-03-08 16:55:00, 2022-03-08 17:05:00}|5          |1    |
+-----------------------------------------------------+----------+-----+
```

Figure 5.5 – Results showing duplication

The window between 17:10 and 17:20 has an aggregate count of 2 for `p_user_id` 6 when, in fact, the source records are duplicates and should be filtered out.

To resolve this problem, incorporating a duplicate check is the recommended solution. This approach leverages the watermark to disregard records that arrive after the specified watermark threshold, while also examining the state store to verify whether the duplicate column values have already been processed. By utilizing this feature, duplicate checks can be performed efficiently against the state store since only the duration of the watermark is stored for comparison. Specifically, in this scenario, the system will retain the data flowing in for the last 10 minutes, discarding any records older than this timeframe.

Let's write some code to deduplicate our data:

```
val resultDF = presentStream
  .withWatermark("present_time","10 minutes").dropDuplicates("p_user_
id","present_time")
  .groupBy(
    window($"present_time", windowDuration = "10 minutes",
slideDuration = "5 minutes"),
    $"p_user_id"
).count()
```

We can now see that our data is deduplicated!

```
+-------------------------------------------------------+---------+-----+
|window                                                 |p_user_id|count|
+-------------------------------------------------------+---------+-----+
|{2022-03-08 17:05:00, 2022-03-08 17:15:00}|5           |2        |     |
|{2022-03-08 17:10:00, 2022-03-08 17:20:00}|6           |1        |     |
|{2022-03-08 17:55:00, 2022-03-08 18:05:00}|6           |1        |     |
|{2022-03-08 16:55:00, 2022-03-08 17:05:00}|6           |1        |     |
|{2022-03-08 17:00:00, 2022-03-08 17:10:00}|5           |2        |     |
|{2022-03-08 18:00:00, 2022-03-08 18:10:00}|6           |1        |     |
|{2022-03-08 17:05:00, 2022-03-08 17:15:00}|6           |1        |     |
|{2022-03-08 17:00:00, 2022-03-08 17:10:00}|6           |1        |     |
|{2022-03-08 17:10:00, 2022-03-08 17:20:00}|5           |1        |     |
|{2022-03-08 16:55:00, 2022-03-08 17:05:00}|5           |1        |     |
+-------------------------------------------------------+---------+-----+
```

Figure 5.6 – Results of deduplication

The last portion of a streaming pipeline is writing the insights to some type of sink for further consumption or action. When writing to a streaming sink, a checkpoint location will be used to track which messages have been processed already to provide fault tolerance guarantees. Some sources, such as file sinks and Delta Lake, provide exactly-once semantics, meaning Spark guarantees each message will be delivered exactly one time to the destination. Other implementations, such as Kafka and for-each-batch, provide at-least-once guarantees, meaning each message is guaranteed to be processed, but it could be processed multiple times.

The following example is reading from a streaming Delta Lake location, renaming a column, and then writing to a streaming sink – in this case, another Delta Lake location. The checkpoint location should be unique per sink and will store all of the necessary information to ensure exactly-once delivery of each record. The trigger option will tell Spark how often to check for new data. This can be set to continuous to always look for new data as soon as one micro-batch finishes, or longer in order to build up more data in the streaming source before processing. Other options include `Trigger.AvailableNow()`, which allows for incremental processing from the source, but will terminate the query when all new data has been processed. This allows for effective data engineering to be done without needing to have compute resources constantly looking for new data:

```
val presentStream = spark.readStream.format("delta").load("s3a://
scala-data-engineering/ads/input/presented")
  .withColumnRenamed("p_ad_id","ad_id")
```

```
val query = presentStream.writeStream
 .trigger(Trigger.ProcessingTime("10 seconds"))
 .format("delta")
 .outputMode("append")
 .option("checkpointLocation","s3a://scala-data-engineering/ads/
checkpoint/silver_presented")
 .start("s3a://scala-data-engineering/ads/output/silver_presented")
query.awaitTermination()
```

Apart from built-in streaming sinks, such as Kafka files, and Delta Lake, Spark can write to arbitrary sinks through the forEachBatch or forEach mechanism.

To illustrate this, a streaming Delta table is written to DynamoDB on AWS. The DynamoDbWriter class must extend ForeachWriter and implement the open, process, and close methods in order to be used in a streaming sink. It can be utilized in a streaming sink as follows:

```
val query =presentStream.writeStream
 .trigger(Trigger.AvailableNow())
 .option("checkpointLocation",s"$prefix/ads/checkpoint/silver_dynamo_
presented")
 .foreach(new DynamoDbWriter)
 .start()
query.awaitTermination()
```

Streaming architectures can come in many different shapes and sizes. Spark structured streaming is extremely flexible in what sources and sinks it can use and what type of processing can be done on the data, and can scale to handle massive amounts of data. Streaming should not be thought of only as a real-time processing engine, but rather as an incremental processing framework that can adjust how often it processes data to business requirements. This can be continuously running or scheduled to run once a day, coupled with a trigger interval of AvailableNow. Taking advantage of streaming architectures will allow developers to process data in real time for time-sensitive applications, or vastly simplify data engineering pipelines that do not require data to be delivered as soon as it is available.

Summary

In this chapter, we have learned about the evolution of storage to manage large volumes of data with distributed file systems. These systems have evolved over time, from data lakes to lakehouses that use cloud object storage to efficiently store data types and volumes in a way that is not possible with data warehouses.

We also learned how to read, write, and modify data stored in these systems. We then learned about streaming systems and the various ways to use them to enrich and store data in an incremental fashion, all of which is fundamental knowledge the Scala data engineer needs to know.

In the next chapter, we'll dive deep into how to further transform and use data.

6

Understanding Data Transformation

One of the main jobs of any data engineer is to transform data in some way to make it usable for **Business Intelligence** (**BI**) applications or for data scientists or analysts. In *Chapter 3*, you learned the basics of a Spark application and how to ingest data.

Now, in this chapter, we are going to dive a bit deeper and look at some advanced topics that are essential for any data engineer to understand when using Spark to build data pipelines.

Here is a list of them:

- Understanding the difference between transformations and actions
- Learning how to aggregate, group, and join data
- Leveraging advanced window functions
- Working with complex dataset types

Technical requirements

All of the code and data for this chapter is located in our GitHub repository at the following location: https://github.com/PacktPublishing/Data-Engineering-with-Scala-and-Spark/tree/main/src/main/scala/com/packt/dewithscala/chapter6.

You also need to add the following dependency to work with spark-xml:

```
libraryDependencies += "com.databricks" %% "spark-xml" % "0.16.0"
```

Understanding the difference between transformations and actions

When working with data and sets of data in Spark with Scala, it's helpful to understand how and when execution takes place on your Spark cluster. Spark by design is lazy, meaning that it doesn't transform your data until absolutely necessary. This is so that it can run a batch of transactions together and apply optimizations to help improve the processing time.

Transformations are code statements that are lazily executed. A ledger of transformations is tracked until Spark sees a code statement called an **action**. The action tells Spark it's time to execute all the transformations. Transformations are code that returns an **RDD** (short for **resilient distributed dataset**), dataset, or DataFrame. An action is code that returns some kind of value using the dataset you are processing.

Examples of action functions are as follows:

- `count`
- `show`
- `write`
- `head`
- `take`

The following are examples of transformation functions:

- `withColumn`
- `drop`
- `explode`
- `select`

Now that we understand the difference between transformations and actions, let's take a look at how to select data from our datasets.

Using Select and SelectExpr

Selecting columns of data to use is an important part of preparing a dataset for further operations, which helps to reduce I/O and thus boosts performance. You should always reduce the size of your datasets to process just what you need.

Following the steps in the *Creating a Spark application using Scala* section in *Chapter 3*, let's create a Scala object for our Spark applications:

```
package com.packt.dewithscala.chapter6

import org.apache.spark.sql._import org.apache.spark.sql.types._
import org.apache.spark.sql.functions._
import org.apache.spark.sql.expressions.Window
import java.sql.Date
import org.apache.log4j.{Level, Logger}

object DatasetTransformations extends App {
  Logger.getLogger("org").setLevel(Level.ERROR)

  val spark: SparkSession = SparkSession
    .builder()
    .master("local[1]")
    .appName("dewithscala")
    .getOrCreate()

  spark.conf.set("spark.sql.shuffle.partitions", 1)
  spark.conf.set("spark.sql.legacy.timeParserPolicy", "Legacy")

  import spark.implicits._

  // We will start writing code after this line

}
```

We imported a few packages; it would be good to cover a few of the most commonly used ones:

- `org.apache.spark.sql` contains various classes, such as `Column`, `Dataset`, and `SparkSession`, along with packages such as `types` and `functions`

- `org.apache.spark.sql.types` contains various Spark types, such as `DateType` and `IntegerType`

- `org.apache.spark.sql.functions` contains various functions used in the transformations, such as `groupBy`, `agg`, `col`, and `withColumn`

Throughout this chapter, we will be using the preceding objects to execute our code. Notice the line `import spark.implicits._`, which is not included with the imports at the top of our object. This is because it requires an instantiated `SparkSession`, so it is after our `spark` declaration. The `spark implicits` import statement gives us access to some syntactic sugar. Sugar is a way to make code easier to read or express as a shortcut to writing the full expression.

For example, in most of our examples, I will not specify columns as `col("columnName")`. Instead, I will use some sugar to express the same statement as `$"columnName"`. Either will work, but expect to see both used when working with Spark and Scala.

Now, to work with the Dataset API, the first thing we'll do is create a `case` class:

```scala
case class NetflixTitle(
    show_id: String,
    stype: String,
    title: String,
    director: String,
    cast: String,
    country: String,
    date_added: Date,
    release_year: Int,
    rating: String,
    duration: String,
    listed_in: String,
    description: String
)
```

The preceding `case` class provides a type for our `Dataset` object. We'll be working with Netflix data from Kaggle. This is a direct link to the data: `https://www.kaggle.com/datasets/shivamb/netflix-shows`.

As a next step, we will now read a file that is available in our GitHub repository as a DataFrame. Let's read it into a DataFrame as follows:

```scala
val df: DataFrame = spark.read
    .option("header", true)
    .csv("src/main/scala/com/packt/dewithscala/chapter6/data/netflix_
titles.csv")
    .na.fill("")
```

Notice that we're using the `header` instances option when reading in the CSV file. This will use the first record in the file as column names for the generated DataFrame. We are also using `.na.fill("")` to replace any null values with an empty string.

Next, we convert the DataFrame into a dataset by using the case class `NetflixTitle` defined previously and using it as the method made available through `import spark.implicits._`:

```scala
val dsNetflixTitles: Dataset[NetflixTitle] =
    df
    .withColumnRenamed("type","stype")
    .withColumn("date_added",
to_date($"date_added", "MMMM dd, yyyy"))
```

```
        .withColumn("release_year",
          $"release_year".cast(IntegerType))
      .as[NetflixTitle]
```

In the preceding example, we're converting the DataFrame into a dataset and fixing a few things. Spark doesn't like columns named `Type` because it's a reserved word. So, we'll change it to `stype` using the `withColumnRenamed` function. You could use `` `type` `` (note the backquotes), but we would strongly discourage it unless absolutely necessary. We also need to cast our `date_added` column to a date because it was read in as a string from the CSV file and will raise an error when it is mapped to the target column, `date_added`, in the `NetflixTitle` case class, which is of the `java.sql.Date` type. We'll use the `to_date` function and pass a date format as the second parameter, which matches what is in our source file. Last, we'll cast the `release_year` column as an integer and type the whole DataFrame as `Dataset[NetflixTitle]` using `.as[NetflixTitle]`. The `as[T]` method is supplied by an implicit object, which we imported into our source code.

Now, running `printSchema()` will give us the schema for our dataset so we can check that our data types are correct:

```
dsNetflixTitles.printSchema()

root
 |-- show_id: string (nullable = false)
 |-- stype: string (nullable = false)
 |-- title: string (nullable = false)
 |-- director: string (nullable = false)
 |-- cast: string (nullable = false)
 |-- country: string (nullable = false)
 |-- date_added: date (nullable = true)
 |-- release_year: integer (nullable = true)
 |-- rating: string (nullable = false)
 |-- duration: string (nullable = false)
 |-- listed_in: string (nullable = false)
 |-- description: string (nullable = false)
```

Everything looks good with our data types! Also note that the types are no longer the Spark data types (such as `IntegerType` and `StringType`) but Scala types instead.

Spark DataFrames and datasets are immutable, meaning that whenever you transform a dataset, you aren't modifying the existing data; you're creating a new dataset based on the previous set of data.

So far in this section, we've looked at how to read a file into Spark as a DataFrame and convert it into a dataset. Now, let's start exploring the various ways in which we can select columns from our dataset:

```
val dfCastMembersSelect: DataFrame =
  dsNetflixTitles.select(
    $"show_id",
    explode(split($"cast", ",")).alias("cast_member")
  )
dfCastMembersSelect.show(10)
```

Consider the preceding code. The cast column in our dsNetflixTitles dataset is a string, which can be empty or contain one or more cast members delimited by commas. This makes it difficult to get any meaningful insights from this field. We need to expand the cast into their own rows, which is what explode(split($"cast", ",")) does.

Our code returns a new DataFrame called dfCastMembersSelect with the select function, using the explode and split functions to break out cast members into their own rows. The split function turns the string into an array of strings. Then, the explode function creates a row for each element in the array. We also include the show_id value so that we can link the cast back to show.

Calling show(10) prints 10 records of the dataset to the console:

```
+-------+-------------------+
|show_id|        cast_member|
+-------+-------------------+
|     s1|                   |
|     s2|        Ama Qamata|
|     s2|       Khosi Ngema|
|     s2|      Gail Mabalane|
|     s2|     Thabang Molaba|
|     s2|   Dillon Windvogel|
|     s2|    Natasha Thahane|
|     s2|        Arno Greeff|
|     s2|  Xolile Tshabalala|
|     s2|    Getmore Sithole|
+-------+-------------------+
```

Now that we have looked at select, let's turn our attention to one of its variants – selectExpr. As the name suggests, it accepts expressions instead of column names, as can be seen from the following example:

```
val dfCastMembersSelectExpr: DataFrame = dsNetflixTitles
  .selectExpr(
    "show_id",
    "explode(split(cast, ',')) as cast_member"
```

```
    )
    .selectExpr("show_id", "trim(cast_member) as cast_member")
  dfCastMembersSelectExpr.show(10,0)
```

Here is its output:

```
+-------+-----------------+
|show_id|cast_member      |
+-------+-----------------+
|s1     |                 |
|s2     |Ama Qamata       |
|s2     |Khosi Ngema      |
|s2     |Gail Mabalane    |
|s2     |Thabang Molaba   |
|s2     |Dillon Windvogel |
|s2     |Natasha Thahane  |
|s2     |Arno Greeff      |
|s2     |Xolile Tshabalala|
|s2     |Getmore Sithole  |
+-------+-----------------+
```

We get the same results, but notice now that we're passing through an SQL expression that returns the values we want. The difference between `select` and `selectExpr` is that the former uses methods built into the DataFrame API while the latter uses Spark SQL. The last thing to note is that we also added `trim` to each cast member to remove white space around the cast member's name.

Both of the preceding methods work and would be easy for anyone with a SQL background to pick up and use. Before moving on, let's perform another similar operation by extracting directors from our dataset:

```
val dfDirectorByShowSelectExpr: DataFrame = dsNetflixTitles
  .selectExpr(
    "show_id",
    "explode(split(director, ',')) as director"
  )
  .selectExpr("show_id", "trim(director) as director")
dfDirectorByShowSelectExpr.show(10)
```

Here is the director data:

```
+-------+---------------+
|show_id|       director|
+-------+---------------+
|     s1|Kirsten Johnson|
|     s2|               |
|     s3|Julien Leclercq|
|     s4|               |
|     s5|               |
|     s6|  Mike Flanagan|
|     s7|  Robert Cullen|
|     s7| José Luis Ucha|
|     s8|   Haile Gerima|
|     s9|Andy Devonshire|
+-------+---------------+
```

For a more Scala-like way of doing the same selection, let's define two case classes, `CastMember` and `CastMembers`, and map over the elements of the `dsNetflixTitles` dataset:

```
Case class CastMember(show_id: String, cast_member: String)
case class CastMembers(show_id: String, cast: Seq[String])
val dsCastMembers: Dataset[CastMember] = dsNetflixTitles
  .map(r => CastMembers(r.show_id, r.cast.split(",")))
  .flatMap({ c =>
    c.cast.map(cm => CastMember(c.show_id, cm.trim()))
  })
dsCastMembers.show(10, 0)
```

Here is the output:

```
+-------+------------------+
|show_id|cast_member       |
+-------+------------------+
|s1     |                  |
|s2     |Ama Qamata        |
|s2     |Khosi Ngema       |
|s2     |Gail Mabalane     |
|s2     |Thabang Molaba    |
|s2     |Dillon Windvogel  |
|s2     |Natasha Thahane   |
|s2     |Arno Greeff       |
|s2     |Xolile Tshabalala |
|s2     |Getmore Sithole   |
+-------+------------------+
```

Again, we get the same results but accomplish our goal in a very different way. Now we're using map and flatMap. Let's unpack what's going on here.

Since we're using the Dataset API, we need to define two case classes to keep track of changes to our data. CastMember contains show_id and an individual cast_member as a string. CastMembers contains show_id but Seq of cast_members. Seq is an ordered iterable collection.

We then call the map method on the dsNetflixTitles dataset to map over each row in the dataset. Each row is transformed into a CastMembers object by returning show_id and using split to turn the CSV string into Seq of strings. Then, flatmap is called to return a dataset of CastMember. We use another map to return each element in Seq of cast members as one CastMember. We also trim the name at this point in the code.

We're now able to use various methods to select and transform our datasets. We'll now learn how to filter and order data.

Filtering and sorting

The ability to reduce the number of records we're working with and sort that data is extremely important for a data engineer. Filtering the records to what we really need is essential to improve the performance of the Spark application. We'll learn how to do that in this section.

Let's use the DataFrames and datasets from the previous examples to explore filtering and sorting.

Here is the code to filter the data:

```
dsCastMembers.filter(r => r.show_id.equals("s2")).show()
```

Here is the filtered data:

```
+--------+--------------------+
|show_id|        cast_member|
+--------+--------------------+
|     s2|        Ama Qamata|
|     s2|        Khosi Ngema|
|     s2|       Gail Mabalane|
|     s2|      Thabang Molaba|
|     s2|    Dillon Windvogel|
|     s2|     Natasha Thahane|
|     s2|         Arno Greeff|
|     s2|  Xolile Tshabalala|
|     s2|     Getmore Sithole|
|     s2|      Cindy Mahlangu|
|     s2|        Ryle De Morny|
|     s2|      Greteli Fincham|
|     s2|Sello Maake Ka-Ncube|
```

```
|      s2|       Odwa Gwanya|
|      s2|    Mekaila Mathys|
|      s2|     Sandi Schultz|
|      s2|    Duane Williams|
|      s2|   Shamilla Miller|
|      s2|   Patrick Mofokeng|
+-------+-------------------+
```

The preceding example filters our cast to just a specific show. We called the `filter` method and defined a value, r, to represent our record. Using r, we can access all the columns of that record and check for the s2 value using equals.

Now, let's look how to filter by a substring, refer to the following code:

```
dsCastMembers.filter(r => r.cast_member.contains("Eric")).show()
```

Here is its output:

```
+-------+-------------------+
|show_id|        cast_member|
+-------+-------------------+
|   s104|          Ken Erics|
|   s128|      Erica Hubbard|
|   s154|    Erica Schroeder|
|   s171|      Erick Sermon|
|   s192|        Eric Lange|
|   s272|        Eric Lange|
|   s280|     Erica Lindbeck|
|   s325|    Erica Schroeder|
|   s353|   Eric Keenleyside|
|   s361|         Eric Dane|
|   s508|       Eric Obinna|
|   s537|        Eric Cheng|
|   s549|         Eric Dane|
|   s585|Eric Christian Olsen|
|   s585|      Eric Jungmann|
|   s595|         Eric Bana|
|   s734|      Erica Mendez|
|   s817|   Eric Keenleyside|
|   s826|         Eric Bana|
|   s849|      Eric Wareheim|
+-------+-------------------+
```

With the preceding filter, we're looking for anyone with `Eric` in their name. Following the same pattern as the previous example, we define `r` as a reference to the records in the dataset and use `contains` to check whether `Eric` exists in the `names` column. `contains` is a case-sensitive function! You could leverage the `lower` or `upper` function with `contains` in the following way to check for any occurrence of `Eric`:

```
lower(r.cast_member).contains("eric")
```

We used dataset filtering in the previous examples, but we can also use the DataFrame API to filter our data in a slightly different way. Here is how:

```
dfCastMembersSelectExpr
  .filter("cast_member like '%Eric%'").show()
dfCastMembersSelectExpr
  .filter($"cast_member".contains("Eric")).show()
```

In the preceding code snippet, both methods return the same results. The first uses a SQL expression while the second uses the `contains` method of the column.

Let's go back to the Dataset API:

```
dsCastMembers
  .filter(r => {
    val id: Int = r.show_id
          .substring(1, r.show_id.length())
          .toInt
    id < 2 || id == 5
  })
  .show()
```

In the preceding example, we're doing a more complex filter. The goal is to return records where `show_id` is less than 2 or `show_id` is equal to 5. There is a slight problem, as `show_id` is a string in the form of `sx`, where `s` is a character and `x` is an integer greater than 0.

We need to do some work to extract the integer from the string so we can perform our filter. We'll work with a Scala anonymous function to do this task. We define `r` as usual, but now we'll also define a code block with the curly brackets { ... }. Within these brackets, we'll create a function to filter our data.

First, we define an `id` value, which will use a substring to parse out the integer value from the `show_id` string. Next, we'll use that value to check for two conditions: the first that `id` is less than 2, and the second that `id` is 5. Either condition can be met to return data. Here are the results:

```
+-------+--------------+
|show_id|   cast_member|
+-------+--------------+
|     s1|              |
```

```
|      s5|      Mayur More|
|      s5|Jitendra Kumar|
|      s5|     Ranjan Raj|
|      s5|       Alam Khan|
|      s5| Ahsaas Channa|
|      s5|Revathi Pillai|
|      s5|       Urvi Singh|
|      s5|      Arun Kumar|
+-------+--------------+
```

We now have a good set of data we can use to generate metrics on cast members. In the next section, we'll learn how to aggregate, group, and join data.

Learning how to aggregate, group, and join data

Another set of basic skills a data engineer needs is the ability to aggregate, group, and join data together. Let's learn how to do this using Scala in Spark!

```
val numDirectorsByShow: DataFrame =
  dfDirectorByShowSelectExpr
    .groupBy($"show_id")
    .agg(
      count($"director").alias("num_director")
    )
numDirectorsByShow.show(10, 0)
```

Here is the output:

```
+-------+------------+
|show_id|num_director|
+-------+------------+
|s1     |1           |
|s2     |1           |
|s3     |1           |
|s4     |1           |
|s5     |1           |
|s6     |1           |
|s7     |2           |
|s8     |1           |
|s9     |1           |
|s10    |1           |
+-------+------------+
```

With the preceding code, we want to identify the number of directors per show. Luckily, we already have a dataset with all of our directors individually in a row by `show_id`. We can use this data to group by `show_id` and use our `count  aggregate` function to count the number of directors per show. Now let's count cast members:

```
val numCastByShow: DataFrame =
  dfCastMembersSelectExpr
    .groupBy($"show_id")
    .agg(
      count($"cast_member").alias("num_cast_member")
    )
numCastByShow.show(10, 0)
```

Here is the output for it:

```
+-------+---------------+
|show_id|num_cast_member|
+-------+---------------+
|s1     |1              |
|s2     |19             |
|s3     |9              |
|s4     |1              |
|s5     |8              |
|s6     |16             |
|s7     |10             |
|s8     |8              |
|s9     |4              |
|s10    |11             |
+-------+---------------+
```

Similarly, we also want to count the cast members per show, so we do so with the preceding code.

Now we have two sets of metrics on our shows, `num_director` and `num_cast_member`, but they are in separate tables. They would be easier to use if we joined them together. So, let's do that now:

```
val dfNetflixTitlesWithNumMetrics: DataFrame = dsNetflixTitles
    .join(numCastByShow, "show_id")
    .join(numDirectorsByShow, "show_id")
```

Our data is now joined and we can perform a few additional calculations:

```
val dfNetflixUSMetrics: DataFrame =
    dfNetflixTitlesWithNumMetrics
      .filter(trim(lower($"country")) === "united states")
```

```
    .groupBy(
      $"rating",
      year($"date_added").alias("year"),
      month($"date_added").alias("month")
    )
    .agg(
      count($"rating")
        .alias("num_shows"),
      avg($"num_director")
        .alias("avg_num_director"),
      avg($"num_cast_member").alias("avg_num_cast_member"),
      max($"num_director").alias("max_num_director"),
      max($"num_cast_member").alias("max_num_cast_member"),
      min($"num_director").alias("min_num_director"),
      min($"num_cast_member").alias("min_num_cast_member")
    )
    .sort($"rating".desc)
  dfNetflixUSMetrics.show(10)
```

In the preceding example, we're first filtering our data to just the United States. Then, we group the data by the show rating and the year and month it was added to Netflix. We're then going to perform a number of aggregations. We want to count the total records and get the average, maximum, and minimum values for the number of directors and cast members per show.

Let's examine the groupBy method. All of the columns specified in the groupBy method will end up in our output dataset. We can also use derived columns in our groupBy key. As stated previously, we're going to use the ratings column, and then use our date_added column with the year and month functions to extract those values from the date.

Next, we're going to aggregate our data. We'll use the count function on the ratings column to count the number of records in the group of records returned by the groupBy key. We also use the avg, max, and min functions to get those values from the same set of records, as shown in the following screenshot:

rating	year	month	num_shows	avg_num_director	avg_num_cast_member	max_num_director	max_num_cast_member	min_num_director	min_num_cast_member
UR	2019	9	1	1.0	10.0	1	10	1	10
TV-Y7-FV	2016	2	1	1.0	8.0	1	8	1	8
TV-Y7	2020	11	1	1.0	12.0	1	12	1	12
TV-Y7	2019	10	2	1.0	12.0	1	17	1	7
TV-Y7	2021	8	1	1.0	6.0	1	6	1	6
TV-Y7	2021	6	1	1.0	8.0	1	8	1	8
TV-Y7	2020	10	3	1.0	8.0	1	9	1	7
TV-Y7	2020	9	2	2.0	6.5	3	8	1	5
TV-Y7	2020	8	3	1.0	9.0	1	10	1	8
TV-Y7	2021	4	1	1.0	10.0	1	10	1	10

Figure 6.1 – Results from our complex group by/aggregation

Aggregation functions such as sum and avg also work with cube and rollUp. These functions are not as frequently used as groupBy, so we did not cover them here. If you are interested, refer to this great post on Stack Overflow: https://stackoverflow.com/questions/37975227/what-is-the-difference-between-cube-rollup-and-groupby-operators.

Spark also has a built-in method called describe that can give us some of these types of metrics:

```
dfNetflixTitlesWithNumMetrics
  .filter(trim(lower($"country")) === "united states")
  .describe("num_cast_member", "num_director")
  .show()
```

Here is the output for it:

```
+-------+------------------+------------------+
|summary|  num_cast_member|      num_director|
+-------+------------------+------------------+
|  count|              2818|              2818|
|   mean| 7.072036905606813|1.1014904187366927|
| stddev| 5.332680221863612|0.5073033316490272|
|    min|                 1|                 1|
|    max|                50|                13|
+-------+------------------+------------------+
```

Before we call describe on the dataset, we'll filter the records down to just the United States and focus on the number of cast members and directors per show. The describe method gives us the count, mean, standard deviation, minimum, and maximum for the columns we choose.

We can also do more advanced analytics using Scala and Spark. In the next section, we'll cover window functions and how to use them.

Leveraging advanced window functions

Window functions are a way to perform calculations on a specific group of records or a sliding subset of records. They can be used to perform cumulative calculations, get values from other records relative to the position of the current record being processed, and perform ranking calculations. They can also use aggregate functions such as count, avg, min, and max. Let's take a look at them now:

```
val windowSpecRatingMonth =
  Window.partitionBy("rating", "month")
        .orderBy("year", "month")
```

Windows are created by defining a window specification. In the preceding example, we defined a window called `windowSpecRatingMonth` by partitioning our records by rating and month and ordering the records in the partition by year and month:

```
val dfWindowedLagLead = dfNetflixUSMetrics
  .withColumn(
    "cast_per_director",
    $"avg_num_cast_member"/$"avg_num_director")
  .withColumn(
    "previous_avg_cast_member",
    lag("avg_num_cast_member", 1)
      .over(windowSpecRatingMonth))
  .withColumn(
    "next_avg_cast_member",
    lead("avg_num_cast_member", 1)
      .over(windowSpecRatingMonth))
  .withColumn(
    "diff_prev_curr_num_cast",
    abs($"avg_num_cast_member" -
        $"previous_avg_cast_member"))
  .drop("max_num_director",
        "min_num_director",
        "avg_num_director")
```

To use the window, we can incorporate it with window functions when creating a derived column using the `withColumn` method on a DataFrame.

In the preceding code, we're using our `dfNetflixUSMetrics` DataFrame from the previous section. We'll create a new column using `withColumn` called `cast_per_director` by dividing the average number of cast members and directors.

Next, we'll use our `window` function with two new columns. The first column using the `window` function will get the previous average number of cast members relative to the current row being processed. We do this using the `lag` function, passing through two parameters, the column we're interested in and 1, which tells the `lag` function to get the value from the previous record. The second function we'll use is the `lead` function. This is similar to our `lag` function, but in this case, it gets the column value we want from the next record. You can see the pattern in the following result set:

```
+------+----+-----+---------------+---------------+-----------+
|rating|year|month|           prev|           curr|       next|
+------+----+-----+---------------+---------------+-----------+
|    PG|2017|    4|           null|            6.0|       13.0|
|    PG|2018|    4|            6.0|           13.0|8.3333333334|
|    PG|2019|    4|           13.0|8.33333333334|      10.75|
```

```
|      PG|2020|      4|8.33333333334|            10.75|             9.0|
|      PG|2021|      4|         10.75|              9.0|           null|
+------+----+-----+-------------+-----------------+------------+
```

Now, let's take a look at how ranking works with windows. We'll define a new window specification and add a new column to our dataset, as follows:

```
val windowSpecRating =
  Window.partitionBy("rating", "year")
        .orderBy($"avg_num_cast_member".desc)
val dfWindowedRank = dfNetflixUSMetrics
  .withColumn("dense_rank", dense_rank()
        .over(windowSpecRating))
```

In our new window, we're partitioning by rating and year and ordering by the average number of cast members. Then, we add a new column to our dataset using `withColumn`, called `dense_rank`. We define this column using the `dense_rank` function and run the ranking over our window specification. The `dense_rank` function doesn't leave any gaps in the ranking. That means in the case where there is a tie for a rank, the next record(s) after the tie would be the next value.

Take a look at the results of our operation:

```
+------+----+-------------------+----------+
|rating|year|avg_num_cast_member|dense_rank|
+------+----+-------------------+----------+
|PG    |2012|2.0                |1         |
|PG    |2013|10.0               |1         |
|PG    |2014|8.0                |1         |
|PG    |2014|5.0                |2         |
|PG    |2015|10.0               |1         |
|PG    |2016|11.0               |1         |
|PG    |2017|10.5               |1         |
|PG    |2017|10.0               |2         |
|PG    |2017|8.0                |3         |
|PG    |2017|8.0                |3         |
|PG    |2017|6.0                |4         |
|PG    |2018|15.0               |1         |
|PG    |2018|13.0               |2         |
|PG    |2018|12.0               |3         |
|PG    |2018|10.5               |4         |
|PG    |2018|10.5               |4         |
|PG    |2018|9.0                |5         |
|PG    |2018|9.0                |5         |
|PG    |2018|8.5                |6         |
```

```
|PG      |2018|6.0                      |7       |
+------+----+--------------------+---------+
```

There are many different types of window functions. Please refer to the following Spark documentation to read more about windows and their functions:

- `https://spark.apache.org/docs/latest/api/python/reference/pyspark.sql/window.html`

- `https://spark.apache.org/docs/latest/api/python/reference/pyspark.sql/functions.html#window-functions`

In the next section, we will learn how to handle complex data types.

Working with complex dataset types

In the real world, we very often have to deal with data that doesn't fit into a standard table format with one value per column in each record. We did see a little of that previously with our `netflix titles` CSV file in our **cast** and **director** columns, but what happens when we run into more complex structures?

In this section, we'll show you how to manage nested data in semi-structured data, such as XML and JSON. Consider the following code:

```scala
val dfDevicesJson = spark.read.json(
"src/main/scala/com/packt/dewithscala/chapter6/data/devices.json")

dfDevicesJson.printSchema()

root
 |-- country: string (nullable = true)
 |-- device_id: string (nullable = true)
 |-- event_ts: timestamp (nullable = true)
 |-- event_type: string (nullable = true)
 |-- id: long (nullable = true)
 |-- line: string (nullable = true)
 |-- manufacturer: string (nullable = true)
 |-- observations: array (nullable = true)
 |    |-- element: double (containsNull = true)
```

Here is the output:

```
+--------------------+
|        observations|
+--------------------+
```

```
|                 [8.3]|
|            [9.9, 6.5]|
|       [4.9, 6.5, 9.0]|
|       [4.2, 8.8, 3.2]|
|                 [5.7]|
| [6.4, 5.2, 5.5, 4.1]|
|                 [3.2]|
|            [7.5, 6.1]|
| [8.0, 9.9, 3.4, 8...|
| [5.1, 1.3, 7.7, 6...|
+--------------------+
```

We've read in some JSON data, which includes a column with an array of values. Specifically, column observations is an *Array of Doubles*. In its current form, it is not very usable, but we can split the nested values into rows and then perform aggregation, as the following code shows.

```
dfDevicesJson
  .select($"id", explode($"observations")
                    .alias("observation"))
  .groupBy("id")
  .agg(
    max($"observation").alias("max_obs"),
    min($"observation").alias("min_obs"),
    avg($"observation").alias("avg_obs"))
```

In the preceding example, we take our observations data and explode it into individual records per element in the array with the ID of the parent record. We can now do a group by and aggregate to collect some metrics on that data.

This is our end result:

```
+---+-------+-------+------------------+
| id|max_obs|min_obs|           avg_obs|
+---+-------+-------+------------------+
|  0|    8.3|    8.3|               8.3|
|  1|    9.9|    6.5|               8.2|
|  2|    9.0|    4.9|               6.8|
|  3|    8.8|    3.2|5.399999999999995|
|  4|    5.7|    5.7|               5.7|
|  5|    6.4|    4.1| 5.300000000000001|
|  6|    3.2|    3.2|               3.2|
|  7|    7.5|    6.1|               6.8|
|  8|   10.0|    3.4| 7.95999999999999|
|  9|    9.2|    1.3|              5.88|
+---+-------+-------+------------------+
```

Now, let's take a look at how we would manage embedded XML data in our JSON file:

```
val dfDevicesXMLInJson = spark.read.json( "src/main/scala/com/packt/
dewithscala/chapter6/data/devicesWithXML.json")


dfDevicesXMLInJson.printSchema()
```

Here is the output:

```
root
 |-- country: string (nullable = true)
 |-- device_id: string (nullable = true)
 |-- event_ts: string (nullable = true)
 |-- event_type: string (nullable = true)
 |-- id: long (nullable = true)
 |-- line: string (nullable = true)
 |-- manufacturer: string (nullable = true)
 |-- observations: array (nullable = true)
 |    |-- element: double (containsNull = true)
 |-- xmlObservations: string (nullable = true)
```

We now have a new column called xmlObservations in our data of the string type. This is an XML representation of the observations column, which we now need to parse to produce the same results as our previous code. It's not as easy as it seems, though.

Here is an example of data in the xmlObservations column:

```
|<observations>
  <observation>8.3</observation>
 </observations>
|<observations>
  <observation>9.9</observation>
  <observation>6.5</observation>
 </observations>
```

We'll have to include a library called spark-xml from Databricks:

```
import com.databricks.spark.xml.functions.from_xml
import com.databricks.spark.xml.schema_of_xml
```

These two imports will allow us to use two functions.

As we can see in the following code, the `from_xml` function will parse the XML in the column, and `schema_of_xml` will read the XML value and generate a schema that Spark can use to read the data:

```
val dfXmlFun = dfDevicesXMLInJson
    .withColumn("parsed",from_xml($"xmlObservations",
                 schema_of_xml(dfDevicesXMLInJson
                   .select("xmlObservations").as[String])))


dfXmlFun.printSchema()
```

Here is the output:

```
root
 |-- country: string (nullable = true)
 |-- device_id: string (nullable = true)
 |-- event_ts: string (nullable = true)
 |-- event_type: string (nullable = true)
 |-- id: long (nullable = true)
 |-- line: string (nullable = true)
 |-- manufacturer: string (nullable = true)
 |-- observations: array (nullable = true)
 |    |-- element: double (containsNull = true)
 |-- xmlObservations: string (nullable = true)
 |-- parsed: struct (nullable = true)
 |    |-- observation: array (nullable = true)
 |    |    |-- element: double (containsNull = true)
```

In the preceding code, we use those two functions together with a `withColumn` method to add a new column with the parsed XML. The parsed column is typed as a struct of arrays. We now need to explode out the elements of the array from inside the struct, as the following code shows:

```
dfXmlFun
  .select($"id", explode($"parsed.observation")
                     .alias("observation"))
  .groupBy("id")
  .agg(
    max($"observation").alias("max_obs"),
    min($"observation").alias("min_obs"),
    avg($"observation").alias("avg_obs")
  ).show(10)
```

Here is the output:

```
+---+-------+-------+-------------------+
| id|max_obs|min_obs|            avg_obs|
+---+-------+-------+-------------------+
|  0|    8.3|    8.3|                8.3|
|  1|    9.9|    6.5|                8.2|
|  2|    9.0|    4.9|                6.8|
|  3|    8.8|    3.2|  5.3999999999999995|
|  4|    5.7|    5.7|                5.7|
|  5|    6.4|    4.1|   5.300000000000001|
|  6|    3.2|    3.2|                3.2|
|  7|    7.5|    6.1|                6.8|
|  8|   10.0|    3.4|   7.959999999999999|
|  9|    9.2|    1.3|               5.88|
+---+-------+-------+-------------------+
```

The preceding code is the same as the code that exploded the observations from the JSON file, except for this line:

```
.select($"id", explode($"parsed.observation")
```

When we define the column to be used in the explode action, we have to access the nested array in the struct by using `parsed.observation`.

With this, we conclude the section, where we learned about complex types and saw several examples of how to work with them.

Summary

In this chapter, we learned how to transform our data using Scala with Spark. You now understand the difference between transformations and actions. You've learned how to use `select`, `selectExpr`, `filter`, `join`, and `sort` to reduce data to just what you need for your transformation. You've worked with various types of complex data and generated aggregations using group by and windows. We've covered a lot, and now you'll be able to take what you've learned and apply it to a real-world scenario.

In the next chapter, we are going to cover how to work with various sources and sinks for object data, streaming data, and so on.

Data Profiling and Data Quality

As we work with multiple sources of data, it is quite easy for some bad data to pass through if there are no checks in place. This can lead to serious issues in downstream systems that rely on the accuracy of upstream data to build models, run business-critical applications, and so on. To make our data pipelines resilient, it is imperative that we have data quality checks in place to ensure the data being processed meets the requirements imposed by both business as well as downstream applications.

Six primary data quality dimensions can be measured individually and used to improve the data quality:

- **Completeness**: Does your customer dataset that you plan to use for an upcoming marketing campaign have all of the required attributes filled in?

- **Accuracy**: Are the email addresses and phone numbers accurate for your customer records?

- **Consistency**: Is customer data consistent across systems?

- **Validity**: Do your customer records have valid zip codes?

- **Uniqueness**: Do you have multiple records for the same customer in your dataset?

- **Integrity**: Can your customer data be traced and connected across your organization?

In this chapter, we are going to look at the Deequ library (`https://github.com/awslabs/deequ`), which makes it quite easy to define data quality checks, perform analysis, suggest constraints based on the data, store metrics for future reference, and so on. It is an open source library originally developed by Amazon to address various data quality needs.

In this chapter, we are going to cover the following topics:

- Understanding components of Deequ

- Performing data analysis

- Leveraging automatic constraint suggestion

- Defining constraints
- Storing metrics using `MetricsRepository`
- Detecting anomalies

Technical requirements

If you have not done so already, we recommend you follow the steps covered in *Chapter 2* to install VS Code or IntelliJ along with the required plugins to run Scala programs. You also need to add the following dependency to work with Deequ:

```
libraryDependencies +=
"com.amazon.deequ" %
"deequ" % "2.0.4-spark-3.3"
```

Though you can use data of your choice as you follow along, we will be using the tables we loaded into the MySQL database covered in *Chapter 4*. If you have not done so already, you may want to review the steps covered there.

Understanding components of Deequ

Deequ provides a lot of features to make data quality checks easy. The following diagram shows the major components:

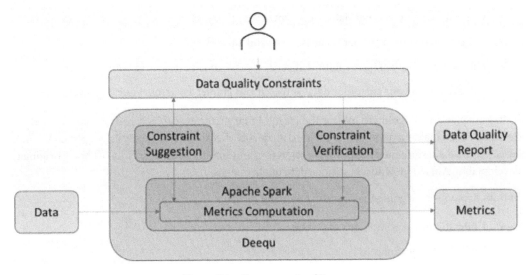

Figure 7.1 – Components of Deequ

We can observe the following components:

- **Metrics computation**: Deequ calculates metrics for data quality, such as completeness, maximum, and so on. You can directly access the raw metrics computed on the data.

- **Constraint verification**: By defining a set of data quality constraints, Deequ automatically derives the necessary metrics to be computed on the data, ensuring constraint validation.

- **Constraint suggestion**: You have the option to utilize Deequ's automated constraint suggestion methods to infer valuable constraints or define your own customized data quality constraints.

In the background, Deequ uses Apache Spark for metrics computation, and thus it is fast and efficient. In the upcoming sections, we are going to cover these features.

Performing data analysis

Deequ offers capabilities to generate statistics called metrics on data. For example, we can use Deequ to provide us with the number of records in a dataset, tell us whether a particular column is unique, give us the degree of correlation between columns, and so on. Deequ offers this functionality with case classes such as `ApproxCountDistinct`, `Completeness`, `Correlation`, and so on, defined in the `com.amazon.deequ.analyzers` package. For a complete list of metrics along with their definitions, please refer to `https://aws.amazon.com/blogs/big-data/test-data-quality-at-scale-with-deequ/`.

In the following example, we will be using the flight data that we loaded into a MySQL table named `flights`. We analyze the `flights` data to check the count of records, whether the `airline` column contains any `NULL` value, an approximate distinct count of `origin_airport`, and so on. The result set is then converted into a dataframe and finally printed on the screen:

package com.packt.dewithscala.chapter7

```
package com.packt.dewithscala.chapter7

import com.packt.dewithscala.utils._

import com.amazon.deequ.analyzers.runners._
import com.amazon.deequ.analyzers.runners.AnalyzerContext.
successMetricsAsDataFrame
import com.amazon.deequ.analyzers._

import org.apache.spark.sql._
import org.apache.spark.sql.functions._

object DataAnalysis extends App {
```

```scala
  val session: SparkSession = Spark.initSparkSession("de-with-scala")

  val db: Database = Database("my_db")

  val df: DataFrame = db
    .multiPartitionRead(
      session = session,
      dbTable = "my_db.flights",
      partitionCol = "day_of_week",
      upperBound = "7",
      lowerBound = "1",
      7
    )
    .filter(col("airline") === lit("US"))

  val analysisResult: AnalyzerContext = AnalysisRunner
    .onData(df)
    .addAnalyzer(Size())
    .addAnalyzer(Completeness("airline"))
    .addAnalyzer(ApproxCountDistinct("origin_airport"))
    .addAnalyzer(Correlation("departure_delay", "arrival_delay"))
    .addAnalyzer(Compliance("no arrival delay", "arrival_delay <= 0"))
    .run()

  successMetricsAsDataFrame(session, analysisResult).show(false)

}
```

Example 7.1

Here is the output:

entity	instance	name	value
Column	no arrival delay	Compliance	0.6161084970938279
Mutlicolumn	departure_delay,arrival_delay	Correlation	0.8913439368652909
Column	origin_airport	ApproxCountDistinct	74.0
Dataset	*	Size	198715.0
Column	airline	Completeness	1.0

Figure 7.2 – Analysis result

From the previous output, we can understand the following:

- The dataframe has 198715 records

- The airline column does not have any NULL value (Completeness is 1.0)

- The correlation between departure_delay and arrival_delay is 89%

- 61.6% of the flights were on time or ahead of time

- There are approximately 74 distinct values for the origin_airport column

As you can see, getting to these metrics was quite simple. And there are quite a few analyzers that Deequ offers besides what we just looked at.

In this section, we looked at how we can leverage Deequ to run analysis on our data. In the next section, we are going to look at how Deequ can automatically suggest constraints that we can then use to define checks for what we expect the dataset to hold.

Leveraging automatic constraint suggestion

Deequ provides a powerful feature where it can analyze the data and suggest constraints that can be applied as checks. To see how it works, we will be using the flights data once again. In *Chapter 4*, we defined an interface to work with databases that we are going to use to create a dataframe. We will then pass the dataframe into ConstraintSuggestionRunner in order for Deequ to suggest constraints.

Here is the complete code for it:

```
package com.packt.dewithscala.chapter7

import com.packt.dewithscala.utils._

import com.amazon.deequ.suggestions.ConstraintSuggestionResult
import com.amazon.deequ.suggestions.ConstraintSuggestionRunner
import com.amazon.deequ.suggestions.Rules

import org.apache.spark.sql.functions._
import org.apache.spark.sql.SparkSession
import org.apache.spark.sql.DataFrame

object ConstraintSuggestion extends App {

  val session: SparkSession = Spark.initSparkSession("de-with-scala")

  val db: Database = Database("my_db")
```

```
val df: DataFrame = db
  .multiPartitionRead(
    session = session,
    dbTable = "my_db.flights",
    partitionCol = "day_of_week",
    upperBound = "7",
    lowerBound = "1",
    7
  )
  .filter(col("airline") === lit("US"))

// constraint suggestions
val suggestionsResult: ConstraintSuggestionResult =
  ConstraintSuggestionRunner()
    .onData(df)
    .addConstraintRules(Rules.DEFAULT)
    .run

suggestionsResult.constraintSuggestions.foreach {
  case (column, suggestions) =>
    suggestions.foreach { suggestion =>
      println(
        s"Constraint suggestion for '$column':\t${suggestion.
description}\n" +
          s"The corresponding scala code is ${suggestion.
codeForConstraint}"
      )
    }
}

}
```

Example 7.2

The following snippet shows the truncated output:

```
[info] Constraint suggestion for 'wheels_on':    'wheels_on' is not
null
[info] The corresponding scala code is .isComplete("wheels_on")
[info] Constraint suggestion for 'departure_delay':
'departure_delay' is not null
[info] The corresponding scala code is .isComplete("departure_delay")
[info] Constraint suggestion for 'origin_airport':    'origin_airport'
is not null
```

```
[info] The corresponding scala code is .isComplete("origin_airport")
[info] Constraint suggestion for 'origin_airport':    'origin_airport'
has value range 'CLT', 'PHX', 'PHL', 'DCA', 'BOS', 'LGA', 'MCO',
'LAX', 'TPA', 'ORD', 'FLL', 'DFW', 'LAS', 'ATL', 'SFO', 'IAH', 'PIT',
'DEN', 'MSP', 'EWR', 'BWI', 'PBI', 'RSW', 'MIA', 'RDU', 'SAN', 'SEA',
'DTW', 'JFK', 'JAX', 'SLC', 'MCI' for at least 89.0% of values
[info] The corresponding scala code is .isContainedIn("origin_
airport", Array("CLT", "PHX", "PHL", "DCA", "BOS", "LGA", "MCO",
"LAX", "TPA", "ORD", "FLL", "DFW", "LAS", "ATL", "SFO", "IAH", "PIT",
"DEN", "MSP", "EWR", "BWI", "PBI", "RSW", "MIA", "RDU", "SAN", "SEA",
"DTW", "JFK", "JAX", "SLC", "MCI"), _ >= 0.89, Some("It should be
above 0.89!")) [info] Constraint suggestion for 'day_of_week': 'day_
of_week' is not null
[info] The corresponding scala code is .isComplete("day_of_week")
[info] Constraint suggestion for 'day_of_week': 'day_of_week' has
value range '5', '4', '1', '2', '3', '7', '6'
[info] The corresponding scala code is .isContainedIn("day_of_week",
Array("5", "4", "1", "2", "3", "7", "6"))
[info] Constraint suggestion for 'day_of_week': 'day_of_week' has no
negative values
[info] The corresponding scala code is .isNonNegative("day_of_week")
```

The preceding snippet contains details of the constraints suggested by Deequ along with the corresponding code to be used to define it.

- The `wheels_on` column does not have any null value. So, you may want to define a not-null check on that column, using is `Complete("wheels_on")` which Deequ helpfully printed to the console

- For 89% of the records, `origin_airport` has one of the listed values

- The `day_of_week` column has to have a value between 1 and 7, and so on

In this section, we looked at how Deequ can suggest constraints. In the next section, we will see how we can use those to define actual checks to be run on the dataset.

Defining constraints

In the previous section, we looked at examples of how Deequ can automatically suggest constraints as well as how we can gather various metrics around data. We will now define the actual constraints that we expect the dataframe to pass. In the following code, we define the following constraints that we expect the `flights` data to pass:

- The `airline` column should not contain any NULL values

- The `flight_number` column should not contain any NULL values

- The `cancelled` column should contain only 0 or 1

- The distance column should not contain any negative value

- The cancellation_reason column should contain only A, B, C, or D

If all of the checks pass, then we print data looks good on the console; else, we print the constraint along with the result status.

Here is the code for it.

As a first step, we will create a dataframe using the flights table we loaded in MySQL:

```
val session = Spark.initSparkSession("de-with-scala")
val db      = Database("my_db")
val df = db
.multiPartitionRead(
  session = session,
  dbTable = "my_db.flights",
  partitionCol = "day_of_week",
  upperBound = "7",
  lowerBound = "1",
  7
)
.filter(col("airline") === lit("US"))
```

Example 7.3

With the dataframe now defined, we can define the constraints that we want our dataframe to hold:

```
val verificationResult = VerificationSuite()
.onData(df)
.addCheck(
  Check(CheckLevel.Error, "checks on flights data")
    .isComplete("airline")
    .isComplete("flight_number")
    .isContainedIn("cancelled", Array("0", "1"))
    .isNonNegative("distance")          .isContainedIn("cancellation_
reason", Array("A", "B", "C", "D"))  )
  .run()
```

Example 7.4

Finally, we can print the results:

```
verificationResult.status match {
case CheckStatus.Success => println("data looks good")
case _ =>
  val constraintResults = verificationResult.checkResults.flatMap
```

```
{        case (_, checkResult) => checkResult.constraintResults
  }
  constraintResults
    .filter(_.status != ConstraintStatus.Success)
    .foreach { checkResult =>
      println(
        s"for ${checkResult.constraint} the check result was
${checkResult.status}"
      )
      println(checkResult.message.getOrElse(""))
    }
}
```

Example 7.5

Running this code prints the following to the console:

```
[info] for ComplianceConstraint(Compliance(cancellation_reason
contained in A,B,C,D,`cancellation_reason` IS NULL OR `cancellation_
reason` IN ('A','B','C','D'),None)) the check result was Failure
[info] Value: 0.020466497244797825 does not meet the constraint
requirement!
```

The reason for this failure is that `cancellation_reason` contains blanks as well. In fact the message, `Value: 0.020466497244797825` does not meet the constraint requirement and shows that only 2% of the records pass the check.

In this section, we looked at how we can define constraints that we expect our dataset to hold. In the next section, we will look at mechanisms to actually store the metrics collected by Deequ.

Storing metrics using MetricsRepository

Deequ allows us to store the metrics we calculate on a dataframe using `MetricsRepository`. Deequ provides facilities to create both in-memory and file-based repositories. File-based repositories support local filesystems, **Simple Storage Service (S3)**, and **Hadoop Distributed File System (HDFS)**. Persisting data quality metrics allow us to run analysis to see trends and spot any volatility in the data.

Creating an in-memory repository is simple, as the next example shows:

```
val inMemoryRepo = new InMemoryMetricsRepository()
```

Example 7.6

Similarly, we can create a file-based repository as follows:

```
val fileRepo = FileSystemMetricsRepository(sparkSession, filePath)
```

Example 7.7

The metrics for each run are stored using a key of type `ResultKey`. `ResultKey` is defined as a case class with the following signature:

```
case class ResultKey(dataSetDate: Long, tags: Map[String, String] =
Map.empty)
```

Example 7.8

Here is an example key of type `ResultKey` that we will use in our example:

```
val key = ResultKey(System.currentTimeMillis(), Map("tag" ->
"metricsRepository"))
```

Example 7.9

For our example, we will use the `flights` data that we have used in earlier sections. We will define the constraints that we want the data to hold and store the corresponding metrics in a repository that we will query.

There are a few ways to query the results stored in the metrics repository, as the following example illustrates. As earlier, we will start with defining the dataframe:

```
val session = Spark.initSparkSession("de-with-scala")
val db        = Database("my_db")
val df = db
.multiPartitionRead(
  session = session,
  dbTable = "my_db.flights",
  partitionCol = "day_of_week",
  upperBound = "7",
  lowerBound = "1",
  7
)
.filter(col("airline") === lit("US"))
```

Example 7.10

We will then define a metrics repository using a temporary file:

```
val session: SparkSession = Spark.initSparkSession("de-with-scala")

val db: Database = Database("my_db")

val df: DataFrame = db
  .multiPartitionRead(
```

```
    session = session,
    dbTable = "my_db.flights",
    partitionCol = "day_of_week",
    upperBound = "7",
    lowerBound = "1",
    7
)
.filter(col("airline") === lit("US"))
```

Example 7.11

In the next step, we will create a `VerificationResult` class using `MetricsRepository`:

```
val verificationResult = VerificationSuite()
.onData(df)
.addCheck(
  Check(CheckLevel.Error, "checks on flights data")
    .isComplete("airline")
    .isComplete("flight_number")
    .isContainedIn("cancelled", Array("0", "1"))
    .isNonNegative("distance")        .isContainedIn("cancellation_
reason", Array("A", "B", "C", "D"))
    )
.useRepository(fileRepo)
.saveOrAppendResult(key)
.run()
```

Example 7.12

Finally, we can query the metrics repository and see the results:

```
// get all of the metrics since last 100 secs
val metricsAsDF = fileRepo
.load()
.after(System.currentTimeMillis() - 100000)
.getSuccessMetricsAsDataFrame(session)

metricsAsDF.show()
// get metrics by the resultKey
val metricsAsMap = fileRepo
.loadByKey(key)
.get
.metricMap
metricsAsMap.foreach { case (a, b) =>
println(s"For '${b.instance}' ${b.name} is ${b.value.get}")
```

```
}

// get metrics by tag
val metricsJSON =
fileRepo
  .load()
  .withTagValues(Map("tag" -> "metricsRepository"))
  .getSuccessMetricsAsJson()
println(metricsJSON)
```

Example 7.13

`metricsAsDF.show()` will print the metrics in a tabular format:

```
+------+-----------------+------------+-------------------+-------------+-----------------+
|entity|         instance|        name|              value| dataset_date|              tag|
+------+-----------------+------------+-------------------+-------------+-----------------+
|Column|distance is non-n...|  Compliance|                1.0|1683725262618|metricsRepository|
|Column|    flight_number|Completeness|                1.0|1683725262618|metricsRepository|
|Column|cancelled contain...|  Compliance|                1.0|1683725262618|metricsRepository|
|Column|cancellation reas...|  Compliance|0.020466497244797825|1683725262618|metricsRepository|
|Column|          airline|Completeness|                1.0|1683725262618|metricsRepository|
+------+-----------------+------------+-------------------+-------------+-----------------+
```

Figure 7.3 – Metrics as a dataframe

`metricsAsMap.foreach` will print the metrics:

```
For 'distance is non-negative' Compliance is 1.0
For 'flight_number' Completeness is 1.0
For 'cancelled contained in 0,1' Compliance is 1.0
For 'cancellation_reason contained in A,B,C,D' Compliance is 0.020466497244797825
For 'airline' Completeness is 1.0
```

Figure 7.4 – Printing metrics using foreach

`println(metricsJSON)` will print out the metrics as JSON:

```
[{"name":"Compliance","tag":"metricsRepository","dataset_
date":1683725262618,"instance":"distance is non-negative","enti-
ty":"Column","value":1.0},{"name":"Completeness","tag":"metricsRepos-
itory","dataset_date":1683725262618,"instance":"flight_number","en-
tity":"Column","value":1.0},{"name":"Compliance","tag":"metricsRepos-
itory","dataset_date":1683725262618,"instance":"cancelled contained
in 0,1","entity":"Column","value":1.0},{"name":"Compliance","tag":"-
metricsRepository","dataset_date":1683725262618,"instance":"can-
cellation_reason contained in A,B,C,D","entity":"Column","value":
0.020466497244797825},{"name":"Completeness","tag":"metricsRepos-
itory","dataset_date":1683725262618,"instance":"airline","enti-
ty":"Column","value":1.0}]
```

In this section, we looked at how we can use `MetricsRepository` to store various metrics collected by Deequ. In the next section, we will look at how these stored metrics are then used to detect anomalies in our data.

Detecting anomalies

Deequ supports anomaly detection in data by using metrics stored in `MetricsRepository`, which we covered in the previous section. For example, we can create a rule to check whether the number of records has increased by 50% compared to the previous run. If it has, then the check will fail.

To show you how it works, we will use a fictitious scenario where we receive a batch of products to be added to the inventory each day. We want to check whether the number of products we receive on any given day has increased by 50% compared to the last run. For this example, we will use an in-memory repository to store the metrics. As we have done earlier, let's define the dataframes we will use in this example:

```scala
val session = Spark.initSparkSession("de-with-scala")
import session.implicits._
val yesterdayDF = Seq((1, "Product 1", 100), (2, "Product 2", 50)).
toDF(
  "product_id",
  "product_name",
  "cost_per_unit"
)
 val todayDF = Seq(
(3, "Product 3", 70),
(4, "Product 4", 120),
(5, "Product 5", 65),
(6, "Product 6", 40)
).toDF("product_id", "product_name", "cost_per_unit")
```

Example 7.14

We will then define an in-memory metrics repository and two result keys:

```scala
val repository = new InMemoryMetricsRepository()
val yesterdayKey = ResultKey(
System.currentTimeMillis() - 24 * 60 * 60 * 1000,
Map("tag" -> "yesterday")
)
val todayKey = ResultKey(
System.currentTimeMillis(),
Map("tag" -> "now")
)
```

Example 7.15

We then run anomaly checks, first on yesterday's data using the in-memory repository to store metrics collected by Deequ:

```
VerificationSuite()
.onData(yesterdayDF)
.useRepository(repository)
.saveOrAppendResult(yesterdayKey)
.addAnomalyCheck(
  RelativeRateOfChangeStrategy(maxRateIncrease = Some(1.5)),
  Size()
)
.run()
```

Example 7.16

Finally, we define a check using the same metrics repository and then print the results:

```
val verificationResult = VerificationSuite()
.onData(todayDF)
.useRepository(repository)
.saveOrAppendResult(todayKey)
.addAnomalyCheck(
  RelativeRateOfChangeStrategy(maxRateIncrease = Some(1.5)),
  Size()
)
.run()
verificationResult.status match {
case CheckStatus.Success => println("data looks good")
case _ =>
  val constraintResults = verificationResult.checkResults.flatMap {
    case (_, checkResult) => checkResult.constraintResults
  }
  constraintResults
    .filter(_.status != ConstraintStatus.Success)
    .foreach { checkResult =>
      println(
        s"for ${checkResult.constraint} the check result was
${checkResult.status}"
      )
      println(checkResult.message.getOrElse(""))
    }
}
```

Example 7.17

Once run, it will print the following output to your terminal:

```
[info] for AnomalyConstraint(Size(None)) the check result was Failure
[info] Value: 4.0 does not meet the constraint requirement!
```

In this section, we looked at anomaly detection offered by Deequ. It uses metrics stored in `MetricsRepository` from previous runs to compare with the current run and check any anomalies in the data. Even though we just looked at `RelativeRateOfChangeStrategy`, there are various other options such as `SimpleThresholdStrategy`, `AbsoluteChangeStrategy`, and so on to support various use cases.

Summary

We began this chapter by outlining why it is imperative to have data quality checks in place for any data pipeline. We then introduced the Deequ library developed by Amazon and its various components. Deequ uses Spark at its core, thereby leveraging the distributed processing that comes with it. We then took a deep dive into the various functionalities offered by Deequ, such as the automatic suggestion of constraints, defining constraints, metrics repositories, and so on.

In the next chapter, we are going to look at code health and maintainability, along with **test-driven development** (**TDD**), which is vital for a scalable and easily maintainable code base.

Part 3 – Software Engineering Best Practices for Data Engineering in Scala

In this part, *Chapter 8* focuses on software development best practices in data engineering, emphasizing TDD, unit and integration tests, code coverage, static analysis, and code style importance for consistency and security. *Chapter 9* introduces CI/CD concepts in Scala projects via GitHub, automating testing and deployment for rapid iteration and enhanced quality control.

This part has the following chapters:

- *Chapter 8, Test-Driven Development, Code Health, and Maintainability*
- *Chapter 9, CI/CD with GitHub*

8

Test-Driven Development, Code Health, and Maintainability

In this chapter, we are going to look at some software development best practices and learn how to apply them to data engineering. The topics covered in the chapter will go a long way to helping you identify defects early, write code in a consistent way, and address potential security vulnerabilities as part of development. For example, **test-driven development** (**TDD**) requires building test cases first before we write the actual application code. Since we start with test cases, this helps to write the application code in a way that can be easily used to run the test cases. Another example is code formatting. Each of us has our own ways of writing programs and having consistency among application code written by different developers helps to reduce the time that it would otherwise take to adapt to a particular coding style.

Since a single chapter cannot cover such a vast topic in detail, we are going to provide a high-level overview of some of the techniques and tools. Specifically, we are going to focus on the following topics:

- Introducing TDD
- Running static code analysis
- Understanding linting and code style

Technical requirements

You need to have Scala installed locally and should be able to update the build. You also need to have Docker installed on your machine. If you have not done so already, please refer to *Chapter 2* for detailed steps.

Introducing TDD

TDD is a topic that is broad and deserves its own book. However, we will cover the basics so that you can apply TDD to your Scala data engineering projects.

One essential aspect of TDD in data engineering is testing the data transformations and manipulations within the pipelines you create. This involves creating unit tests that verify the correctness and accuracy of data transformations, aggregations, filters, and other data manipulation operations. Unit tests also ensure the code you create or change doesn't break any existing processes that were previously created by you or anyone else on your team.

To accomplish this, it is important to develop code that is easily testable. You can do this by creating functions that perform one action and then composing multiple functions together to build your applications. Doing so will help to maintain code health and maintainability because you have small functions that make refactoring those functions easy.

Integration tests also play a crucial role in TDD for data engineering, as they focus on verifying the interactions and behavior of different components within a data pipeline. Integration tests are designed to validate the seamless integration and collaboration between various modules, services, or systems involved in data processing.

A typical Scala project will separate the Scala application and test code. Our book's GitHub repository is a good example to follow. Refer to the following figure:

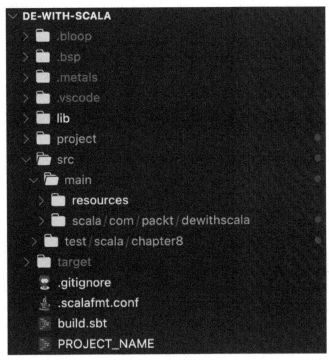

Figure 8.1 – Typical Scala project with a test directory

Now, let's take a closer look at unit tests in Scala.

Creating unit tests

Unit testing is an important part of TDD, as mentioned in the earlier section.

Let's use math to illustrate this concept. Suppose you want to write an application to add and multiply integers together. There are an infinite number of ways to do this, but we'll focus on small functions and compositions to make this happen.

We want to write a program to evaluate the following expression:

```
f(x) = 2(3+4x)
```

To do this, we'll create two functions, one to add two integers together, and another one to multiply two integers together. We will call them `add` and `multiply`, and both will accept two integer parameters. We'll then have another function that will compose the `add` and `multiply` functions to calculate our expression.

Before we even start writing code, we need to think about how we are going to test our functions. Unit tests will have to be written for each function that we create and will be used in our CI/CD and local testing processes to make sure that our new code doesn't break existing code in our application.

For our `add` and `multiply` functions, we need to write unit tests to make sure they are working properly. It's important to write these tests first, and then create functions that will be tested. This ensures that you identify all cases and write code to test for those cases and that your function will also handle those cases.

We'll use the ScalaTest testing framework to write our unit test, which will check that our `add` and `multiply` functions handle the following cases:

- Add 1 and 2 and check that the result is 3
- Add 2 and 0 and check that the result is 2
- Add -1 and -2 and check that the result is -3
- Multiply 1 and 2 and check that the result is 2
- Multiply 2 and 0 and check that the result is 0
- Multiply -1 and -2 and check that the result is 2
- `f(3)` results in 30

Here is how we do it:

1. We will be using ScalaTest for unit testing and need to add the required dependencies to Dependencies.scala as shown here:

```
libraryDependencies += "org.scalactic" %% "scalactic" % "3.2.16"
libraryDependencies += "org.scalatest" %% "scalatest" % "3.2.16"
% "test"
```

2. The tests will be written in a Scala class in the src/test/scala/chapter8 folder in the book's Git repository. We'll create a file called IntroToTDDTest.scala, which will initially contain the following code:

```
package com.packt.dewithscala.chapter8
import org.scalatest.funsuite.AnyFunSuite
class IntroToTDDTest extends AnyFunSuite {
}
```

3. We'll specify the package and import the AnyFunSuite class, which contains the test method we'll use in our unit tests.

4. Then we'll define the IntroToTDDTest class, which will extend AnyFunSuite so that we can use the methods in the AnyFunSuite class in our code. Now let's write our unit tests:

```
// Tests for add function
test("Add two positive numbers") {
  assert(IntroToTDD.add(1, 2) == 3)
}
test("Add zero to a number") {
  assert(IntroToTDD.add(2, 0) == 2)
}
test("Add two negative numbers") {
  assert(IntroToTDD.add(-1, -2) == -3)
}
// Tests for multiply function
test("Multiply two positive numbers") {
  assert(IntroToTDD.multiply(1, 2) == 2)
}
test("Multiply a number by zero") {
  assert(IntroToTDD.multiply(2, 0) == 0)
}
test("Multiply two negative numbers") {
  assert(IntroToTDD.multiply(-1, -2) == 2)
}
```

```
test("f(3) results in 30") {
  assert(IntroToTDD.f(3) == 30)
}
```

The `test` method takes a parameter that is the test name. This will be displayed in our console when we run our unit tests.

5. We then use the `assert` method against our `add` and `multiply` functions to check that we get the expected results.

    Now that we have our tests written, let's create our `add` and `multiply` functions.

    Our code will be written in a Scala class in our `src/main/scala/com/packt/dewithscala/chapter8` folder in our book project. We'll create the `IntroToTDD.scala` file and create an object with the same name that extends the App trait:

    ```
    package com.packt.dewithscala.chapter8
    object IntroToTDD extends App {

    }
    ```

6. Now, let's create our `add` and `multiply` functions!

    ```
    def add(a: Integer, b: Integer): Integer = a + b
    def multiply(c: Integer, d: Integer): Integer = c * d
    ```

7. Then, using function composition, we can write our application in the following way:

    ```
    def f(x: Integer): Integer = multiply(2, (add(3, multiply(4,
    x))))
    println("The output of f(3) is " + f(3))
    ```

    Now that we have our functions created, we can run our unit tests. Since we're using sbt, we can start sbt in our terminal by running the sbt command. Then run the test command in sbt to check whether our tests succeed or not.

```
[SBT] (erictome) : de-with-scala ⇒ test
[info] compiling 1 Scala source to /Users/eric.tome/Documents/vscodePr
[info] IntroToTDDTest:
[info] - Add two positive numbers
[info] - Add zero to a number
[info] - Add two negative numbers
[info] - Multiply two positive numbers
[info] - Multiply a number by zero
[info] - Multiply two negative numbers
[info] - f(3) results in 30
[info] Run completed in 1 second, 402 milliseconds.
[info] Total number of tests run: 7
[info] Suites: completed 1, aborted 0
[info] Tests: succeeded 7, failed 0, canceled 0, ignored 0, pending 0
[info] All tests passed.
```

Figure 8.2 – Running unit tests in sbt

The output shows the number of tests run and how many of them succeeded, and in case of failures, it will print which test cases failed.

We now understand unit tests. Let's move on to integration testing.

Performing integration testing

In the context of data engineering, integration tests typically target the end-to-end functionality of the data pipeline, ensuring that data flows correctly from the source to the destination while passing through intermediate processing stages. These tests help identify any issues or inconsistencies that may arise due to the integration of different components, such as data source connectors, data transformation logic, database systems, or third-party services.

Integration tests in data engineering often involve setting up representative or simulated data scenarios to mimic real-world data processing scenarios. This can include creating test datasets with specific characteristics, such as data volumes, data formats, data distributions, and data quality variations. These test datasets help validate the compatibility and correctness of the data pipeline under different data conditions.

When implementing integration tests in TDD for data engineering, it's essential to consider the following aspects:

- **Data sources and sinks**: Integration tests should verify the compatibility and integrity of the data pipeline with different data sources and sinks, including databases, file systems, message queues, or external APIs. These tests ensure that data is correctly ingested, transformed, and stored in the desired output formats.

- **End-to-end data flow**: Integration tests should cover the complete end-to-end data flow, from the moment data enters the pipeline until it reaches its final destination. This includes validating data transformations, aggregations, filters, enrichment, and any other intermediate processing steps.

- **Data consistency and validations**: Integration tests should include checks and validations to ensure data consistency and integrity at various stages of the pipeline. This can involve comparing the output data against expected results or predefined rules to identify any discrepancies or data quality issues.

- **Error handling and fault tolerance**: Integration tests should assess the pipeline's ability to handle errors and failures gracefully. This includes simulating failure scenarios, such as network outages, server crashes, or data source unavailability, and verifying that the pipeline can recover and resume operation correctly.

- **Performance and Scalability**: Integration tests can also incorporate performance and scalability aspects to validate the pipeline's ability to handle large volumes of data efficiently. This can involve measuring response times, throughput, or resource utilization to ensure that the pipeline can handle expected data loads without compromising performance.

By incorporating integration tests into the TDD process, data engineers can gain confidence in the reliability, stability, and correctness of their data pipelines. Integration tests help identify potential integration issues, data inconsistencies, or performance bottlenecks early in the development cycle, allowing for timely fixes and improvements. Ultimately, these tests contribute to building robust, efficient, and high-quality data pipelines in data engineering projects.

We'll now move on to code coverage, which is essentially to gauge the health of your code base. It shows the extent to which your source code is covered through unit test cases.

Checking code coverage

Code coverage is a metric that measures the extent to which the source code of a program has been executed during testing. This helps you to understand whether you have test cases written for your code base and identify those code snippets that do not have test coverage. This helps to determine which part of the code base will have checks in place to capture potential errors stemming from future updates and which will not.

To enable code coverage analysis in Scala, you typically need to use a code coverage tool or plugin. One popular tool for Scala code coverage is called **scoverage**. You can find more information on scoverage in its Git repository, located here: `https://github.com/scoverage/scalac-scoverage-plugin`.

Here are the general steps to enable and use `scoverage` for code coverage analysis:

1. Add the `scoverage` plugin to your Scala project's build configuration. This can be done using build tools such as `sbt`, which we are using for this book. Add the following line to your `plugins.sbt` file:

   ```
   addSbtPlugin("org.scoverage" % "sbt-scoverage" % "1.9.1")
   ```

2. Enable code coverage instrumentation in your build configuration. In `sbt`, you can add the following line to your `build.sbt` file:

   ```
   coverageEnabled := true
   ```

   This step ensures that the Scala compiler instructs your code to collect coverage information.

3. Compile your Scala code using the `Scalac` compiler as you normally would. For example, using `sbt`, you can run the `compile` task.

4. Execute `tests` in sbt to run your tests and generate coverage data.

5. Execute `coverageReport` in sbt. This task will generate an HTML report that shows the coverage information for your code base. The report is typically located in the following directory:

   ```
   ../de-with-scala/target/scala-2.12/scoverage-report/index.html
   ```

6. Open the generated report in a web browser to view the code coverage results. The report provides detailed information about which lines, branches, and statements were covered by the tests or program execution. Refer to the following screenshot:

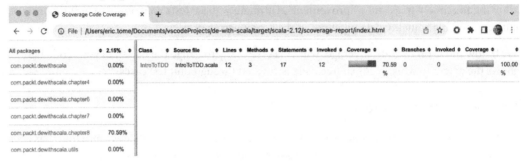

Figure 8.3 – Example coverage report

By following these steps and using a code coverage tool such as `scoverage`, you can analyze how much of your Scala code is being exercised during testing and identify areas that may need additional testing or improvement. You can see in *Figure 8.3* that the tests we created for our `IntroToTDD` class covered 70.59% of our code.

There are many other tools available for calculating coverage using Scala. The specific steps for each tool may vary, but the general concept of enabling code coverage instrumentation, running tests, and generating a report remains the same.

In this section, we looked at code coverage at a high level. In the next section, we are going to look at static code analysis.

Running static code analysis

Static code analysis is a debugging method that is performed without running the code. With application security taking center stage, it is very important to catch potential vulnerabilities early in the development phase and address them as you build your application code. Static code analysis helps developers catch issues such as the following:

- Coding standard violations
- Security vulnerabilities
- Programming errors

There are several tools available for static code analysis. For this book, we are going to look at SonarQube, which can analyze over 30 different programming languages and is one of the most widely adopted tools for static code analysis.

Installing SonarQube locally

The easiest way to install SonarQube is to launch it as a Docker container using the following command:

```
docker run -d --name sonarqube -e SONAR_ES_BOOTSTRAP_CHECKS_
DISABLE=true -p 9000:9000 sonarqube:latest
```

Once installed, open `http://localhost:9000` and log in using admin as the username and password. It will prompt you to change the password. Once you're done, it will take you to the home page:

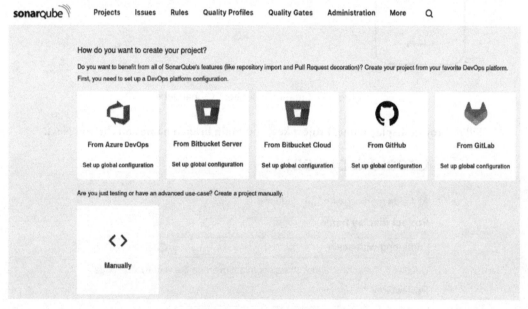

Figure 8.4 – SonarQube UI

Creating a project

The next step is to create a project from the UI:

1. Go to the **Projects** tab and click on **Manually** as shown here:

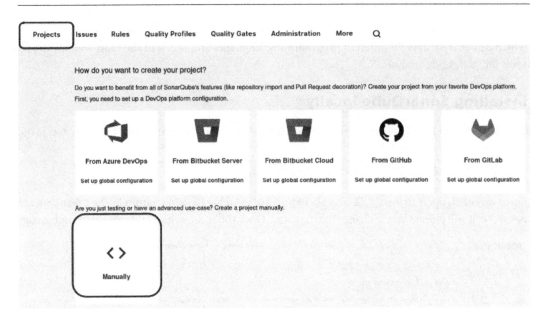

Figure 8.5 – Creating a project in SonarQube

2.   Fill in **Project display name**, **Project key**, and **Main branch name** and click on **Next**:

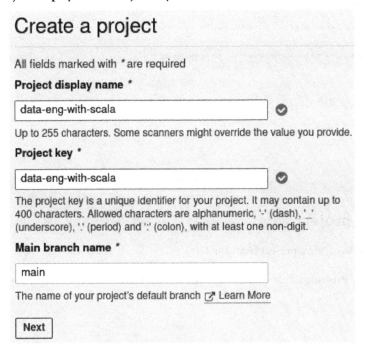

Figure 8.6 – Setting the project name

3. Select the setting for what defines new code for you. We will use the default setting:

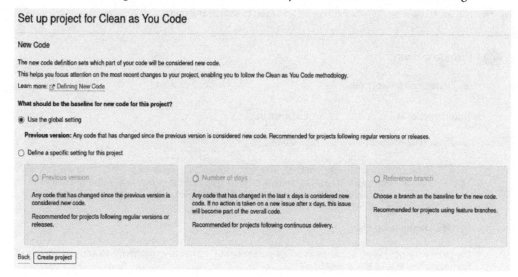

Figure 8.7 – Setting new code

4. On the **Overview** tab, click on **Locally,** as shown here:

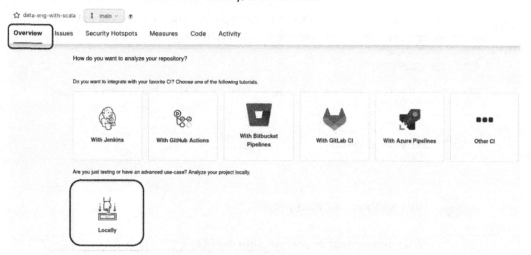

Figure 8.8 – Loading a project locally

5. Generate a project token. This token will be used to identify you.

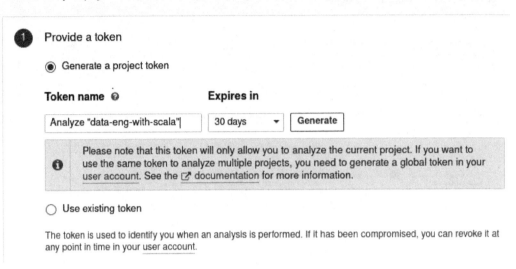

Figure 8.9 – Generating a token

6.   To run the analysis, click on **Other Cl**. It will then prompt you to select your operating system and, based on your selection, list out the steps to run the analysis.

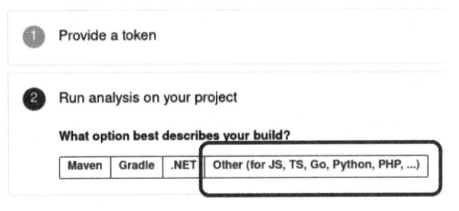

Figure 8.10 – Choosing the project type

For example, to run analysis on a Linux machine, the steps included are as follows:

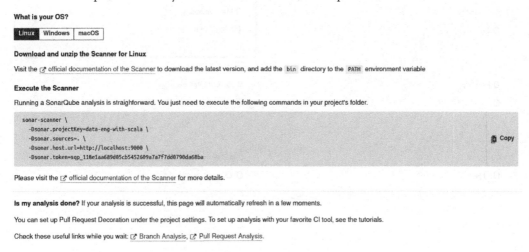

Figure 8.11 – Steps to run analysis locally on Linux

Running SonarScanner

After the UI is configured, we can run **SonarScanner** locally by downloading the ZIP file and extracting the CLI, as outlined in the previous section. However, an easier option is to run the scanner as a Docker container, as shown here:

```
docker run \
--rm \
--network=host \
-e SONAR_HOST_URL="http://localhost:9000" \
-e SONAR_SCANNER_OPTS="-Dsonar.projectKey=data-eng-with-scala" \
-e SONAR_TOKEN=sqp_118e1aa689d05cb5452609a7a7f7dd0790da68ba \
-v /home/rupam/vscode/de-with-scala/:/usr/src \
sonarsource/sonar-scanner-cli
```

This will run the scanner and, once it is done scanning, you will be able to see the results on the UI. Here is an example of how the UI looks like after the scanner runs:

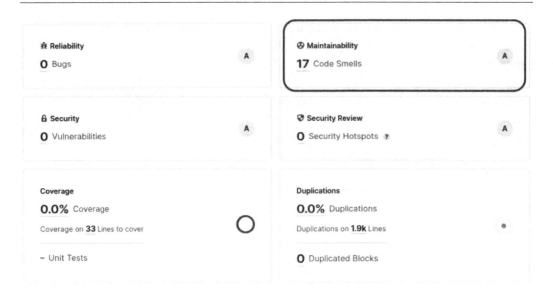

Figure 8.12 – Code analysis overview

If you click on **Maintainability**, it will list out all of the issues identified during static code analysis:

Figure 8.13 – Listing code smells

If you click on an issue, it will provide you with the details. In the example, the issue violates a predefined naming convention, **scala:S117**:

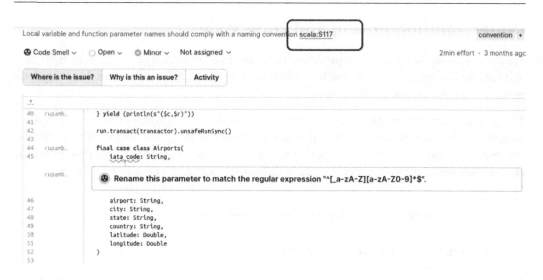

Figure 8.14 – Issue detail

If you click on the link, it will provide you with the details of the rule, as shown here:

Figure 8.15 – Details of built-in rule violated in Figure 8.12

In this section, we looked at static code analysis and reviewed the steps to install SonarQube locally, run SonarScan to analyze the code, and publish the results to the SonarQube UI. We also looked at how to get details about the issue reported by SonarQube and the steps to mitigate them. Now that we have looked at how to run static code analysis, in the next section, we will focus on code style and linting.

Understanding linting and code style

Scala is a type-safe language. By type safety, we mean Scala enforces type checks at compile time and thus enables programmers to catch and fix type errors early. A Scala program that compiles is guaranteed to run without any type errors.

Though type safety enforced by Scala is of immense help, there are still cases where a program will compile but has inherent flaws that the type checker will not call out. This is where linting tools come into play. They highlight potential bugs by analyzing the source code. Please note that there is no clear delineation between a linter and a static code analysis tool and they can be used to complement each other.

We will look at WartRemover, which is a Scala linting tool, next.

Linting code with WartRemover

There are several linting tools available to use. In this section, we are going to look at **WartRemover** and some of its predefined checks. We need to first add WartRemover to `Plugins.sbt`. Here is the code for it:

```
addSbtPlugin("org.wartremover" % "sbt-wartremover" % "3.1.3")
```

By default, all linting errors and warnings are turned off and we need to enable them in `build.sbt`. To report all built-in warts as errors, use the following:

```
wartremoverErrors ++= Warts.all
```

If you instead want to see them as warnings, use the following:

```
wartremoverWarnings ++= Warts.all
```

Another option is to report all of the warts deemed unsafe as errors while flagging the rest as warnings:

```
wartremoverErrors ++= Warts.unsafe
wartremoverWarnings ++= wartremover.Warts.allBut(wartremover.Warts.
unsafe: _*)
```

If you want to select specific warts to be reported, you can do that too, as follows:

```
wartremoverWarnings ++= Seq(Wart.Null, Wart.OptionPartial) //select
specific warts
```

Here are some of the examples of warts:

```
    // [wartremover:PublicInference] Public member must have an explicit
type ascription
    val publicVal = 1
    // [wartremover:Null] null is disabled
```

```
private val aNull = null
// Option#get is disabled - use Option#fold insteadbloop
private val optionPartial = Some(1).get
def isNonNegative(x: Int): Boolean = x match {
case i if i >= 0 => true
case _          => false
}
// [wartremover:NonUnitStatements] Statements must return Unit
isNonNegative(10)
// [wartremover:Var] var is disabled
private var x = 1
```

> **Note**
>
> For a complete list of built-in warts, refer to the WartRemover documentation: `https://www.wartremover.org/doc/warts.html`.

We can also exclude code from checks by using the `SuppressWarnings` annotation. For example, we can suppress a few of the preceding checks as follows:

```
@SuppressWarnings(Array("org.wartremover.warts.PublicInference"))
val publicVal = 1
// [wartremover:Null] null is disabled
@SuppressWarnings(Array("org.wartremover.warts.Null"))
private val aNull = null

// Option#get is disabled - use Option#fold insteadbloop
@SuppressWarnings(Array("org.wartremover.warts.OptionPartial"))
private val optionPartial = Some(1).get
```

In the preceding example, `wartremover` will throw warnings for both `null` and `Some(1).get` as both of these can lead to runtime failures.

In this section, we looked at WartRemover, which can highlight stylistic as well as possible runtime errors. In the next section, we are going to look at code formatting.

Formatting code using scalafmt

In this section, we are going to look at `Scalafmt`, which is used for code formatting. `Scalafmt` can be used from the editor, the build tool (`sbt`), or the terminal. Please refer to the steps outlined in *Installation Scalafmt* (`https://scalameta.org/scalafmt/docs/installation.html`) for installation. We won't be using it as an `sbt` plugin but will use it from the IDE instead.

For both IDEA and VS Code, to enable `Scalafmt`, we need to create a `.scalafmt.conf` file in the root folder. Both these tools will recognize the configuration and use the configurations defined in this file when formatting code.

Configuration in `.scalafmt.conf` is defined in **HOCON** (short for **Human-Optimized Config Object Notation**) format, which is a superset of JSON. As an example, here is a simple set of configurations:

```
version = "3.5.3"
runner.dialect = scala212
align.preset = more
maxColumn = 80
assumeStandardLibraryStripMargin = true
align.stripMargin = true
```

The following are descriptions of some of these options:

- `version` specifies the formatter version to be used
- `runner.dialect` specifies the Scala version that formatter is to be used for
- `align.preset` aligns various tokens and supports none, some, more, and most as values
- `maxColumn` specifies the number of characters per line and so on

For a detailed list of configurations, refer to **Configuration Scalafmt** here: `https://scalameta.org/scalafmt/docs/configuration.html`.

In this section, we looked at code linting, which can alert you when your code does not follow Scala best practices and could potentially lead to errors at runtime. We also looked at `Scalafmt`, which provides a lot of configurations to format code according to your taste.

Summary

In this chapter, we looked at various software engineering best practices, such as TDD, unit and integration testing, code coverage, static code analysis, and code style and formatting. We have seen how TDD helps with building code that is easy to test and maintain, how code coverage gives you an understanding of how much of your code base has unit tests written, and how static code analysis can help you address potential vulnerabilities. Though we have shown how to run these tests and checks locally, we usually want to run them in our Git repositories or CI/CD tools.

In the next chapter, we are going to look at CI/CD with GitHub.

9

CI/CD with GitHub

In this chapter, we will introduce **Continuous Integration/Continuous Delivery (CI/CD)** and how to apply CI/CD in your Scala data engineering project using GitHub. CI/CD is a set of best practices and tools that automate the development, testing, and deployment of data pipelines and workflows. It involves the continuous integration of code changes, automated testing, version control, and continuous delivery of pipeline deployments. The goal of CI/CD is to streamline the development process by enabling rapid iteration, reducing errors, and ensuring consistent quality.

We will cover the following main topics:

- Introducing CI/CD and GitHub
- Working with GitHub
- Deploying pipelines
- Understanding GitHub Actions

Technical requirements

Install the following command-line tools:

- Git CLI: https://git-scm.com/book/en/v2/Getting-Started-Installing-Git
- GitHub CLI: https://cli.github.com/

Introducing CI/CD and GitHub

One of the most common platforms for implementing CI/CD and collaborating on code is GitHub. GitHub and its ecosystem provide a variety of tools to manage your data engineering project from development to deployment to production.

In this section, let's cover how CI and CD work on GitHub.

Understanding Continuous Integration (CI)

The core concept of CI on GitHub revolves around continuously integrating code changes from multiple contributors into a shared repository. Whenever developers push changes to the repository, automated build and test processes are triggered. This enables teams to detect integration issues, conflicts, and errors early on, promoting a more stable and coherent code base. Through the use of GitHub Actions or third-party CI tools such as Jenkins or CircleCI, developers can define custom workflows to automate the build and test stages, ensuring code integrity. We will cover GitHub Actions later in this chapter.

Understanding Continuous Delivery (CD)

The complementary aspect of CD in GitHub focuses on the continuous delivery of software changes to various environments. CD pipelines in GitHub allow developers to define the steps and configurations required to package and deploy their applications. With each successful build and test run, the CD pipeline can automatically push the changes to staging or production environments, following predefined rules and conditions. This approach enables faster feedback loops, shorter release cycles, and a more iterative and agile software development process.

Understanding the big picture of CI/CD

Adopting CI/CD in GitHub can significantly enhance the efficiency and reliability of software development projects. It promotes collaboration, reduces manual errors, and increases the speed of delivering high-quality code. While the developer workflow and tooling may differ depending on your organization, the high-level process can be summarized as follows:

1. You will clone a Git repository to your local machine or cloud environment (such as **Databricks Repos**).

2. You will then create a feature branch (more on this later).

3. Now, it's time to start writing code. You may edit existing code to change a process or you may write new code for a new pipeline.

4. Once you are satisfied with the changes, you will commit your code and push the changes to a remote branch.

5. One or more commits may be bundled together into a *pull* request. This is a request for merging your code changes into the main branch.

6. There is typically a manual review by another engineer, with other types of automated code checks, such as static code analysis and unit and integration testing. If all checks are passed, then the pull request can be merged into the main branch. If not, then you will go back to *step 3* to fix any issues that were uncovered during the PR process.

7.   On a *merge* request, a process can be automated to move the updated code artifact to production. Depending on the type of process, you may need to add automation to stop current running processes, update the code artifact, and restart the process. The following is a pictorial representation of the flow:

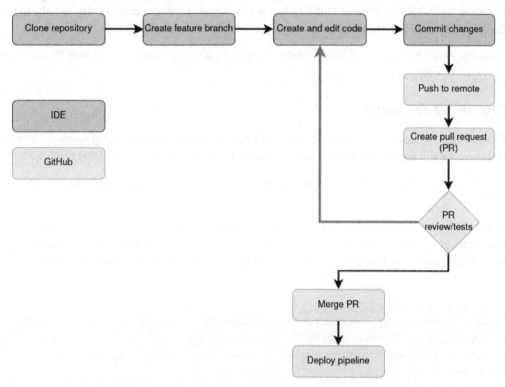

Figure 9.1 – High-level CI/CD process

Now that we have looked at the high-level flow, we will cover working with GitHub from a local development environment.

Working with GitHub

There are many different ways to interact with GitHub. You can use an IDE's interface or extensions, a web user interface, or a **command-line interface** (**CLI**). We'll focus on the Git and GitHub CLIs for this portion of the book.

The Git CLI, or `git`, is the command-line tool that interacts directly with the Git version control system. It provides a set of commands to manage the entire lifecycle of a Git repository, such as creating repositories, initializing a new repository, cloning repositories, managing branches, committing changes, merging branches, and more. It is installed on your local machine and can be used with any Git-compliant repository.

The GitHub CLI, or gh, is a command-line tool provided by GitHub that extends Git's functionality with additional features and allows you to interact with GitHub repositories directly from the command line. It also offers commands for creating repositories; cloning repositories; managing pull requests, issues, and workflows; creating and managing GitHub Actions; interacting with GitHub's API; and more. The main benefit of the GitHub CLI is that it enhances developer productivity by reducing the need to switch between the command line and the GitHub web interface.

Now that we understand the difference between the two tools, let's move on to using them to work with our code repository.

Cloning a repository

To work with our code, we will need a copy of the remote repository on our local machine. To make this copy, we will use the following clone command from a directory on our local machine:

```
git clone https://github.com/data-engineering-in-scala/de-with-scala.
git
```

In the preceding command, we are using GitHub CLI to clone the repository located at https://github.com/data-engineering-in-scala/de-with-scala.git. The following is an example of what running the command would look like after making a directory for our projects:

```
>mkdir book_projects
>cd book_projects
>git clone git@github.com:data-engineering-in-scala/de-with-scala.git
Cloning into 'de-with-scala'...
remote: Enumerating objects: 230, done.
remote: Counting objects: 100% (230/230), done.
remote: Compressing objects: 100% (121/121), done.
remote: Total 230 (delta 72), reused 199 (delta 47), pack-reused 0
Receiving objects: 100% (230/230), 3.59 MiB | 437.00 KiB/s, done.
Resolving deltas: 100% (72/72), done.
```

We now have a local copy of our code that we can work with. Let's move on to working with feature branches.

Understanding branches

Feature branches provide you with the opportunity to work on new features, address issues, or explore innovative concepts within a confined space of your repository. Each branch is derived from an existing one, with the main branch often serving as the starting point for creating a new branch. Let's create a new branch and verify that we are using the new branch by using the following CLI commands:

```
git checkout -b my_new_branch
git status
```

The checkout command is going to create a new branch with the name we have given it. In this case, my_new_branch. We also used the -b flag, which will immediately switch our context to the new branch. We also ran the status command, just to verify that we are working in the new branch.

Here is our example output from running the preceding commands:

```
>git checkout -b my_new_branch
Switched to a new branch 'my_new_branch'
>git status
On branch my_new_branch
nothing to commit, working tree clean
```

Now that we have a new branch and have switched to it, any changes we make to our code will be reflected only in this branch. Changes that are made locally are saved locally until we commit and push code to the remote branch. Next, we'll start working with our branch.

Writing, committing, and pushing code

We'll now illustrate how to write code, commit it, and push the results to our GitHub repository. Let's start by creating a test case for a function that returns the initials of a person from two strings, a first and last name. Consider the following code:

```
package com.packt.dewithscala.chapter9

import org.scalatest.funsuite.AnyFunSuite

class Chapter9Test extends AnyFunSuite {
  test("Pass two strings expect correct result") {
    assert(Chapter9.initials("Eric", "Tome") == "ET")
  }
}
```

We create the preceding code in our testing directory located here: src/test/scala/chapter9. The test checks that the correct results are returned. Given the strings Eric and Tome, we assert that ET will be returned by the function. Now we need to write our function:

```
package com.packt.dewithscala.chapter9

object Chapter9 {
  def initials(firstName: String, lastName: String): String =
    s"${firstName.substring(0, 1)}${lastName.take(1)}"
}
```

In the preceding code, we have our function, which we will use in some transformation process. It's a simple function that takes the first character of the two string parameters and returns a new string with both characters concatenated together. We create it in the following directory: `src/main/scala/com/packt/dewithscala/chapter9`.

As a developer, you always want to run your unit tests locally to make sure your code changes won't break any existing code. When running `sbt test`, we get the following results:

```
[info] IntroToTDDTest:
[info] - Add two positive numbers
[info] - Add zero to a number
[info] - Add two negative numbers
[info] - Multiply two positive numbers
[info] - Multiply a number by zero
[info] - Multiply two negative numbers
[info] - f(3) results in 30
[info] Chapter9Test:
[info] - Pass two strings expect correct result
[info] Run completed in 1 second, 465 milliseconds.
[info] Total number of tests run: 8
[info] Suites: completed 2, aborted 0
[info] Tests: succeeded 8, failed 0, canceled 0, ignored 0, pending 0
[info] All tests passed.
[success] Total time: 9 s, completed Jul 5, 2023 4:41:16 PM
```

Figure 9.2 – Unit test results from the sbt test

Since all of our tests passed, we can feel confident to commit and push these changes into our remote repository.

First, we need to stage and commit our changes to our local branch by running the following commands:

```
git add .
git commit -m "chapter9 - added initials function"
```

This results in the following being returned to the terminal:

```
> git add .
> git commit -m "chapter9 - added initials function"
Databricks pre-commit GitHooks V2
Running secret scanning on changes staged for commit.
[erictome ba74421] chapter9 - added initials function
 2 files changed, 15 insertions(+)
 create mode 100644 src/main/scala/com/packt/dewithscala/chapter9/Chapter9.scala
 create mode 100644 src/test/scala/chapter9/Chapter9Test.scala
```

Figure 9.3 – git commit results

The `git add` command will stage changes that we want to commit, and then we can call the `git commit` command using the `-m` flag to pass through the name of the commit. You always want to write a commit message that is meaningful and concise. As you can see from *Figure 8.3*, we've committed our two new files to our local branch. But we need to push these files to our remote branch in our Git repository.

To do this, we run the following command:

```
git push --set-upstream <origin> <branch-name>
```

After running the command, our remote feature branch is now in sync with all the commits we have in our local environment. At this point, we're ready to create a pull request, which will merge our code changes from our feature branch into our main production branch.

Creating pull requests

Now that you've pushed some commits into your working branch in GitHub, you need some way to merge those changes into the main branch that is used for your production deployments. The way that we do this is with pull requests.

Pull requests offer the ability to make the collaborative development process smoother and more organized. They help maintain a clear separation between the main code base and the proposed changes, reducing the risk of conflicts and unexpected errors. Additionally, pull requests encourage peer review, fostering a culture of collaboration and knowledge-sharing within the development community. During these reviews, a developer will take feedback on their work and refine their code until it meets the repository or project quality standards. By leveraging GitHub's pull request system, teams can effectively manage code changes, keep track of contributions, and ensure that only high-quality code is integrated into the project.

Let's create a pull request from the code pushed into our repository. The first thing to do is to pull in any changes to the main branch into your feature branch to make sure any changes to that branch can be resolved before you submit your pull request:

```
git merge origin/main
```

The preceding command takes the latest code from the remote main branch and merges it into your working branch. You now may need to make changes to fix any merge conflicts and commit those fixes to your remote working branch.

Once you have made your last commit, you can merge your changes from your feature branch into the main branch by creating a pull request. We're going to use the gh CLI to do this. In your terminal, use the following command:

```
gh pr create -title "pull request title" -body "pull request body"
```

The preceding command creates a pull request (pr create) with the specific title (-title flag) and description that you provide (-body flag). After the PR is created, you need to find a reviewer to validate your code, discuss any changes required, make any necessary changes, and, if approved, merge the code into the main branch. We'll discuss this more in the next section.

Reviewing and merging pull requests

Effective code collaboration requires a disciplined approach to ensure the quality and integrity of the code base. Therefore, no code should be merged into the main branch unless it successfully passes all tests, adheres to proper linting standards, and undergoes thorough review. This process serves as a safeguard against introducing bugs and maintains a clean and reliable code base. Reviewers play a vital role in this process by dedicating time to understanding the proposed changes and providing constructive feedback. The aim is not to hastily approve pull requests but to offer meaningful insights, avoiding the mere rubber-stamping of PRs. Although receiving critique on one's code can be challenging, it's essential to maintain a polite and respectful environment, as constructive criticism is crucial for growth and improvement in software development.

Reviewers will generally use the GitHub web **user interface** (**UI**) to review a pull request. In the UI, you can comment on specific lines of code in a file that has been changed and request changes or approve a pull request. Generally, the developer and reviewer(s) will use the UI to communicate about the pull request, but you may want to schedule a meeting to quickly sync on any changes required.

Automated processes can kick in when a developer pushes commits or creates and merges pull requests. On GitHub, these automated CI/CD processes are called **Actions**, which will be discussed in the next section.

Understanding GitHub Actions

GitHub provides a wide range of tools and features to support CI/CD workflows. It offers a powerful marketplace of pre-built CI/CD actions, allowing developers to easily integrate popular tools and services into their workflows. GitHub Actions also enables the creation of custom workflows using YAML-based configuration files, providing flexibility and control over the entire CI/CD pipeline. By leveraging these tools, developers can automate code formatting, run unit tests, perform code reviews, and deploy applications seamlessly.

The following sections introduce the components of GitHub Actions with a running example.

Workflows

Workflows are the top-level objects under GitHub Actions. They provide a logical grouping of all of the jobs that you plan to run as part of the CI/CD pipeline and have associated trigger events. These are defined in the `.gihub/workflows/` directory in your project root folder. A typical workflow looks like the following:

```
name: Sample Workflow
on: push
jobs:
  #list of jobs
```

A workflow can be triggered for a wide variety of events. For the complete list, refer to the official documentation: `https://docs.github.com/en/actions/using-workflows/events-that-trigger-workflows#about-events-that-trigger-workflows`.

Jobs

A workflow consists of jobs that outline the tasks to be performed in each step, along with the specific host where these steps will be executed. A workflow can have multiple jobs; for example, one job that runs unit tests and another that deploys the code into an artifact repository. Building on the earlier example, we can add the details for the jobs shown as follows:

```
jobs:
  test:
  runs-on: ubuntu-latest
  steps:
    #list of steps

  publish:
      needs: test
  runs-on: ubuntu-latest
  steps:
    #list of steps
```

Using `runs-on`, we define the host machine the steps are going to be executed on. You have the choice of either using GitHub-hosted runners or bringing your own. For a complete list of GitHub-hosted runners and their configurations, refer to the official documentation: `https://docs.github.com/en/actions/using-github-hosted-runners/about-github-hosted-runners#supported-runners-and-hardware-resources`.

Using `needs`, we define the dependencies among jobs. For example, the preceding template requires the `test` job to complete before `build` can commence. If no dependency is specified, then all of the jobs in a workflow run in parallel.

Steps

Steps define the actual work to be done by the job. A step can use *actions* available on GitHub Marketplace or can *run* a command. We will build upon the example shown earlier for *workflows* and *jobs* by adding steps. We will run unit tests first and, if they succeed, publish the artifacts to `ARTIFACTORY` as the following example shows:

```
name: Sample Workflow
on: push
jobs:
  test:
```

```
    runs-on: ubuntu-latest
    steps:
      - name: Download code
        uses: actions/checkout@v3
      - name: Setup sbt
        uses: actions/setup-java@v3
        with:
          java-version: "11"
          distribution: "temurin"
          cache: "sbt"
      - name: Run tests
        run: sbt test


  publish:
    needs: test
    runs-on: ubuntu-latest
    steps:
      - name: download code
        uses: actions/checkout@v3
      - name: Setup sbt
        uses: actions/setup-java@v3
        with:
          java-version: "11"
          distribution: "temurin"
          cache: "sbt"
      - name: Publish artifact
        run: sbt publish
        env:
          ARTIFACTORYUSER: ${{ secrets.ARTIFACTORYUSER}}
          ARTIFACTORYTOKEN: ${{ secrets.ARTIFACTORYTOKEN}}
```

The first job is test and it comprises three steps:

1. Download the source code.

2. Install sbt.

3. Run the unit tests.

The second job, publish, runs only upon successful completion of test and also has three steps:

1. Download the source code.

2. Install sbt.

3. Publish to artifactory.

For the last step, we created `artifactory` using a trial account on Jfrog, but the steps will be very similar if you are using an enterprise repository. Also, note that there are secrets read as environment variables. It should be noted that you should define them as secrets instead of variables since the latter gets printed as plain text in the log. The secrets can be created by going to **Settings | Action secrets and Variables** in your GitHub repository:

Actions secrets and variables

Secrets and variables allow you to manage reusable configuration data. Secrets are **encrypted** and are used for sensitive data. Learn more about encrypted secrets. Variables are shown as plain text and are used for **non-sensitive** data. Learn more about variables.

Anyone with collaborator access to this repository can use these secrets and variables for actions. They are not passed to workflows that are triggered by a pull request from a fork.

Secrets	Variables		New repository secret

Repository secrets

🔒 ARTIFACTORYTOKEN	Updated 1 hour ago	✏️ 🗑️
🔒 ARTIFACTORYUSER	Updated 1 hour ago	✏️ 🗑️

Figure 9.4 – Adding secrets to the repository

After you commit the changes and push the code, the workflow will trigger. The following screenshot shows two jobs that ran in sequence:

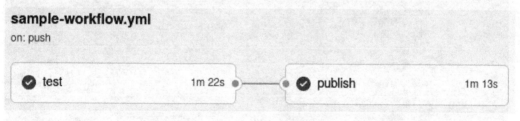

Figure 9.5 – Workflow run

In order to look at the log for each of the steps, click on one of the jobs. The following screenshot shows the steps as well as the log for the `publish` job:

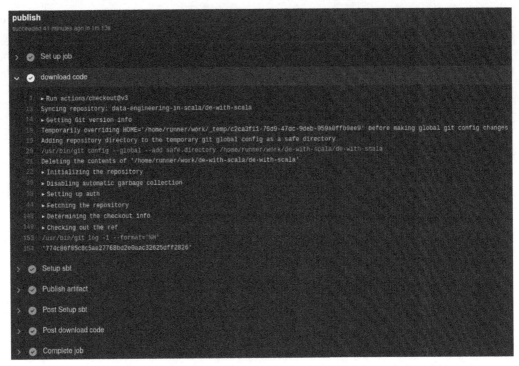

Figure 9.6 – Steps for the publish job

Also, the following is a truncated output of the `publish` step, which shows the artifacts were pushed to artifactory:

```
350  [info]  published de-with-scala_2.12 to https://dataengineeringwithscala.jfrog.io
     /artifactory/de-with-scala-sbt-dev-local/com/packt/de-with-scala/de-with-scala_2.12
     /0.0.0+1-774c86f8/de-with-scala_2.12-0.0.0+1-774c86f8.jar
351  [info]  published de-with-scala_2.12 to https://dataengineeringwithscala.jfrog.io
     /artifactory/de-with-scala-sbt-dev-local/com/packt/de-with-scala/de-with-scala_2.12
     /0.0.0+1-774c86f8/de-with-scala_2.12-0.0.0+1-774c86f8-sources.jar
352  [info]  published de-with-scala_2.12 to https://dataengineeringwithscala.jfrog.io
     /artifactory/de-with-scala-sbt-dev-local/com/packt/de-with-scala/de-with-scala_2.12
     /0.0.0+1-774c86f8/de-with-scala_2.12-0.0.0+1-774c86f8-javadoc.jar
353  [success] Total time: 30 s, completed Jul 25, 2023, 2:47:20 PM
```

Figure 9.7 – Log showing artifacts were published

And we can indeed locate them in artifactory, as shown in the following screenshot:

Name	Last Modified	Size	Download Link
../			
de-with-scala_2.12-0.0.0+1-774c86f8-javadoc.jar	25-07-23 20:17:20 +0530	1.2 MB	de-with-scala_2.12-0.0.0+1-774c86f8-javadoc.jar
de-with-scala_2.12-0.0.0+1-774c86f8-sources.jar	25-07-23 20:17:19 +0530	15.9 KB	de-with-scala_2.12-0.0.0+1-774c86f8-sources.jar
de-with-scala_2.12-0.0.0+1-774c86f8.jar	25-07-23 20:17:19 +0530	180.3 KB	de-with-scala_2.12-0.0.0+1-774c86f8.jar

Figure 9.8 – Artifacts uploaded to JFrog artifactory

In this section, we looked at how we can use GitHub Actions to simplify our CI/CD pipelines. Though we looked at unit testing and the publishing of artifacts, this can easily be extended to build an enterprise-grade CI/CD pipeline by integrating static code scanning, building Docker images, and so on. What makes GitHub Actions so powerful is its descriptive pipeline definition and the vast choice of events and configuration. For example, you can define workflows that trigger based on events on specific branches and so on.

Summary

In this chapter, we learned how to take our code changes and manage them in a collaborative environment while maintaining the code quality and health of our code base. We did this by learning how to work with GitHub by committing and merging code using the Git and GitHub CLIs. We also learned how to use GitHub Actions to promote code from development to production.

In the next chapter, we are going to look at the orchestration of data engineering pipelines through various open source tools.

Part 4 – Productionalizing Data Engineering Pipelines – Orchestration and Tuning

In this part, *Chapter 10* delves into data pipeline orchestration, focusing on seamless task coordination and failure handling. It introduces tools such as Apache Airflow, Argo, Databricks Workflows, and Azure Data Factory. *Chapter 11* highlights the Spark UI's significance in performance optimization, covering the basics, tuning, resource optimization, and data handling techniques such as skewing, indexing, and partitioning.

This part has the following chapters:

- *Chapter 10, Data Pipeline Orchestration*
- *Chapter 11, Performance Tuning*

10

Data Pipeline Orchestration

Once you have defined the business logic and transformations on your data, you need a reliable way to stitch them all together. If there is a failure, you should be notified and be able to easily identify the tasks that failed before you analyze them. This is where data pipeline orchestration comes in. It refers to the coordination and management of tasks in data transformation through well-defined dependencies between them. There are many business reasons for orchestration, but consider the following simple example. You need a report delivered daily and you need to process the data for that report each day. This requires orchestration.

In this chapter, we are going to look at some of the most common tools and techniques used for data pipeline orchestration. Two of them, Airflow and Argo, are open source, whereas Databricks workflows and Azure Data Factory are proprietary software. You can determine which one is best suited for your orchestration needs.

We will be covering the following topics in this chapter:

- Understanding the basics of orchestration
- Understanding the core features of Apache Airflow
- Working with Argo Workflows
- Using Databricks Workflows
- Leveraging Azure Data Factory

Technical requirements

You need Python (between 3.7 and 3.10) on your machine to run Airflow. If you do not have it installed, you can download Python from `https://www.python.org/downloads/`. You also need minikube which we will use to run Argo. You can find the installation steps outlined here, `https://minikube.sigs.k8s.io/docs/start/`.

Understanding the basics of orchestration

Once you have written and tested your transformations, you need a way to define dependencies among the various steps of your data engineering pipelines, define a strategy to deal with failures, and so on. This is where orchestration comes in. It allows you to define the strategy of data pipeline execution. For example, which conditions must be met before the job starts, which transformations are going to run in parallel, what happens when a job fails (do you want to try after a certain interval or ignore it? Should the pipeline be aborted?), and so on. It is important to get it right to ensure optimal performance and cost savings.

In the following sections, we are going to look at some of the popular orchestration tools in the industry.

Understanding core features of Apache Airflow

Apache Airflow is an open source platform that provides a comprehensive solution for orchestrating complex data pipelines. Born out of the need to manage Airbnb's data workflows, Airflow has gained widespread adoption due to its flexibility, scalability, and active community support and is now one of the most widely used orchestration platforms.

Airflow uses concepts such as DAGs and operators, which are the fundamental building blocks that you need to work with when developing an orchestration solution using Airflow:

- **Directed Acyclic Graphs (DAGs)**: At the heart of Airflow's orchestration philosophy are DAGs. A DAG is a collection of tasks with defined dependencies, where the direction of dependencies forms a directed graph, and there are no cycles. Each node in the graph represents a task, while edges denote the order in which tasks should be executed.

- **Operators**: Tasks within an Airflow DAG are implemented using operators. An operator defines a single, atomic task in the pipeline. Airflow provides a variety of built-in operators catering to diverse data engineering needs, such as `PythonOperator` for executing arbitrary Python code, `BashOperator` for running shell commands, and more.

- **Task dependencies**: Task dependencies are established using Python code, wherein tasks are linked together to form a DAG. Dependencies determine the order of task execution and can be defined explicitly or by using the `>>` and `<<` operators.

- **Scheduling**: Airflow's scheduler automates the execution of tasks based on their defined dependencies and schedules. Tasks can be triggered on a fixed schedule, at specified intervals, or even in response to external events.

One of the key features of Airflow is extensibility, which is what we will look at next.

Apache Airflow's extensibility

One of Apache Airflow's standout features is its robust extensibility and customization options. This allows data engineers to modify the platform to fit their specific data processing needs and integrate it effortlessly into their existing data workflows. A key example of Airflow's adaptability is its support for custom operators. Though Airflow provides a variety of built-in operators for standard tasks, unique challenges sometimes require specialized logic. By subclassing the base operator classes, you can design custom operators that cater to complex business logic, data transformations, or external system interactions, leading to reusable and modular components.

Consider the need to extract data from a unique API and deposit it into a data warehouse. A custom operator lets engineers streamline API authentication, data gathering, and transformation, simplifying the process and encouraging code reusability across various pipelines.

Custom operators are powerful. However, Airflow offers other features as well to serve various data engineering use cases. Let's understand them in the following section.

Extending beyond operators

But it's not just about operators. Airflow's adaptability also encompasses hooks and sensors. Hooks offer a standardized way to connect with external systems, such as databases or cloud platforms. Crafting custom hooks allows smooth integration of Airflow with a diverse set of data sources. Sensors, meanwhile, enable pipelines to respond to external triggers. For instance, a pipeline might halt until a specific file becomes accessible in a directory. A custom sensor lets engineers dictate the logic, ensuring the pipeline runs only under the right conditions.

Moreover, Airflow's extensibility isn't limited to individual projects. It fosters broader community collaboration. By adding custom operators, hooks, sensors, and other extensions to the Airflow community, engineers can expand the platform's capabilities and offer solutions to shared obstacles.

In the dynamic realm of data engineering, Apache Airflow's adaptability ensures that engineers possess the tools and versatility to adjust to evolving demands, harmonize with existing infrastructures, and craft optimized, bespoke data pipelines. Whether enhancing core functions, merging with external systems, or giving back to the open source sphere, Airflow's extensibility offers a commanding grasp over your data orchestration journey.

Having looked at various ways you can extend the functionalities of Airflow, let's now take a high-level tour of monitoring.

Monitoring and UI

In the realm of data pipeline orchestration, visibility and control are paramount. Apache Airflow excels in this regard by offering a comprehensive web-based **user interface** (**UI**) that empowers data engineers and operators to monitor, manage, and optimize their data pipelines effectively. The Airflow web UI is a central hub that provides an intuitive and user-friendly interface for interacting with your orchestrated pipelines. With its visually appealing and informative layout, the UI offers a wealth of features that enhance your monitoring and management capabilities.

Upon logging in to the Airflow UI, users are greeted with an overview of DAGs. This snapshot gives an instant view of pipeline health, execution statuses, and schedules. Users can quickly identify any potential bottlenecks or issues that may arise during pipeline execution. The UI offers a granular breakdown of task execution within each DAG. It displays the current status, start and end times, execution duration, and any logs generated during task execution. This level of detail enables data engineers to monitor task progress, identify delays, and troubleshoot errors efficiently. The Gantt chart visualization provides an interactive representation of task dependencies and their execution timelines. This visual aid allows users to comprehend the flow and concurrency of tasks, aiding in the optimization of task scheduling and resource allocation. Airflow's UI incorporates comprehensive log tracking for each task, allowing data engineers to delve into the details of task execution. Logs can be filtered, searched, and sorted, facilitating effective troubleshooting and performance analysis. For DAGs with multiple instances, the UI maintains a record of each instance's execution history. This facilitates the easy comparison and analysis of different runs, enabling data engineers to track changes in task behavior over time.

Hosting and deployment options

When implementing Apache Airflow for data pipeline orchestration, data engineers have several options for hosting and deployment. The choice of hosting solution depends on factors such as scalability, resource requirements, security, and organizational preferences. The following sections are some potential ways to host Apache Airflow.

Self-hosting

Data engineering teams with robust infrastructure and technical expertise may opt for self-hosting Airflow. This involves setting up Airflow on-premises or on a cloud-based **virtual machine** (**VM**) or container. While self-hosting provides maximum control and customization, it requires diligent management of server resources, security configurations, and scaling challenges.

Cloud platforms

Cloud providers such as **Amazon Web Services** (**AWS**), **Microsoft Azure**, and **Google Cloud Platform** (**GCP**) offer managed services specifically designed for Apache Airflow. These managed services abstract away much of the infrastructure management overhead, enabling data engineers to focus on designing and running pipelines. Cloud-hosted Airflow solutions often integrate seamlessly with other cloud services, allowing data pipelines to interact with various data sources and storage solutions.

Managed services

Beyond cloud platforms, there are third-party managed services that specialize in hosting Apache Airflow. These services offer the convenience of a fully managed solution while allowing data engineers to leverage Airflow's capabilities without the need for extensive infrastructure management. Managed services typically provide features such as automatic scaling, high availability, and simplified deployment.

Kubernetes orchestration

For organizations embracing containerization and microservices architecture, deploying Airflow on Kubernetes is a viable option. Kubernetes provides powerful orchestration and scaling capabilities, allowing data engineers to manage Airflow containers efficiently. This approach offers flexibility, resource optimization, and easier integration with other containerized services.

Making the right choice

The decision of how to host Apache Airflow depends on a combination of technical considerations, organizational preferences, and available resources. As you embark on your journey of data pipeline orchestration, carefully evaluate the hosting options that align with your team's expertise and the specific needs of your data engineering projects. Apache Airflow's versatility and adaptability ensure that, regardless of your chosen hosting method, you can harness its capabilities to build and manage robust, efficient, and scalable data pipelines.

Installing Airflow locally

In order to install airflow locally, a Python environment is required. With a working Python environment that is between 3.7 and 3.10, a user can execute the following commands to install Airflow, initialize the local database, and create an `admin` user:

```
pip install apache-airflow
export AIRFLOW_HOME=$(pwd)
airflow db init
airflow users create --role Admin --username admin --email admin
--firstname admin --lastname admin --password admin
```

These commands will result in producing the following files in the directory where they were run:

- `airflow.cfg`
- `airflow.db`
- `webserver_config.py`

After these initialization commands are complete, it is time to start the webserver and scheduler. Open a new command window for each of the following components.

Make sure to change to the same directory where the initialization commands were run, or provide the full path to the `AIRFLOW_HOME` variables:

```
export AIRFLOW_HOME=$(pwd)
airflow webserver

export AIRFLOW_HOME=$(pwd)
airflow scheduler
```

After both of these commands are executed, the webserver can be visited from a browser at `http://localhost:8080`, where a user can see the home screen once they are authenticated, as seen in *Figure 10.1*:

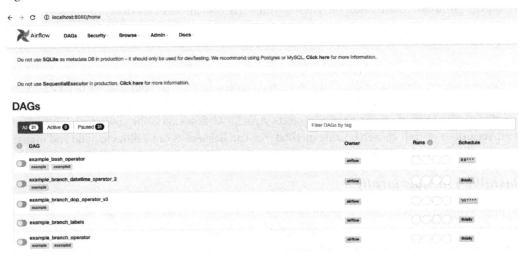

Figure 10.1 – Airflow home screen

The `example_bash_operator` operator can be used as a quick start into how tasks are executed by switching the toggle next to the DAG in *Figure 10.2*:

Figure 10.2 – Starting a DAG

Once the DAG completes, the user can explore the different visualizations of how it was executed in *Figure 10.3*:

Figure 10.3 – Tasks in a DAG

Now, we move to the next feature.

Designing data pipelines with Airflow

Designing efficient and robust data pipelines with Apache Airflow requires careful consideration of various factors. Employing best practices ensures that your pipelines are well organized, maintainable, and performant. Each task should encapsulate a specific unit of work, making it easier to develop, test, and troubleshoot. Embrace abstraction by creating custom operators and sensors for common tasks, promoting code reuse, and simplifying pipeline construction. Use variables, connections, and configuration files to store sensitive information, such as credentials, and pipeline-specific settings. Parameterize your DAGs to make them adaptable to different environments (development, testing, and production) and scenarios. Design your tasks to be idempotent, meaning they can be safely retried without causing duplicate or erroneous data. Ensure that tasks can be rerun if needed without negatively impacting downstream processes. Implement logging and error handling within tasks to maintain a clear audit trail of data processing steps. Store your DAG definitions and any custom operators, hooks, or sensors in version-controlled repositories. This practice facilitates collaboration among team members, helps track changes over time, and ensures a reliable history of your pipeline configurations. Adopt a robust deployment strategy, such as promoting DAGs through different environments using automation and continuous integration tools.

In this section, we looked at Apache Airflow, one of the most popular open source orchestration tools, and its various components and capabilities. In the next section, we are going to look at another open source tool – Argo Workflows.

Working with Argo Workflows

Argo Workflows is an open source orchestration tool for jobs running on Kubernetes. It is implemented as a Kubernetes **custom resource definition** (**CRD**). Each step in Argo Workflows runs as a container on a Kubernetes platform. In this section, we are going to take a look at the capabilities offered by Argo Workflows starting with installation on your local machine.

Installing Argo Workflows

For the purposes of this chapter, we will set up Argo locally. There are two steps you need to take before we can start looking at Argo:

1. Install `minikube`. Please refer to the steps outlined in `https://minikube.sigs.k8s.io/docs/start/` to install `minikube`.

2. Install the `kubectl` CLI to interact with minikube by following the steps outlined in `https://kubernetes.io/docs/tasks/tools/#kubectl`.

Once you have `minikube` and `kubectl` installed, you can proceed with configuring two separate Argo components that we are going to use in this section:

*   Argo server and controller

*   Argo CLI

To install the Argo server and controller, you can run the following commands against your locally installed `minikube`:

```
minikube start
kubectl create namespace argo
kubectl apply -n argo -f https://github.com/argoproj/argo-workflows/
releases/download/v3.4.8/install.yaml #replace v3.4.8 with the
latest available version. Refer to https://github.com/argoproj/argo-
workflows/releases
```

To install the Argo CLI on Mac and Linux, follow the steps outlined in the Mac and Linux sections of `https://github.com/argoproj/argo-workflows/releases`. For Windows, download `argo-windows-amd64.exe.gz` from the **Assets** section and perform the following steps:

1. Rename `argo-windows-amd64.exe` to `argo.exe`.

2. Create `C:\argo-cli` and place `argo.exe` in there.

3. Open the environment variables setting and add the folder to **System Variables** | **PATH**.

4. To test whether `argo cli` is working, open cmd and type `argo version`.

Understanding the core components of Argo Workflows

The following are the core concepts that you need to be familiar with when creating an Argo workflow:

- **Workflow**: The workflow is the most important resource in Argo and serves two purposes:

  - It defines the workflow to be executed

  - It stores the state of the workflow

- **Workflow spec**: The `Workflow.spec` field defines the workflow. It comprises a list of templates and an entry point. Templates define instructions to be executed whereas the entry point defines which template will be executed first.

- **Templates**: Templates define the tasks to be executed. There are two categories of templates:

  - **Template definitions**: Template definitions define the work to be done. They are of four types: `container`, `script`, `resource`, and `suspend`.

  - **Template invocators**: Template invocators are used to call other templates. They are of two types: `dag` and `steps`.

In this book, we are going to look at `resource` and `dag`. When creating an Argo workflow for a Spark application, job specifications are laid out within resource template definitions as steps. And finally, those steps are invoked through a DAG in which the dependencies among individual steps are defined.

Taking a short detour

Before we can run a Spark application on our `minikube` cluster, you need to configure Spark by following these steps:

1. The first step is to create a namespace to run Spark applications:

   ```
   minikube start #start minikube
   kubectl config use-context minikube #it is a good practice to
   explicitly set the context
   kubectl create ns spark-app #create a spark-app namespace
   kubectl config set-context --current --namespace=spark-app
   #switch to spark-app namespace
   ```

2. Next, we need to install the Spark operator on our local cluster. In order to do that, you first need to install Helm by following the steps outlined here: `https://helm.sh/docs/intro/install/`.

3. Next, you need to install the Spark operator by using Helm charts:

   ```
   helm repo add spark-operator https://googlecloudplatform.github.
   io/spark-on-k8s-operator
   helm install my-release spark-operator/spark-operator
   --namespace spark-operator --create-namespace
   ```

4. Then, you need to create the service account needed by the Spark application and create a cluster role binding. This is required for the service account to be able to create executor pods:

```
kubectl create serviceaccount spark
kubectl create clusterrolebinding spark-role
--clusterrole=cluster-admin --serviceaccount=spark-app:spark
--namespace=spark-app
```

5. With these steps completed, you can run your Spark application by applying the following manifest:

```
apiVersion: "sparkoperator.k8s.io/v1beta2"
kind: SparkApplication
metadata:
  name: "spark-pi"
  namespace: spark-app
spec:
  timeToLiveSeconds: 3600
  type: Scala
  mode: cluster
  image: apache/spark:v3.3.1
  imagePullPolicy: IfNotPresent
  mainClass: org.apache.spark.examples.SparkPi
  mainApplicationFile: "local://///opt/spark/examples/jars/
spark-examples_2.12-3.3.1.jar"
  sparkConf:
    spark.kubernetes.authenticate.driver.serviceAccountName:
spark
  sparkVersion: 3.0.0
  driver:
    memory: 1G
  executor:
    instances: 1
    cores: 1
    memory: 1G
```

6. In order to run the Spark application, save the preceding content in a file called `spark-pi.yaml` and run the following:

```
kubectl apply -f ./spark-pi.yaml
sparkapplication.sparkoperator.k8s.io/spark-pi created
```

7. You can check the status of your Spark application using the following command:

```
kubectl get sparkapp spark-pi -n spark-app
```

This is what you will see:

```
NAME         STATUS       ATTEMPTS    START               FINIS
H                     AGE
spark-pi    COMPLETED    1           2023-08-18T12:34:06Z    2023-08-1
8T12:34:19Z    5m49s
```

8. In order to check the evaluated value of pi, you can check the driver log:

```
kubectl logs spark-pi-driver -n spark-app | grep ^Pi
Pi is roughly 3.145675728378642
```

Next, we move to the Argo workflow.

Creating an Argo workflow

For the purposes of this chapter, we will create a simple workflow that consists of the following steps:

1. Print a message at the start of the workflow.

2. Run a Spark job.

3. Print a message at the end of the workflow.

Based on what we have covered so far in this chapter, the basic workflow structure will look like the following:

```
apiVersion: argoproj.io/v1alpha1 #k8s apiVersion
kind: Workflow #k8s resource kind
metadata:
  generateName: example-workflow- #helps to avoid name conflict
  namespace: spark-app #k8s namespace this workflow is going to run on
spec:
  entrypoint: dag-seq #workflow will start with the dag-seq
  templates:
    - name: print-start-message
      container:
        #template type container. will be used to print a message

    - name: calculate-pi
      resource:
        #template type resource. will be used to launch a spark job

    - name: print-termination-message
      container:
        #template type container. will be used to print a message
```

```
        - name: dag-seq
          dag: #template type dag
            tasks:
              - name: start-message #name of the task
                template: print-start-message #name of the tamplate to be
used

              - name: launch-spark-job
                depends: start-message #launch-spark-job starts after
start-message
                template: calculate-pi

              - name: termination-message
                depends: launch-spark-job
                template: print-termination-message
```

All we need to do is to provide details for the individual templates. To print messages, we will use the busybox image available in Docker Hub. The following is the complete workflow:

```
apiVersion: argoproj.io/v1alpha1 #k8s apiVersion
kind: Workflow #k8s resource kind
metadata:
  generateName: example-workflow- #helps to avoid name conflict
  namespace: spark-app #k8s namespace this workflow is going to run on
spec:
  entrypoint: dag-seq #workflow will start with the dag-seq
  templates:
    - name: print-start-message
      container:
        image: busybox
        imagePullPolicy: IfNotPresent
        command: [echo]
        args: ["Starting Argo Workflow!"]

    - name: calculate-pi
      resource:
        action: create
        successCondition: status.applicationState.state = COMPLETED
        failureCondition: status.applicationState.state = FAILED
        manifest: |
          apiVersion: "sparkoperator.k8s.io/v1beta2"
          kind: SparkApplication
          metadata:
            generateName: "spark-pi-"
```

```
              namespace: spark-app
          spec:
            timeToLiveSeconds: 3600
            type: Scala
            mode: cluster
            image: apache/spark:v3.3.1
            imagePullPolicy: IfNotPresent
            mainClass: org.apache.spark.examples.SparkPi
            mainApplicationFile: "local://////opt/spark/examples/jars/
spark-examples_2.12-3.3.1.jar"
            sparkConf:
              spark.kubernetes.authenticate.driver.serviceAccountName:
spark
            sparkVersion: 3.0.0
            driver:
              memory: 1G
            executor:
              instances: 1
              cores: 1
              memory: 1G

    - name: print-termination-message
      container:
        image: busybox
        imagePullPolicy: IfNotPresent
        command: [echo]
        args: ["Congratulations! Argo Workflow ran sucessfully!"]

    - name: dag-seq
      dag:
        tasks:
          - name: start-message #name of the task
            template: print-start-message #name of the tamplate to be
used

          - name: launch-spark-job
            depends: start-message #launch-spark-job starts after
start-message
            template: calculate-pi

          - name: termination-message
            depends: launch-spark-job
            template: print-termination-message
```

You can save the preceding content in a file and then start the workflow using `argo submit` as follows:

```
argo submit my-first-workflow.yaml --serviceaccount=spark -n spark-app
--watch
```

Note that we are using the `spark` service account we created in the previous section. Without a service account with proper roles, the Spark application will not run. We also used the `watch` flag, which will keep track of the progress and print it on your screen. Once the workflow is complete, it should look like the following:

```
Name:                example-workflow-252jj
Namespace:           spark-app
ServiceAccount:      spark
Status:              Succeeded
Conditions:
 PodRunning          False
 Completed           True
Created:             Fri Aug 18 21:17:49 +0530 (53 seconds ago)
Started:             Fri Aug 18 21:17:49 +0530 (53 seconds ago)
Finished:            Fri Aug 18 21:18:42 +0530 (now)
Duration:            53 seconds
Progress:            3/3
ResourcesDuration:   27s*(100Mi memory),27s*(1 cpu)

STEP                      TEMPLATE                   PODNAME                                                        DURATION  MESSAGE
 ✔ example-workflow-252jj  dag-seq
  ├─ start-message         print-start-message       example-workflow-252jj-print-start-message-62597978            3s
  ├─ launch-spark-job      calculate-pi              example-workflow-252jj-calculate-pi-2727560289                 22s
  └─ termination-message   print-termination-message example-workflow-252jj-print-termination-message-152001688     3s
```

Figure 10.4 – Argo workflow status

Argo also provides `CronWorkflow`, which provides the ability to run workflows in a preset schedule. For example, if you want to schedule the workflow to run every hour, you can create a `cron` workflow as follows:

```
apiVersion: argoproj.io/v1alpha1 #k8s apiVersion
kind: CronWorkflow #k8s resource kind
metadata:
 generateName: example-cron-workflow- #to avoid name conflict
 namespace: spark-app #k8s namespace this workflow is going to run on
spec:
  schedule: "0 * * * *"
  timeZone:  Etc/UTC
  workflowSpec:  #workflow spec
   entrypoint: dag-seq #workflow will start with the dag-seq
   templates:
    - name: print-start-message
    container:
      image: busybox
      imagePullPolicy: IfNotPresent
      command: [echo]
      args: ["Starting Argo Workflow!"]
   #rest of the workflow
```

Note that the `.spec` section of the workflow goes unaltered to the `.workflowSpec` section in `CronWorkflow`.

To create a `CronWorkflow instance`, use `cron create` instead of `submit` as shown in the following example:

```
argo cron create my-first-cron-workflow.yaml --serviceaccount=spark -n
spark-app
Name:                      example-cron-workflow-n7wgx
Namespace:                 spark-app
Created:                   Fri Aug 18 22:31:18 +0530 (now)
Schedule:                  0 * * * *
Suspended:                 false
Timezone:                  Etc/UTC
NextScheduledTime:         Fri Aug 18 23:30:00 +0530 (58 minutes
from now) (assumes workflow-controller is in UTC)
```

In this section, we looked at Argo Workflows, how to install and configure it locally, its various components, and how we can run Spark applications using a workflow. Finally, we looked at creating Cron workflows, which allow us to trigger workflows following a specified schedule. The declarative nature of Argo Workflows makes it easy for developers to quickly learn functionalities and implement changes without having to write a lot of code.

In the next section, we are going to look at Databricks Workflows, which is not an open source tool and is available to applications running on Databricks. Given the immense popularity of Databricks in this space, we want to provide a quick tour of its orchestration capabilities.

Using Databricks Workflows

Databricks Workflows is a fully managed cloud orchestration service available to all Databricks customers. It simplifies the creation of pipeline orchestration for the following types of tasks:

- Databricks notebooks
- Python Script/Wheel
- JAR
- Spark Submit
- Databricks SQL – dashboards, queries, alerts, or files
- Delta Live Table pipelines
- dbt

We will focus on using a `spark submit` task to run a Scala JAR. The first thing we have to do is create an assembly or `fat jar`, which will include all the dependencies of our project in our JAR.

To do this, we will add the following code to our `build.sbt` file:

```
assemblyJarName in assembly := "de-with-scala-assembly-1.0.jar"
assemblyMergeStrategy in assembly := {
case PathList("META-INF", _*) => MergeStrategy.discard
case _ => MergeStrategy.first
}
```

The first line is to specify the name of the `.jar file` to be created. The next block will provide a merge strategy to manage duplicate asserts in our dependencies. After the preceding code is added to our project, we can create the `.jar file` by running the following code in our terminal.

We also need to add the `sbt-assembly` dependency. Create a new file called `assembly.sbt` in the `project` folder and add the following line to the file:

```
addSbtPlugin("com.eed3si9n" % "sbt-assembly" % "0.15.0")
```

It will look something like this:

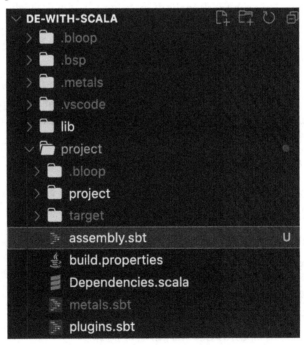

Figure 10.5 – Folder structure with assembly.sbt

Now that we have added `sbt-assembly` to our project, we can run it using the following code:

```
sbt reload
sbt assembly
```

The preceding commands will create the .jar file in our target directory in our main project:

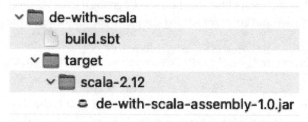

Figure 10.6 – Local location of .jar file

In the Databricks' Data Explorer, click on the +**Add** button and upload the .jar file to a location in the **Databricks File System** (**DBFS**). We need to add the .jar file to DBFS so that we can call it from our workflow task as shown here:

Upload Data to DBFS

DBFS Target Directory ❷

/FileStore | erictome | **Select**

Files uploaded to DBFS are accessible by everyone who has access to this workspace. Learn more

Files ❷

de-with-scala-
assembly-
1.0.jar

0.2 GB
Remove file

✔File uploaded to /FileStore/erictome/de_with_scala_assembly_1_0.jar

Done

Figure 10.7 – Databricks Databricks' Explorer DBFS upload dialog

After the file is uploaded, make sure to note the DBFS path to the file. Here is the path from our example: dbfs:/FileStore/erictome/de_with_scala_assembly_1_0.jar.

Now, we'll click on **Workflows** in the Databricks UI and then select **Create Job**. There will be a job and an unnamed task that is created for you. Edit this by giving it a name, select **Spark Submit** for the type, choose a jobs cluster, and enter something similar to the following in the parameters:

```
["--class","com.packt.dewithscala.chapter6.
SparkTransformations","dbfs:/FileStore/ erictome/de_with_scala_
assembly_1_0.jar"]
```

The first parameter specifies that we will be using a class. The next is the class we will be executing. Lastly, you'll notice we're using the DBFS location of the JAR we uploaded earlier. Refer to the following screenshot to see what this looks like in the UI:

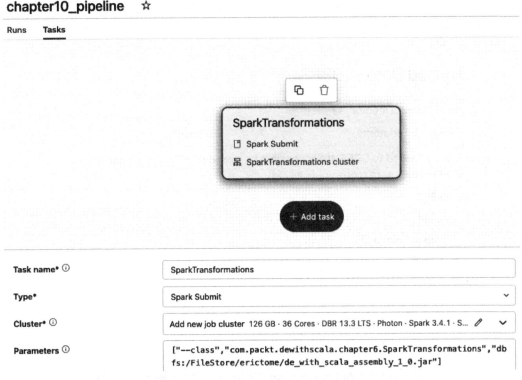

Figure 10.8 – Spark Submit task example

Make sure to click **Save Task**, and now we have created a job with one task. At this point, we can select **Run now** to test run our process:

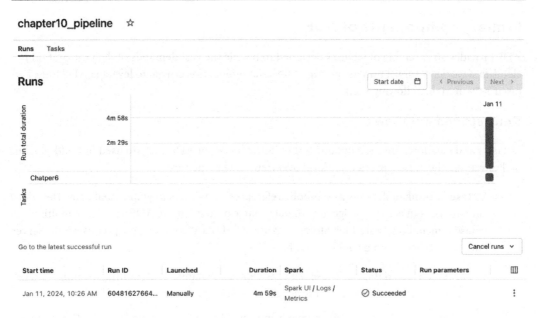

Figure 10.9 – Successful Workflow run!

You should see the preceding result after a successful run. Once you have confirmed it is working, you can do any of the following:

- Add additional tasks
- Conditionally execute those tasks with dependencies on other tasks
- Create a schedule
- Set up notifications via email, pager duty, Slack, and so on

Databricks Workflows provides an easy, built-in way to manage the orchestration of complex data engineering pipelines without having to maintain and pay for third-party orchestration. We've barely scratched the surface of its capabilities, but you can use what we have learned to get started. For information, please refer to https://docs.databricks.com/en/workflows/index.html.

Next, we'll discuss using Azure Data Factory for native orchestration to the Microsoft Azure cloud.

Leveraging Azure Data Factory

Azure Data Factory (**ADF**) evolved from the on-premises version called Data Management Gateway. Recognizing the shift to cloud computing, Microsoft revamped and launched ADF to serve the growing demand for cloud data solutions. ADF is built on the philosophy of "code-free" data integration. It emphasizes visual tools, allowing users to build, deploy, and manage data transformation processes without needing to write extensive code. In this section, we are going to look at the capabilities offered by ADF and see how it can simplify building pipeline orchestration.

Primary components of ADF

ADF provides an ensemble of features designed to handle the vast demands of data integration in a cloud-first world. A robust understanding of these components is crucial to leverage ADF fully. Let's discuss them in the following sections.

Datasets and dataflows

Datasets and dataflows are the fundamental building blocks of ADF that are used to build pipeline orchestration. The following is a high-level overview of what they are:

- **Datasets**: Think of datasets as symbolic references or pointers to your actual data. They don't contain data but act as a bridge to your data source or destination. ADF supports a multitude of datasets, including Azure Blob Storage, Azure SQL Data Warehouse, on-premises SQL Server, and many others, with a couple listed here:

  - **Parameterized datasets**: These datasets allows a dynamic content link, meaning you can pass parameters to determine the specific dataset at runtime

  - **Schema mapping**: ADF can automatically map schema from source to destination, reducing manual configuration

- **Dataflows**: While datasets point to data, dataflows define how data should be transformed. It's a visually designed **ETL** (short for **Extract, Transform, Load**) or **ELT** (short for **Extract, Load, Transform**) process. Within a dataflow, we have the following:

  - **Transformations**: These can be column-level (such as concatenation or conversion) or row-level (such as filtering or sorting).

  - **Debugging and testing**: You can preview the data at any transformational step, ensuring the desired changes are in effect.

Linked services

A linked service encapsulates connection information needed for ADF to access external resources. In essence, it's the "how" of accessing your data. To find out more, please refer to the following list:

- **Secure integration**: Linked services support integration runtimes, ensuring that your data remains within a specified region or even within your on-premises environment

- **Multiple data stores**: ADF supports a vast array of linked services, such as relational, non-relational, big data, and more

Pipelines

A pipeline is a logical grouping of activities that together perform a task. It's the heart and soul of ADF. Let's take a look at a pipeline's components:

- **Activities**: These are the processing steps in a pipeline. They can be data movement activities or data transformation activities. For instance, you might copy data from an on-premises SQL Server (data movement) and then run a Hive script on Azure HDInsight to process it (data transformation).

- **Control flow**: Pipelines can have a sequence, conditions, loops, and more. This provides granular control over the orchestration of activities.

- **Concurrency and throttling**: Pipelines allow you to manage how many activities can run simultaneously, ensuring optimal performance and cost management.

Triggers

While pipelines define *what* and *how*, triggers define *when*. The following are the types of triggers available in ADF:

- **Schedule triggers**: Execute pipelines on a wall-clock schedule, such as daily or weekly.

- **Event-based triggers**: React to an event, such as when a file is created or deleted in Azure Blob Storage.

- **Tumbling window triggers**: These are especially useful for handling large datasets. They allow the repeated execution of a pipeline within a specified time window.

Integration Runtimes (IRs)

IRs determine the *where* of data movement and compute. They provide the bridge between the public network space and private network space. Some of the available options are listed here:

- **Azure IR**: For public, globally available data movement.

- **Self-hosted IR**: For private, on-premises data or even private networks in Azure. It enables hybrid scenarios.

- **Azure-SSIS IR**: This allows you to natively execute **SQL Server Integration Services** (**SSIS**) packages in ADF, ensuring continuity for businesses migrating from SSIS.

In this section, we looked at **ADF**, which is quite popular among organizations running their data engineering workloads on the Azure cloud.

Summary

In this chapter, we looked at pipeline orchestration, which is a key component of data engineering. We looked at various options – both open source and paid – that should allow you to evaluate the solution that works best for your data engineering needs. We looked at Airflow and Argo, which are open source tools that are quite popular among developers. We then looked at Databricks Workflows as well as ADF, which are managed solutions and provide a lot of functionalities and seamless integration with other services running in the cloud.

In the next chapter, we are going to look at performance tuning, which is extremely important for ensuring your data engineering workloads run efficiently and are cost effective.

11
Performance Tuning

In the world of big data processing, Apache Spark has emerged as a powerful and versatile framework. Its ability to handle large-scale data processing tasks, coupled with its speed and ease of use, has made it a favorite among data engineers and analysts. However, as data volumes grow and processing demands become more complex, ensuring optimal performance becomes paramount. The Spark **user interface (UI)** plays a crucial role in this pursuit, offering insights and metrics that can guide performance tuning efforts by helping to identify undersized or oversized compute and issues with data.

In this chapter, we will delve into the intricacies of the Spark UI and explore how it can be leveraged to fine-tune the performance of your Spark applications.

We will cover the following topics:

- Introducing the Spark UI
- Leveraging the Spark UI for performance tuning
- Right-sizing compute resources
- Understanding data skewing, indexing, and partitioning

Introducing the Spark UI

At its core, the Spark UI is a web-based interface that provides a comprehensive view of the internal workings of your Spark application. It offers detailed information about various aspects of your application's execution, from a high-level overview down to the specifics of individual tasks and stages. The Spark UI is an invaluable tool for diagnosing bottlenecks, identifying resource utilization, and gaining a deeper understanding of the runtime behavior of your Spark jobs. It is also an integral part of the Spark ecosystem as it's designed to give you unparalleled visibility into the execution of your Spark applications. Whether you're working on a small cluster or a sprawling data center, the Spark UI offers a unified interface to monitor, analyze, and optimize the performance of your Spark workloads.

Let's learn how to navigate the Spark UI.

Navigating the Spark UI

Accessing the Spark UI is typically straightforward. When you submit a Spark application, the framework automatically launches a web server that hosts the UI. By default, the UI can be accessed at `http://<driver-node>:4040`, where `<driver-node>` is the hostname or IP address of your Spark driver node. In hosted Spark platforms, such as Databricks, the UI can be accessed through the cluster compute page, as shown in *Figure 11.1*:

Figure 11.1 – Example of the Spark UI

As the application progresses, the UI is continuously updated to reflect real-time information. The Spark UI's web-based interface is designed with user-friendliness in mind, making it accessible to both novice and experienced users. Navigating the UI provides you with a wealth of information, empowering you to make informed decisions about performance optimization.

Let's explore some key components of the Spark UI by taking a look at the **Jobs** tab.

The Jobs tab – overview of job execution

The **Jobs** tab serves as a launching point for understanding the execution flow of your Spark application. Here, you can find a summary of submitted jobs, each accompanied by essential details such as start time, duration, number of stages, and current status. Clicking on a specific job opens a detailed view that exposes the inner workings of the job:

Figure 11.2 – Example of the Jobs tab

Within the detailed view, you'll find a **directed acyclic graph (DAG)** visualization that illustrates the stages and tasks comprising the job. This visual representation provides insights into the data flow and dependencies between different computational steps. Additionally, statistics related to input and output data sizes can shed light on the data processing load at each stage.

The Stages tab – digging into task execution

The **Stages** tab offers a more granular perspective into the execution of individual stages within your Spark jobs. Stages represent logical subdivisions of your job's computation, and the tab provides essential insights into the tasks that comprise each stage:

Figure 11.3 – Example of the Stages tab

As you delve into the details of a stage, you can access vital metrics such as task runtimes, input data sizes, and shuffle data sizes. The ability to monitor shuffle data is particularly valuable as shuffling can often be a performance-intensive operation. By identifying stages with significant shuffle data sizes, you can focus your optimization efforts on minimizing data shuffling and improving overall job efficiency.

The Executors tab – monitoring resource usage

The **Executors** tab is your gateway to understanding how resources are allocated and utilized across the Spark cluster. Executors are worker nodes that are responsible for executing tasks, and this tab provides real-time insights into their performance.

In this tab, you'll find a wealth of metrics related to CPU usage, memory consumption, and garbage collection. These metrics are critical for diagnosing resource bottlenecks and ensuring that your Spark application operates within the defined resource limits. By keeping a watchful eye on metrics such as **Used On-Heap Memory** and **Used Off-Heap Memory**, you can preemptively address memory-related issues and optimize memory utilization.

The Storage tab – tracking cached data

Caching data in memory is a common optimization technique in Spark, and the **Storage** tab offers visibility into the data that's cached either in memory or on disk. Efficient caching can lead to substantial performance improvements by minimizing the need to recompute data between stages:

| Jobs | Stages | Storage | Environment | Executors | SQL / DataFrame | JDBC/ODBC Server | Structured Streaming | Connect |

Storage

Parquet IO Cache

Host	Disk Usage	Max Disk Usage Limit	Percent Disk Usage	Metadata Cache Size	Max Metadata Cache Size Limit	Percent Metadata Usage	Data Read from IO Cache (Cache Hits, Compressed)	Data Written to IO Cache (Compressed)	Cache Misses (Compressed)	Cache Misses	True Cache Misses	Rescheduling Cache Misses	Cache Hit Ratio	Number of Local Scan Tasks	Number of Rescheduled Scan Tasks
10.139.64.132	1248.7 MiB	489.0 GiB	0 %	0.0 B	6.0 GiB	0 %	5.1 MiB	1247.7 MiB	1247.7 MiB	1248.7 MiB	24.6 KiB		0 %	235	19
Total	1248.7 MiB	489.0 GiB	0 %	0.0 B	6.0 GiB	0 %	5.1 MiB	1247.7 MiB	1247.7 MiB	1248.7 MiB	24.6 KiB		0 %	235	19

Data Read from External Filesystem (All Formats)	Data Read from IO Cache (Cache Hits, Compressed)	Data Written to IO Cache (Compressed)	Cache Misses (Compressed)	True Cache Misses	Rescheduling Cache Misses	Cache Hit Ratio	Number of Local Scan Tasks	Number of Rescheduled Scan Tasks	Cache Metadata Manager Peak Disk Usage
38.4 GiB	5.1 MiB	24.5 GiB	24.5 GiB	24.5 GiB	49.0 KiB	0 %	502	23	7.0 KiB

Figure 11.4 – Example of the Storage tab

This tab provides insights into the storage levels, sizes, and replication factors of cached data. By monitoring cached data, you can ensure that your caching strategies align with the memory resources available and the access patterns of your Spark application.

The Environment tab – JVM metrics and configuration

Under the hood, Apache Spark relies on **Java Virtual Machine** (**JVM**) for execution. The **Environment** tab delves into the JVM metrics, system properties, and environment variables that influence your Spark application's behavior. In this tab, you'll find a trove of information about memory usage, garbage collection patterns, and system configurations. For instance, monitoring metrics such as **Heap Memory Usage** and **GC Time** can reveal memory management inefficiencies and help you fine-tune JVM settings to optimize performance.

The SQL tab – analyzing Spark SQL queries

For applications that leverage Spark SQL, the **SQL** tab provides a specialized view into the execution of SQL queries. Spark SQL enables you to query structured data using SQL syntax, and this tab enables you to dissect query execution plans and associated performance metrics.

By examining the logical and physical query plans, you can identify potential optimization opportunities. For example, complex joins or costly operations can be spotted and addressed using techniques such as indexing, partitioning, or query restructuring. This tab empowers you to optimize Spark SQL workloads for maximum efficiency and responsiveness.

Now, let's learn how to leverage the Spark UI for performance tuning.

Leveraging the Spark UI for performance tuning

The Spark UI is not a passive monitoring tool; it is a powerful instrument for driving performance improvements across your Spark applications. Let's look at how to effectively leverage the UI for performance tuning.

Identifying performance bottlenecks

When embarking on performance tuning, the **Jobs** and **Stages** tabs serve as your initial checkpoints. Begin by scrutinizing the **Jobs** tab to identify jobs with prolonged runtimes or unusually high shuffle data sizes. These are indicative of potential performance bottlenecks that warrant deeper investigation.

Navigate to the **Stages** tab to further dissect the problematic stages. Pay close attention to tasks with extended runtimes or excessive data shuffling. Such insights will guide your efforts to optimize critical stages and alleviate performance constraints.

Optimizing data shuffling

Data shuffling is a resource-intensive operation that can significantly impact performance. By closely examining the shuffle read and write metrics on the **Stages** tab, you can pinpoint stages that are responsible for substantial data shuffling.

Consider strategies such as tuning the partitioning of data or optimizing join operations to reduce the need for shuffling. Reducing data movement between nodes can lead to faster execution times and more efficient resource utilization.

Memory management and garbage collection

Efficient memory management is paramount to Spark application performance. The **Executors** tab offers invaluable insights into memory usage and garbage collection behavior.

Monitor metrics such as **Used On-Heap Memory** and **Used Off-Heap Memory** to identify memory bottlenecks. Excessive garbage collection or frequent memory spills can degrade performance. Adjusting memory configurations, such as heap sizes and off-heap memory allocation, can help mitigate these issues and enhance overall stability.

Scaling resources

The **Executors** tab not only assists in diagnosing resource utilization but also aids in scaling your cluster appropriately. If you consistently observe executors running out of memory or facing resource constraints, it may be necessary to scale up your cluster by adding more nodes or increasing the resources that are allocated to each executor.

By making informed decisions about cluster size and resource allocation, you can ensure that your Spark application operates within optimal resource bounds, thereby delivering consistent and reliable performance.

Analyzing SQL query performance

For Spark applications that utilize Spark SQL, the **SQL** tab is an indispensable resource for query optimization. Dive into the execution plans of your SQL queries to identify costly operations, suboptimal join strategies, or inefficient data access patterns.

Leverage this tab to fine-tune SQL queries by applying appropriate indexing, partitioning, or caching strategies. By optimizing SQL query execution, you can unlock substantial performance gains and expedite data processing tasks.

Let's move and understand how to right-size computing resources.

Right-sizing compute resources

One of the critical factors that affects the performance and cost-effectiveness of Apache Spark applications is the size and type of compute resources used. Right-sizing your Spark cluster can result in significant improvements in processing speed and cost efficiency.

This section dives deep into the concept of right-sizing compute resources for Apache Spark and provides guidelines to achieve the best balance between performance and cost.

Understanding the basics

Before diving into right-sizing, it's essential to understand the fundamental components that are part of a Spark cluster:

- **Executor**: The JVM process is initiated on a worker node and is responsible for executing tasks and storing data in memory or disk storage. Each task runs on a single executor.

- **Memory**: This shows how much RAM is available on each node.

- **Core**: This is a computational unit available to the executor. Memory on each node is generally split between each core and each core is typically an executor.

- **Disk**: This shows how much disk space is available for spilling from memory. This will come into play when large shuffles cannot be held entirely in memory.

- **Network**: This shows the network throughput that is available to each node. This will affect how quickly the cluster can read from object storage and shuffle data between nodes.

It is important to right-size a cluster to gain optimal performance while balancing cost. Generally speaking, the cost-to-performance calculation is linear, meaning that the more compute that is added, the faster it will process.

Adding more compute to a cluster will typically keep costs flat while improving the performance of the job. However, adding too much compute will have diminishing returns. It is important to test workloads with a few options to ensure a balance between fulfilling service-level agreements and avoiding resource wastage. Coupling this with widely available autoscaling functionality will allow engineers to approach this problem with more simplicity. In some instances, bottlenecks will occur because one of the components needs to be changed to handle specific scenarios. If these components are correctly allocated, then the cluster can be set up to start with a minimum threshold of nodes. The maximum number of nodes should be set high to allow for scaling to automatically handle unexpected larger workloads. By following these principles, engineers can spend minimal time fine-tuning their compute resources.

Now, let's take a look at the different components that we can optimize.

Executors, cores, and memory

Executors can be configured to have different core and memory allocations. However, the vast majority of use cases can take a simplistic approach to have the same number of executors to core ratio. It is usually not worth the tuning effort to configure more cores being allocated to an executor and time is better spent on other optimizations. The best optimization to look at in this category is the memory-to-core ratio. For large shuffle workloads, a higher memory-to-core ratio is advantageous to avoid shuffle spills to disk. This causes data to have to go through a serialization process and significantly slows down processing time.

Disk

The disk component largely comes into play with large shuffle operations (joins, aggregations, and so on). When there is not enough memory in the cluster, data will be spilled to disk. This is one of the biggest problems that will slow a pipeline down but is sometimes unavoidable during very large shuffles such as a join between two large tables. Disk storage can be network-attached, or physically attached storage. Network storage has the benefit of being able to be elastically resized to accommodate unexpectedly larger volumes and is generally cheaper. The drawback is that I/O will be slower. Physically attached storage is fixed in size and more costly but comes with the benefit of dramatically faster I/O speeds. For general workloads, network-attached storage will suffice, and enabling it to elastically scale should be done when workloads are known to spike up periodically. When disk spill is known to happen, then choosing physically attached storage will be the correct decision.

Network

In the cloud, networking can be given up to a certain throughput or dedicated bandwidth. This component choice will affect reading from object storage as well as shuffle efficiency in the cluster. Dedicated bandwidth will allow uninterrupted fast network speeds, which are critical for large shuffle operations.

Monitoring and tools

There are two main groups of tools that we use to monitor our Spark applications and the components mentioned previously:

- **The Spark UI**: This provides comprehensive details on job stages, tasks, executor memory, and shuffling

- **External monitoring tools**: Tools such as Grafana, Prometheus, and Datadog can offer insights into JVM metrics, CPU, memory usage, and more

Right-sizing compute resources for Apache Spark is a blend of art and science. While the aforementioned guidelines provide a structured approach, often, the nuances of specific use cases necessitate iterative testing and tuning. Always monitor your Spark applications, be ready to adapt, and strive for a balance between performance and cost-effectiveness.

In the next section, we'll cover optimization from a data perspective.

Understanding data skewing, indexing, and partitioning

Like with any data processing system, all of the greatest hardware will only produce mediocre results. There is no magic bullet that will solve poor data layouts. The fastest disk, processing chips, and network will not negate the need to plan for well-thought-out indexing and partitioning strategies. Data skew can sneak into processing pipelines or queries and bring them to a crawl. These three critical aspects need to be planned for and monitored to prevent degradation to data processing and querying. We'll learn more about them in the following sections.

Data skew

Data skew is a common problem when utilizing distributed data systems such as Apache Spark. It will show up when some processing partitions are significantly larger than others, resulting in some tasks finishing quickly while waiting for others to complete. This can result in under-utilized compute, long processing times, and out-of-memory errors. Joins are some of the most common tasks to suffer from data skew and can be the hardest to discover and troubleshoot. Skew occurs because a key being joined on has a significantly higher count than other join keys, and Spark will co-locate data from each side of the join for a given key on a single executor. If one of these keys has an order of magnitude more values to process than other executors, it will lag because it has more work to do.

Often, data skew will be identified during development, but there are many times when skewing can show up in post-production. When a certain product becomes much more popular than others, an orders table can become more heavily weighted to a particular item number. Seasonal influxes can cause certain products to have a short-lived spike that can cause delayed pipelines during critical selling seasons. Catching these impacts or avoiding them altogether is critical to healthy pipelines.

Identifying data skew can be done through the Spark UI. By looking at the stages of a job, an engineer can see that most tasks finish quickly compared to other tasks that take more than twice as long as others. Some techniques to solve a data skew are as follows:

- Broadcast join
- Salting
- **Adaptive Query Execution** (AQE)

Broadcast joins can be used if the table(s) being joined are small enough to fit in memory. These tables will be sent to each executor and eliminate the need to shuffle the larger table because each executor has a copy to use for comparison. This is by far the most efficient way to handle skew, but it comes with many disadvantages. Not all tables are small enough to broadcast, which could severely limit the use of this strategy. The broadcast tables could also be unpredictable sizes, leaving the pipeline in an unpredictable state. Use the broadcast technique only when the tables are relatively static.

Salting involves adding a random value, or *salt*, to the key that is causing data skew. By adding this salt, you are essentially creating multiple copies of the same key, which helps distribute the data more evenly across partitions. The following example shows a skewed distribution of joining DataFrames:

```
df1:
+-------+------+
| userID|value1|
+-------+------+
|    123|   A  |
|    123|   B  |
|    123|   C  |
|    456|   D  |
|    789|   E  |
+-------+------+


df2:
+-------+------+
| userID|value2|
+-------+------+
|    123|   X  |
|    123|   Y  |
|    456|   Z  |
+-------+------+
```

Instead of performing a skewed join, an engineer can add *salt* to the join keys to distribute them better while maintaining the same result:

```
df1 (salted):
+-------+------+
| userID|value1|
+-------+------+
| 123_1 |   A  |
| 123_2 |   B  |
| 123_3 |   C  |
| 456   |   D  |
| 789   |   E  |
+-------+------+


df2 (salted):
+-------+------+
| userID|value2|
+-------+------+
| 123_1 |   X  |
| 123_2 |   X  |
| 123_3 |   X  |
| 123_1 |   Y  |
| 123_2 |   Y  |
| 123_3 |   Y  |
| 456   |   Z  |
+-------+------+
```

Luckily, in Spark 3.x, AQE introduced the ability to automatically detect and handle skew joins in most scenarios. See *Figure 11.3* to understand how to discover this in the Spark UI:

Figure 11.5 – Automatic skew join detection

If a pipeline is utilizing Spark 3.x, then most of the time, data skew can be an afterthought. In general, it is a good idea to monitor pipelines and alert jobs that are taking longer to complete than expected. Operations teams can be alerted to these scenarios and take appropriate action before a larger outage is incurred.

Indexing and partitioning

When working on data pipelines with Spark, the vast majority of data lives on some kind of object storage in the cloud. Just like in traditional databases, the key to efficient queries lies in the ability to read the least amount of data to resolve a query or transformation.

In a data lake or lakehouse, the ability to co-locate data together will be the driving force to limit scans. Without this co-location, queries will end up performing full scans of all the files in a table to satisfy a query.

Delta Lake currently provides two core mechanisms for achieving this goal. Partitioning is a tried and true method for sending the same data values to the same set of files. This is useful when a low cardinality column is utilized for the partitioning column, such as a date, a sensor ID, or sometimes a product ID. Z-ordering is the equivalent of cluster indexing and is the second method for co-locating data in the same set of files. This technique can be used on low or high-cardinality columns.

Partitioning is a great technique to use for coarse-grained data skipping. It is commonly used with a date field (without a timestamp) because there are only a finite number of days in a dataset and it is a common filter column when running queries.

When a query asks for a certain date or range of dates, the query can immediately skip all other partitions and only read the files within the dates that were asked for. This can significantly reduce the data that's scanned and improve the performance of the query. Partitioning can easily run into problems when it's applied to columns that have a high cardinality.

Take, for example, partitioning a table on a timestamp. Each record that's coming in can have a slightly different timestamp, resulting in each partition holding only a few records. Instead of a table having 365 partitions for a date partition, this table could now have more than 31 million partitions. When asking for a single date and partitioned by date, the query could read as little as a single file and be extremely efficient on I/O. By taking this to a timestamp partition, the query could read upwards of 86 thousand files, resulting in many more trips to storage for the same amount of data. This is what is known as **over-partitioning** and it can occur if the column that's been chosen for partitioning results in far too many partitions. Over-partitioning can also result from picking too many partition columns. A general rule is that a table should not be considered for partitioning unless it is over a terabyte.

Z-ordering is a feature of Delta Lake that allows for further data skipping on top of a coarse-grained partition or even as a standalone feature. The Z-order feature allows an engineer to specify one-to-many columns for Spark to cluster together in each file and order them so that there are ranges of values in each file. This ensures that a sensor ID in a file can range from something such as 5 to 10 and only values within this range will be located in the file. Without Z-order, the file could contain sensor ID values of, say, 5, 99, 16, 3, and 10. Delta Lake will collect statistics on this file and understand that the minimum value is 3 and the maximum value is 99. If a query wants a sensor ID of 6, then it will have to open this file and scan the contents, even though 6 is not located there. When using Z-order, Spark will sort the files and make sure each file has a finite range. In the previous example, it could modify the file to only have a sensor ID of 5 to 10 and make sure that all sensor ID values of 6 are included in this file. Now that they have been sorted and co-located, the query will only have to open a single file, thus reducing the scan volume significantly.

The performance of a query is highly dependent on the data layout in storage and memory. Data skewing can have major implications on how quickly a pipeline can be completed because a small number of executors are doing more than their fair share of work. This work needs to be distributed properly so that each executor can contribute evenly.

In this section, we explored techniques such as broadcast joins, salting, and leveraging AQE to help achieve this goal. The other major factor of efficiency is limiting how much data needs to be scanned from storage. Properly applying partitioning strategies can significantly reduce the number of files scanned, but is only applicable to coarse-grained columns such as date. To achieve similar results for higher cardinality columns, features such as Z-order should be used to co-locate data in the same files. File statistics should also be leveraged so that you can quickly skip data that is not relevant to queries. As a general rule, monitoring should be in place to ensure operations teams receive early warnings when pipeline performance has degraded past an acceptable level.

Summary

Through the Spark UI, you can unveil the hidden dimensions of your Spark workloads, transforming them from code into orchestrated symphonies of efficiency, speed, and precision. In this chapter, we covered how to access the Spark UI and how to use it to profile and troubleshoot potential performance issues.

In this and the previous chapters, we covered all the basics you'll need to build pipelines in Scala and Spark. In the next two chapters, we'll put this all together and build batch and streaming processes for real-world use cases.

Part 5 – End-to-End Data Pipelines

In this part, *Chapter 12* utilizes your previously acquired skills to create a batch pipeline, highlighting batch processing's importance in data engineering. The topics covered include a typical business use case, ingestion, transformation, quality checks, and orchestration.

Chapter 13 constructs a streaming pipeline, emphasizing real-time data ingestion via Azure Event Hubs, configured as Apache Kafka for Spark integration. It utilizes Spark's Structured Streaming and Scala and covers topics such as use case understanding, data ingestion, transformation, serving layer loading, and orchestration, aiming to prepare you for similar pipeline implementation in your organization.

This part has the following chapters:

- *Chapter 12, Building Batch Pipelines Using Spark and Scala*
- *Chapter 13, Building Streaming Pipelines Using Spark and Scala*

Building Batch Pipelines Using Spark and Scala

The goal of this chapter is to combine all the things we've learned so far to build a batch pipeline. The ability to handle large volumes of data efficiently and reliably in batch mode is an essential skill for data engineers. A batch pipeline is simply a process that ingests, transforms, and stores a set of data at a scheduled time or in an ad hoc fashion. Apache Spark, with its powerful capabilities for distributed data processing, and Scala, as a versatile and expressive programming language, provide an ideal foundation for constructing robust batch pipelines. This chapter will equip you with the knowledge and tools to harness the full potential of batch processing in the big data landscape.

In this chapter, we're going to cover the following main topics:

- Understanding our use case and data
- Understanding the **medallion architecture**
- Ingesting data in batch
- Transforming data and checking quality
- Loading to a serving layer
- Orchestrating our pipeline

Understanding our business use case

The scenario is that you're working on a data engineering project for a business stakeholder. That stakeholder is your marketing department. They want to track the effectiveness of marketing campaign conversion events. Let's quickly define marketing campaigns and conversion events.

A marketing campaign is a coordinated and strategic effort by a business or organization to promote a specific product, service, event, or message to a target audience. It typically involves a series of planned activities, channels, and content designed to achieve predefined marketing objectives, such as increasing brand awareness, generating leads, or driving sales. Marketing campaigns often have set timeframes and utilize various marketing channels, including digital advertising, social media, email marketing, and traditional advertising, to reach and engage the intended audience.

Marketing conversion events refer to specific actions or behaviors that a user or potential customer takes in response to marketing efforts. These events are critical indicators of the effectiveness of a marketing campaign and can vary depending on the marketing goals and objectives. Marketing professionals use these events to track user interactions and measure the success of their marketing strategies.

It's critical for marketers to measure success so they can change the course or spending strategies of their campaigns and it's your job as a data engineer to get them the data they need to perform that analysis.

Now, let's try to understand more about our specific use case and how we are going to help our marketers.

What's our marketing use case?

We'll need to understand a little bit more about what exactly our marketing department is trying to do. We're also going to have to understand what data we're trying to collect, and what data we already have in our current systems. Understanding the domain knowledge helps you to become a better data engineer and it's important you take the time to understand your organization's business.

Your marketing department wants to track the following conversion events by marketing campaign, geography, and time:

- **Purchase**: A purchase conversion event occurs when a user completes a transaction by buying a product or service, indicating a successful revenue-generating action for a business

- **Survey response**: A survey response represents a user actively engaging with a survey or questionnaire, providing feedback or data in response to specific questions or prompts

- **Event registration**: Event registration signifies a user's intention to attend a specific event, such as a webinar, seminar, or conference, by signing up in advance

- **Follow social media**: When a user chooses to follow social media, they opt to receive updates, posts, and content from a brand or individual on social media platforms such as Facebook, X (formerly Twitter), or Instagram

- **Read content**: Read content occurs when a user consumes and engages with written or visual content, such as articles, blog posts, or news stories

- **Download content**: Download content indicates a user actively retrieving digital assets such as e-books, whitepapers, or software for personal use

You should always ask your stakeholders what they want to do with their data. The marketing department has identified the following metrics it wants to track in the data:

- The number of conversion events by country name and product group for each day
- The number of conversion events by product group for each day
- Which conversion events are being driven the most by product group, ranked highest to lowest

Let's move on to understanding our data so we can identify how to solve this business problem.

Understanding the data

After speaking with our marketing team, and the operations team that is collecting our data, we now know that the new data coming in will be conversion event data. We already have data on our geographies and marketing campaigns, and descriptive data on our conversion events.

Let's first look at the data we already have in our systems. The first table we have is a country geography table with the following schema:

Column	Type
country_id	bigint
country_name	string
iso_3_char	string
iso_2_char	string

Figure 12.1 – Country dimension schema

Let's take a look at some sample data from this table so we know what's in it:

country_id	country_name	iso_3_char	iso_2_char
1	Aruba	ABW	AW
2	Afghanistan	AFG	AF
3	Angola	AGO	AO
4	Anguilla	AIA	AI
5	Albania	ALB	AL

Figure 12.2 – Sample country dimension data

In *Figure 12.3* we have a conversion events table. It has the following schema:

Column	Type
conversion_event_id	bigint
conversion_event	string

Figure 12.3 – Conversion event dimension schema

Let's take a look at some sample data from this table so we know what's in it:

conversion_event_id	conversion_event
1	Purchase
2	Survey Response
3	Event Registration
4	Follow Social Media
5	Read Content
6	Download Content

Figure 12.4 – Sample conversion event dimension data

The table in *Figure 12.5* is the marketing campaigns table. It has the following schema:

Column	Type
campaign_id	bigint
campaign_code	string
product_group	string

Figure 12.5 – Marketing campaign dimension schema

Let's look at some sample data from this table so we know what's in it:

campaign_id	campaign_code	product_group
1	social_media_02	Application
2	digital_mkting_01	Application
3	digital_mkting_02	Application
4	webinar_01	Training
5	social_media_01	Social Team

Figure 12.6 – Sample marketing campaign dimension data

Now that we have an understanding of the data in our existing systems, let's take a look at the data that we will be ingesting:

```
{

"country": "GB",

"marketing_campaign":

"digital_mkting_02",

"event_info": {

  "event_type": "Follow Social Media",

  "event_ts": "2021-08-08T17:33:00.000Z"

}

}
```

The preceding JSON is a sample of the data coming from our operations team. The first element is a two-character country code. First, we need to check that we can join our internal data to the values we see in this dataset. We can see that we can join the data to our country table with the two-character ISO country code. To join the data to our marketing campaign table, we'll use the campaign code column. Last, for event types, we'll have to get the data from the JSON array, and then join it to our conversion event table on the conversion event column.

Recall the following from the previous section our marketing metrics:

- The number of conversion events by country name and product group for each day

- The number of conversion events by product group for each day

- Which conversion events are being driven the most by product group, ranked highest to lowest

Let's put together a dimensional model that will allow us to get those metrics now that we understand our data structure and values.

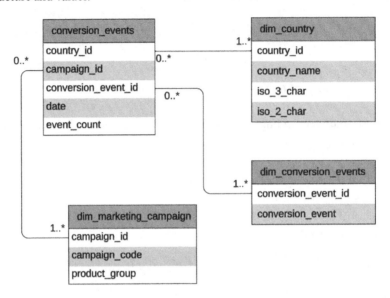

Figure 12.7 – ERD diagram for our conversion event model

Figure 12.7 represents an **Entity Relationship Diagram** (**ERD**) for the dimensional model we will create to satisfy the reporting requirements provided by our marketing team. We'll be using the existing tables, taking our input data, and doing some transformations and look-ups to add the right dimensional keys. The diagram represents the physical data model with relationships. It shows the end state that we want to get to for serving the data to our stakeholders.

Now, let's talk a little bit about how to get there.

Understanding the medallion architecture

The process of bringing in data, transforming it, and then preparing it for usage is the main focus of this section. There are many different logical models for this process, with various naming conventions. However, Databricks has proposed the medallion architecture, which can serve as a good model for you to use when thinking about data engineering pipelines. Let's dive into it.

The medallion architecture, as shown in the following figure, is a data processing architecture that leverages a multi-layered approach to organize, refine, and deliver data for analytics and decision-making purposes. Each layer in this architecture serves a specific function and contributes to the overall data pipeline.

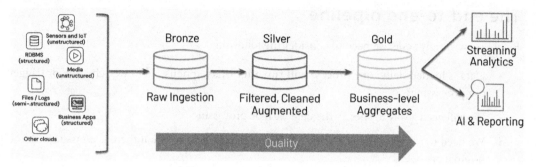

Figure 12.8 – The medallion architecture

Let us understand each layer in this architecture:

- **The Bronze layer**: At the foundation of the medallion architecture is the **Bronze** layer. This layer is responsible for data ingestion and acts as the initial landing zone for raw data. Raw data from various sources, such as databases, cloud storage accounts, event buses, or external APIs, is collected, stored, and cataloged in the Bronze layer. It serves as an immutable data lake where data is retained in its original form, preserving a historical record of all incoming data.

- **The Silver layer**: The **Silver** layer is the next layer in the process and focuses on data transformation and refinement. Data engineers and data scientists use this layer to clean, restructure, and transform the raw data into a format that is more suitable for analysis. Data quality checks and validations are performed at this stage to ensure the data's accuracy and consistency. Once data is processed in the **Silver** layer, it becomes a reliable source for downstream analytics and reporting.

- **The Gold layer**: The **Gold** layer represents the final stage of data processing in the medallion architecture. In this layer, data is curated and optimized for business intelligence and reporting purposes. It is highly structured, enriched, and aggregated to support complex analytical queries and dashboards. The **Gold** layer provides a trusted and business-ready dataset that stakeholders can use confidently for making critical decisions.

By incorporating the **Bronze**, **Silver**, and **Gold** layers, the medallion architecture ensures a systematic and controlled flow of data from its raw form to a refined, business-ready state. This tiered approach allows organizations to manage data efficiently, maintain data lineage, and ensure data quality while providing the flexibility to cater to various data-processing requirements, including batch and real-time data processing.

The ERD diagram from the previous section can be considered our Gold layer. We understand our source data and our serving or Gold layer, so now let's take a look at how we get from the source through to the Bronze, Silver, and finally our Gold layer.

The end-to-end pipeline

Before we write any code, we need to consider the following:

- Data is loaded daily; our process will run after this happens... Do we schedule or trigger our processing?

- We will need a way to specify the date we'll be processing

- We need to consider the possibility of having to reprocess a date if there is an issue with the original dataset

- Do we need to write a mechanism to process more than one day?

- Do we need to write a mechanism to reprocess the whole dataset?

- What data quality rules should be put in place?

- How and where are we going to transform our data?

Here's a high-level overview of how we can structure our Spark/Scala application to meet these requirements:

- **Scheduling or triggering**: We can use a scheduling tool such as ADF, Argo, Apache Airflow, or cron jobs to trigger our Spark application daily after data loading is complete. We'll show an example in Argo in the *Orchestrating our batch process* section later in this chapter.

- **Specifying processing date**: Write the Spark application to accept a date parameter that specifies the date to be processed.

- **Reprocessing capability**: Implement error-handling and data-reprocessing logic within our Spark application. We could store information about processed dates and rerun the processing for specific dates if needed.

- **Processing multiple days**: Extend our code to process multiple days by accepting a date range or a list of dates as input parameters. This allows for batch processing of multiple dates.

- **Reprocessing the whole dataset**: Create a separate option in our Spark application to trigger a full dataset reprocessing if required. Ensure it clears any existing data for those dates.

- **Data quality rules**: Implement data quality checks in the Silver layer of our data processing pipeline. Define rules to validate data completeness, consistency, and accuracy. Log and handle data quality issues accordingly.

- **Data transformation**: Use Spark's DataFrame API to perform data transformations in our Silver and Gold layers. Define clear transformation steps and apply them to the loaded data. We will create functions or methods to encapsulate these transformations.

Now that we have a plan in place, let's move on to data ingestion.

Ingesting the data

The first step in our pipeline is to ingest data from JSON files and establish a robust data process that efficiently processes and stores this data within our data platform. The initial destination for the incoming data will be our Bronze layer.

Our data, originating from our operations department, arrives in JSON format. As part of our data ingestion process, we will collect these JSON files and store the data in them in its original, unaltered state within the Bronze layer. This retention of raw data ensures that we maintain an immutable historical record of all incoming data, which can be invaluable for traceability, auditing, and data lineage purposes. Our operations department will be landing the data in a storage location for us once a day in a folder specific to that day; for example, `/<storage_location/event_date=<yyyy-mm-dd>`.

To further enhance the capabilities and manageability of our data, we will leverage the Delta Lake (Delta) format within the Bronze layer. Delta is a powerful data storage and versioning technology that integrates seamlessly with any Spark process. It brings features such as **Atomicity, Consistency, Isolation, Durability** (**ACID**) transactions, time travel, and schema enforcement to our data lake. By choosing Delta, we ensure that the data in the Bronze layer is not only stored efficiently but also benefits from advanced functionalities that simplify data processing and enhance data quality. This approach sets a strong foundation for subsequent data transformation and refinement processes in the Silver and Gold layers of our data architecture.

We will exclude portions of the code that are scaffolding for the application and focus on the code that's relevant to our pipeline processing. You can find the full set of code on our GitHub repository. Let's break down each function and its purpose now.

The `readJson` function reads JSON data for a specified date from a source directory (stored as files in the location your operations team has defined) and returns it as a DataFrame:

```
// Function to read JSON data for a given date
def readJson(date: String): DataFrame = {
  spark.read.json(s"${source}event_date=${date}/")
}
```

The `writeDelta` function writes a DataFrame to a Bronze Delta table named `conversion_events`. The reprocess parameter determines whether the table should be appended to or overwritten based on the value of `reprocess`:

```
// Function to write DataFrame to a Delta Lake table
def writeDelta(reprocess: Boolean, df: DataFrame) = {
  df.write
    .format("delta")
    .mode(reprocess match {
      case false => "append"
      case _     => "overwrite"
    })
    .save(s"${target}conversion_events")
}
```

The `ingest` function ingests JSON data for multiple dates that are specified in the command line. It starts with the DataFrame for the first date and then iteratively unions (concatenates) the data for subsequent dates, effectively combining data for all specified dates into a single DataFrame:

```
// Function to ingest and union JSON data for multiple dates
def ingest(reprocess: Boolean, dates: String*) = {
  dates.tail.foldLeft(readJson(dates.head)) { (acc, date) =>
    acc union readJson(date)
  }
}
```

The main part of the following code does the following:

- Parses command-line arguments to determine whether to reprocess data and which dates to process.

- Calls the `ingest` function to combine data for all specified dates.

- Calls the `writeDelta` function to write the combined data into a Delta Lake table:

```
// The first parameter should be a boolean, 2...n are dates to be
processed in format yyyy-mm-dd
val reprocess: Boolean = args(0).toBoolean
val dates = args.tail

writeDelta(reprocess, ingest(reprocess, args.tail: _*))
```

Overall, this code is used to process JSON data for specific dates, aggregate it into a single DataFrame, and write it into a Delta table in our Bronze layer. Now, let's take a look at our Silver layer.

Transforming the data

Our Silver layer code will process our conversion events data, flattening the information there, and joining it to our dimensional tables. We're focused on restructuring the data so it can be used in our Gold layer while cleaning and standardizing the naming conventions in our data platform.

We'll start by creating a function to help read our data into a DataFrame.

```
def read(formatType: String, sourceLocation: String): DataFrame = {
    formatType match {
        case "delta" => spark.read.format(formatType).
load(s"${sourceLocation}")
        case "csv" =>
          spark.read
            .format(formatType)
            .options(Map("delimiter" -> ",", "header" -> "true"))
            .load(s"${sourceLocation}")
    }
  }
```

This function reads data from a specified source location based on the given `formatType` format and location. It supports two formats: `delta` and `csv`. For `delta`, it directly loads data using `spark.read.format(formatType).load(sourceLocation)`. For `csv`, it specifies options such as the delimiter and header before loading the data. Typically, our dimensional data will not be stored in CSV files, but we use this format in this exercise purely for demonstration purposes:

```
val bronzeConversionEvents: DataFrame = read("delta", sourceCE)

val dimConversionEvents: DataFrame = read("csv", sourceDimCE)

val dimCountry: DataFrame = read("csv", sourceDimCountry)

val dimCampaigns: DataFrame = read("csv", sourceDimCampaigns)
```

Four DataFrames (`bronzeConversionEvents`, `dimConversionEvents`, `dimCountry`, and `dimCampaigns`) are loaded from different source locations using the `read` function:

```
val explodedBronzeCE: DataFrame = bronzeConversionEvents
    .withColumn("date", to_date(col("event_info.event_ts")))
    .withColumn("event_type", col("event_info.event_type"))
```

Now, we're going to do some transformations on the conversion event data. The explodedBronzeCE DataFrame is created by adding two new columns (date and event_type) to the bronzeConversionEvents DataFrame using withColumn. The date column is derived from the event_info.event_ts column, and the event_type column is renamed.

Next, we're going to join our ingested data with our existing dimensional data:

```
val joinedData: DataFrame = explodedBronzeCE
    .join(
      dimConversionEvents,
      col("conversion_event") === col("event_type"),
      "left"
    )
    .join(dimCountry, col("iso_2_char") === col("country"), "left")
    .join(
      dimCampaigns,
      col("marketing_campaign") === col("campaign_code"),
      "left"
    )
```

The joinedData DataFrame is created by performing several left joins between explodedBronzeCE, dimConversionEvents, dimCountry, and dimCampaigns DataFrames. We're using left joins because we want all the records from the left table, regardless of a match in the right table. The joins are based on specific columns, for example, conversion_event and event_type, iso_2_char and country, and so on.

At this point, we want to remove the non-standard columns and keep the columns we've brought in via our joins:

```
val silverConversionEvents = joinedData.select(
    "country_id",
    "country_name",
    "iso_3_char",
    "iso_2_char",
    "campaign_id",
    "campaign_code",
    "product_group",
    "conversion_event_id",
    "conversion_event",
    "date"
  )
```

The silverConversionEvents DataFrame is derived from joinedData by selecting a subset of columns using the select method. It includes columns such as country_id, country_name, and iso_3_char.

We now persist our Silver layer by writing it to our storage account:

```
def writeDelta(reprocess: Boolean, df: DataFrame) = {
    df.write
      .format("delta")
      .mode(reprocess match {
        case false => "append"
        case _     => "overwrite"
      })
      .save(s"${target}conversion_events")
  }

  writeDelta(true, silverConversionEvents)
```

The `writeDelta` function is called to write the `silverConversionEvents` DataFrame to a Delta table. In this case, it is set to overwrite the existing data (`writeDelta(true, silverConversionEvents)`), indicating that the table will be replaced with the data in the `silverConversionEvents` DataFrame.

Let's take a look at adding data quality checks to our data to ensure our end users can trust this data in their analysis.

Checking data quality

As mentioned in *Understanding the medallion architecture* section, it is now time to think about the rules and constraints that we would like our data to adhere to. The rules are usually defined by the business team but it is not uncommon for the development team to define those constraints themselves. For our purposes, we want our Bronze layer data to adhere to the following rules:

- At least 50% of the records should be of the `Download Content`, `Event Registration`, or `Survey Response` conversion event types

- At least 90% of the records must have product group specified

- Country name must be present for all records

We will write to the Silver layer only if all of the preceding checks pass.

For this example, we will create `DeequChecks` class that has a `runIfSuccess` method. This method takes a body of code that will be executed only if the constraints defined in the caller evaluate to `true`:

```
package com.packt.dewithscala.chapter12

import com.amazon.deequ._
import com.amazon.deequ.checks.CheckStatus
import com.amazon.deequ.constraints.ConstraintStatus
```

```scala
import org.apache.spark.sql.SparkSession

final case class DeequChecks(
  verificationResult: VerificationResult,
  session: SparkSession
) {

  def runIfSuccess(body: => Unit) = verificationResult.status match {
  case CheckStatus.Success =>
    body
    VerificationResult
      .successMetricsAsDataFrame(session, verificationResult)
      .show(false)
  case _ =>
    val constraintResults =
      verificationResult.checkResults.flatMap { case (_, checkResult)
=>
        checkResult.constraintResults
      }

    val deequValidationError = constraintResults
      .filter(_.status != ConstraintStatus.Success)
      .map { checkResult =>
        s"""|
            |for ${checkResult.constraint} the check result was
${checkResult.status}
            |checkResult.message.getOrElse("")""".stripMargin

      }
      .mkString("\n")

    VerificationResult
      .successMetricsAsDataFrame(session, verificationResult)
      .show(false)

    throw new Exception(deequValidationError)
  }
}
```

To see it in action, let's create a `VerificationResult` object with all of the constraints outlined at the beginning of this section:

```scala
val verificationResult = VerificationSuite()
    .onData(silverConversionEvents)
```

```
      .addCheck(
        Check(CheckLevel.Error, "silver layer checks!")
          .isContainedIn(
            "conversion_event",
            Array("Download Content", "Event Registration", "Survey
Response"),
            _ >= 0.5
          )
          .isComplete("country_name")
          .hasCompleteness("product_group", _ >= .9)
      )
      .run()
```

And then we invoke `runIfSuccess` as follows:

```
DeequChecks(verificationResult, spark)
  .runIfSuccess { writeDelta(true, silverConversionEvents) }
```

The preceding code will print the following to the console, which confirms that all of the constraints were indeed met:

```
+------+--------------------------------------------------------------------------+------------+--------+
|entity|instance                                                                  |name        |value   |
+------+--------------------------------------------------------------------------+------------+--------+
|Column|conversion_event contained in Download Content,Event Registration,Survey Response|Compliance  |0.500019|
|Column|country_name                                                              |Completeness|1.0     |
|Column|product_group                                                             |Completeness|1.0     |
+------+--------------------------------------------------------------------------+------------+--------+
```

Figure 12.9 – Check results as dataframe

Now that our data is trusted and we've applied data quality rules to our Silver processing, let's cover preparing and writing to a serving or Gold layer.

Creating a serving layer

The final step in our pipeline will be a process to write to our serving layer, referred to as the *Gold layer* in a Medallion data architecture. The Gold layer represents the final destination where refined, high-quality data is stored and made available for various analytical, reporting, and business intelligence purposes. In this layer, data undergoes a series of critical transformations to ensure it is reliable, accessible, and sufficiently prepared to support data-driven decision-making within an organization.

We'll focus on modeling our data to fit into our ERD diagram discussed previously in this chapter. Refer to *Figure 12.7* for the full model. The main task of our Gold layer code is to take our Silver layer conversion event data and transform it into the conversion events table. Let's take a look at the code that will do this conversion:

```
val silverConversionEvents: DataFrame =
    spark.read.format("delta").load(silverCE)
```

The first thing we'll do is load our Silver layer conversion events data into a DataFrame named `silverConversionEvents`. Next, we'll use that to transform this code into our Gold layer serving table:

```
val goldConversionEvents: DataFrame =
    silverConversionEvents
        .groupBy(
            col("country_id"),
            col("campaign_id"),
            col("conversion_event_id"),
            col("date")
        )
        .agg(
            count(col("conversion_event")).alias("event_count")
        )
```

In the preceding code, the `silverConversionEvents` DataFrame is transformed and aggregated. It groups the data based on specific columns: `country_id`, `campaign_id`, `conversion_event_id`, and `date`. The `groupBy` operation creates distinct groups based on the unique combinations of these columns.

The `agg` operation is used to calculate the count of `conversion_event` occurrences within each group, and the result is aliased as `event_count`. This means that the resulting DataFrame, `goldConversionEvents`, will have a count of events for each unique combination of the specified columns as shown here:

```
goldConversionEvents.write
    .format("delta")
    .mode("overwrite")
    .save(s"${target}conversion_events")
```

Finally, the code writes the `goldConversionEvents` DataFrame to the Gold layer using the Delta format. It specifies the write mode as `overwrite`, indicating that any existing data in the `conversion_events` Delta Lake table (in the Gold layer) should be replaced with the new data.

The `save` operation specifies the target location for the Gold layer, which is `${target}conversion_events`. The `${target}` represents the path or directory where the Gold layer data is stored.

Since we're using Delta, our data lake can be used as a lakehouse. If needed, the data can then be copied into a data warehouse of your organization's choice.

Next, we'll show how to orchestrate this pipeline using Argo.

Orchestrating our batch process

Now that we have our transformation written, it is time to build our pipeline. For this example, we will use our `minikube` instance that was set up as part of *Installing Argo workflows* section in *Chapter 10*.

Our workflow will print a message to start with, followed by Bronze, Silver, and Gold layer transformations, and finally a pipeline completion message. One important thing to note here is all of these steps will run as separate containers. What that means is data written by the Bronze layer will not be automatically available for Silver. In order to share data among containers, we need to use persistent volumes. There are several ways to do it, but for our example we will use `hostPath`, which is a type of `PersistentVolumes` supported by `minikube`. Please note that `hostPath` does not refer to a directory or file on your local machine, but rather within the `minikube` container. So we need to make the required datasets available so that Spark can find them at runtime.

To locate the minikube container, run `docker ps -f name=minikube`. Using this ID, you can copy any file or directory on your host machine to the `minikube` container. For our example, we will copy files in `chapter12/data` to the `/app` directory within the container. To do that, go to the `chapter12/data` directory in your terminal and run the following:

```
docker cp ./ <containerid>:/app/
```

After the files are copied, you can then mount `/app/` to the driver and executor Pods, as the following workflow illustrates:

```
apiVersion: argoproj.io/v1alpha1 #k8s apiVersion
kind: Workflow #k8s resource kind
metadata:
  generateName: data-pipeline-
  namespace: spark-app
spec:
  entrypoint: dag-seq
  templates:
    - name: print-start-message
      container:
        image: busybox
        imagePullPolicy: Always
        command: [echo]
        args: ["Starting Argo Workflow!"]
    - name: bronze
      resource:
        action: create
        successCondition: status.applicationState.state = COMPLETED
        failureCondition: status.applicationState.state = FAILED
        manifest: |
          apiVersion: "sparkoperator.k8s.io/v1beta2"
```

```yaml
        kind: SparkApplication
        metadata:
          generateName: bronze-
          namespace: spark-app
        spec:
          arguments:
          - "true"
          - ""
          - ""
          - "2023-08-01"
          - "2023-08-02"
          timeToLiveSeconds: 3600
          type: Scala
          mode: cluster
          image: rupambhattacharjee/de-with-scala:latest
          imagePullPolicy: Always
          mainClass: com.packt.dewithscala.chapter12.Bronze
          mainApplicationFile: "local://///app/de-with-scala-
assembly-1.0.jar"
          sparkConf:
            spark.kubernetes.authenticate.driver.serviceAccountName:
spark
          sparkVersion: 3.1.1
          driver:
            memory: 1G
            volumeMounts:
            - name: data
              mountPath: /tmp/data/
          executor:
            instances: 1
            cores: 1
            memory: 1G
            volumeMounts:
              - name: data
                mountPath: /tmp/data/
          volumes:
            - name: data
              hostPath:
                path: /app
                type: Directory
  - name: silver
    resource:
      action: create
      successCondition: status.applicationState.state = COMPLETED
```

```
        failureCondition: status.applicationState.state = FAILED
      manifest: |
        apiVersion: "sparkoperator.k8s.io/v1beta2"
        kind: SparkApplication
        metadata:
          generateName: "silver-"
          namespace: spark-app
        spec:
          arguments:
            - "/tmp/data/"
          timeToLiveSeconds: 3600
          type: Scala
          mode: cluster
          image: rupambhattacharjee/de-with-scala:latest
          imagePullPolicy: Always
          mainClass: com.packt.dewithscala.chapter12.Silver
          mainApplicationFile: "local://////app/de-with-scala-
assembly-1.0.jar"
          sparkConf:
            spark.kubernetes.authenticate.driver.serviceAccountName:
spark
          sparkVersion: 3.1.1
          driver:
            memory: 1G
            volumeMounts:
              - name: data
                mountPath: /tmp/data/
          executor:
            instances: 1
            cores: 1
            memory: 1G
            volumeMounts:
              - name: data
                mountPath: /tmp/data/
          volumes:
            - name: data
              hostPath:
                path: /app
                type: Directory
  - name: gold
    resource:
      action: create
      successCondition: status.applicationState.state = COMPLETED
      failureCondition: status.applicationState.state = FAILED
```

```yaml
    manifest: |
      apiVersion: "sparkoperator.k8s.io/v1beta2"
      kind: SparkApplication
      metadata:
        generateName: "gold-"
        namespace: spark-app
      spec:
        arguments:
          - "/tmp/data/"
        timeToLiveSeconds: 3600
        type: Scala
        mode: cluster
        image: rupambhattacharjee/de-with-scala:latest
        imagePullPolicy: Always
        mainClass: com.packt.dewithscala.chapter12.Gold
        mainApplicationFile: "local://////app/de-with-scala-
assembly-1.0.jar"
        sparkConf:
          spark.kubernetes.authenticate.driver.serviceAccountName:
spark
        sparkVersion: 3.1.1
        volumes:
        - name: task-pv-storage
          persistentVolumeClaim:
            claimName: pvc01
        driver:
          memory: 1G
          volumeMounts:
            - name: data
              mountPath: /tmp/data/
        executor:
          instances: 1
          cores: 1
          memory: 1G
          volumeMounts:
            - name: data
              mountPath: /tmp/data/
        volumes:
          - name: data
            hostPath:
              path: /app
              type: Directory
  - name: print-termination-message
    container:
```

```
      image: busybox
      imagePullPolicy: Always
      command: [echo]
      args: ["Congratulations! Argo Workflow ran sucessfully!"]

- name: dag-seq
  dag:
    tasks:
      - name: start-message
        template: print-start-message
      - name: bronze
        depends: start-message
        template: bronze
      - name: silver
        depends: bronze
        template: silver
      - name: gold
        depends: silver
        template: gold
      - name: termination-message
        depends: gold
        template: print-termination-message
```

You can run the preceding workflow using the following command:

```
argo submit pipeline.yaml --serviceaccount=spark -n spark-app --watch
```

Once you start the workflow, you can monitor the progress on your screen. It should complete within a few minutes and you should see the following:

```
Name:                data-pipeline-95d7z
Namespace:           spark-app
ServiceAccount:      spark
Status:              Succeeded
Conditions:
 PodRunning          False
 Completed           True
Created:             Wed Oct 04 17:54:04 +0530 (4 minutes ago)
Started:             Wed Oct 04 17:54:04 +0530 (4 minutes ago)
Finished:            Wed Oct 04 17:58:22 +0530 (now)
Duration:            4 minutes 18 seconds
Progress:            5/5
ResourcesDuration:   3m32s*(1 cpu),3m32s*(100Mi memory)

STEP                       TEMPLATE                   PODNAME                                                    DURATION  MESSAGE
 ✓ data-pipeline-95d7z     dag-seq
  ├─✓ start-message        print-start-message        data-pipeline-95d7z-print-start-message-62597978           6s
  ├─✓ bronze               bronze                     data-pipeline-95d7z-bronze-2737169672                      1m
  ├─✓ silver               silver                     data-pipeline-95d7z-silver-1033989585                      1m
  ├─✓ gold                 gold                       data-pipeline-95d7z-gold-136267398                         1m
  └─✓ termination-message  print-termination-message  data-pipeline-95d7z-print-termination-message-152001688    6s
```

Figure 12.10 – End-to-end pipeline

In this section, we looked at how we can use Argo to create an end-to-end data pipeline. Though we configured this pipeline to run locally on a minikube cluster, deploying it on your production system would require very few changes.

Summary

In this chapter, we delved into the world of batch data processing, underscoring the importance of efficiently managing and processing large volumes of data, a fundamental skill for data engineers.

You've learned the importance of comprehending the specific use case and data requirements before embarking on a data engineering project. Clarity in your objectives was emphasized as a foundational step. You've also had experience of hands-on techniques to efficiently collect and ingest data in batch mode. Data transformation techniques, including data cleaning, structuring, and quality checking, have been explored in detail. The significance of ensuring data quality for reliable processing has been highlighted. You've also gained an understanding of the final stage of the batch pipeline, where processed data is loaded into a serving layer, often referred to as the Gold layer. This layer is reserved for refined, business-ready data used in analysis and decision-making. Lastly, we covered the orchestration of the entire batch pipeline, guiding you to effectively manage and schedule data-processing workflows.

In conclusion, this chapter has provided you with a comprehensive skill set to excel in building batch data processing pipelines. By combining the power of Apache Spark and Scala, you are well prepared to tackle the challenges of handling vast volumes of data efficiently and reliably, contributing to informed decision-making and data-driven success in your organization.

In the next chapter, we'll cover streaming pipelines!

## 13

Building Streaming Pipelines Using Spark and Scala

The final chapter of this book is another combination of all we've learned, but in this case, we'll be building a streaming pipeline. You can think of streaming as continuous or "real-time" ingestion of data into your analytics system. There are many ways to accomplish this, but usually, this involves an event bus or message queuing system. We'll be using Azure Event Hubs as our streaming ingestion source because it can be configured to appear as Apache Kafka, which Spark can easily use due to its open source connectors. As a data engineer, you need to understand how to handle data efficiently and reliably in real time. Again, we'll leverage Spark, using its structured streaming capabilities, and Scala, as a versatile and expressive programming language. This time, we'll bring Apache Kafka into the picture to provide an event bus for our streaming pipeline.

In this chapter, we're going to cover the following main topics:

- Understanding our business use case
- What's our **Internet of Things (IoT)** use case?
- Ingesting the data
- Transforming the data
- Creating a serving layer
- Orchestrating our streaming process

By the end of this chapter, you will have learned how to fully plan, develop, and implement a streaming pipeline. This will prepare you to do the same in your organization.

Understanding our business use case

Our streaming scenario is based on IoT devices. IoT use cases have become increasingly common in organizations due to their transformative potential by allowing industries to fully understand what's happening with their operations in real-time. IoT sensors and devices help to do this by collecting data snapshots from various sources, allowing industries to monitor and optimize processes more effectively. For example, in manufacturing, IoT-enabled machinery can detect and report issues, reducing downtime and increasing production output. This efficiency improvement not only saves time and resources but also has a direct impact on the bottom line.

An example of this efficiency and cost reduction is predictive maintenance. By analyzing data from sensors embedded in equipment, companies can predict when machinery is likely to fail and schedule maintenance proactively. This proactive approach minimizes unplanned downtime, lowers maintenance costs, and extends the lifespan of assets. Another example is in the energy and utilities sector. IoT devices play a vital role in optimizing resource consumption and reducing waste, leading to environmental benefits and sustainability gains. These applications underscore the importance of IoT in fostering a more sustainable and eco-friendly industrial landscape.

The massive amount of data generated by IoT devices is analyzed to gain valuable insights into operations, customer behavior, and market trends over time. This data-driven decision-making empowers businesses to make informed choices, refine their strategies, and stay competitive in the market. IoT devices can also enable automation in various processes, which not only reduces the risk of human error but also frees up employees to focus on more strategic tasks. In essence, the adoption of IoT in the industry is not merely a technological trend but a strategic imperative for companies looking to stay efficient, competitive, and environmentally responsible in today's fast-paced business environment.

We'll be working on a general use case in IoT where we want to keep track of a device's status. This can be useful to notify customers when their device is down and track the overall reliability of manufacturers' models and the overall health of our fleet of devices.

What's our IoT use case?

We work for a telecommunications company that has various types of devices at customers' homes and businesses. Our devices are all attached to our network, and every minute, we get a status update on each device. The device returns the following statuses:

- **Activation**
- **Deactivation**
- **Plan change**
- **Telecoms activity**
- **Internet activity**
- **Device error**

Our operations team will collect this data from our devices and load each status update as an event in Azure Event Hubs. They have enabled Azure Event Hubs to act as an Apache Kafka surface so that we can use Spark's Kafka connectors to read that data into our data platform for analytics.

The data will be used in three different ways. The first will be an ad hoc analysis against our Silver layer data, which is structured and deduplicated. The second is to identify the total number of device states for each day. The last case is to identify the current state of any device.

Please see *Figure 13.1* for an example of the data we will be ingesting from our IoT devices:

	key	value
1	device_state	{"device_id":"0x100000001281d","country":"CN","event_type":"internet activity","event_ts":"2023-09-30T21:06:10.896Z"}
2	device_state	{"device_id":"0x1000000001f27","country":"IN","event_type":"internet activity","event_ts":"2023-09-30T21:06:10.896Z"}
3	device_state	{"device_id":"0x100000000b149","country":"CN","event_type":"telecoms activity","event_ts":"2023-09-30T21:06:10.896Z"}
4	device_state	{"device_id":"0x1000000011dde","country":"US","event_type":"activation","event_ts":"2023-09-30T21:06:10.896Z"}
5	device_state	{"device_id":"0x100000000f9b5","country":"CN","event_type":"internet activity","event_ts":"2023-09-30T21:06:10.896Z"}

Figure 13.1 – Sample data from our IoT devices

The requirement is to continuously ingest the data and process groups of records in batches every 15 minutes. Now, let's move on to understanding our data so that we know what to do with it.

Understanding the data

As before, we first need to understand our data and how to get access to it for ingestion. The data comes off the devices, and the operations team will feed that data into Azure Event Hubs. Each event in our event hub is stored as a key-value pair with additional metadata information about the message. The operations team is loading the key-value pair, which has a static key of device_state and a value with a JSON string containing four items:

- device_id: This is the unique ID of the deployed device
- country: The country in which this device is operating
- event_type: The status of the device at the time of the message
- event_ts: The timestamp of the message event

We'll need to parse this data into a usable record and perform some deduplication as we're not guaranteed to read this data only once from our Kafka topic. This data will be our Silver layer table. Next, we'll also create two tables from this Silver layer table to put into our Gold layer. Those two tables will be purpose-built for our second and third use cases, as mentioned in the previous section.

Refer to the following diagram for a visual representation of our data:

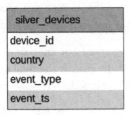

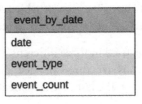

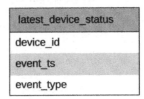

Figure 13.2 – ERD for device tables

Now that we understand our data, let's move on to thinking about how to build our streaming pipeline.

The end-to-end pipeline

Before we write any code, we need to consider the following use case and platform specific requirements:

- We must continuously stream our data from Kafka as it only has a 1-hour retention rate due to cost constraints

- We must continuously append new data to our Bronze layer and clean and deduplicate the data in our Silver layer, but we must not overwrite our bronze data

- The processing from Bronze to Silver and Gold can be scheduled every 15 minutes

- Where are we going to perform our transformations and deduplications?

- We want to be able to upsert our data in our Silver layer in an efficient manner, so we should look at the Delta format

- Where do we do our aggregations?

Here's a high-level overview of how we can structure our Kafka/Spark/Scala application to meet these requirements:

- **Data source and streaming**: The first step is to identify the data source; in this case, Kafka. It's important to note that in our organization, Kafka is configured to have a retention rate of 1 hour. This means that data must be continuously streamed from Kafka to ensure no data is lost. Setting up a reliable and efficient Kafka consumer is crucial to handle this continuous flow of data.

- **Bronze and Silver layers**: The bronze layer is where raw data is continuously appended, and it should not be modified or overwritten. The silver layer is where data is cleaned, deduplicated, and transformed into a more usable format. Decisions need to be made about where and how these processes will take place. Typically, data cleaning and deduplication can occur within the silver layer.

- **Processing schedule**: While data is continuously ingested into bronze, the processing from bronze to silver and then to gold should be scheduled at regular intervals; in this case, every 15 minutes. This schedule ensures that data is continuously refined and made available for downstream processes.

- **Data storage format**: To efficiently upsert data in the silver layer, consider using Delta Lake or similar technologies. Delta Lake provides ACID transactions, time travel, and versioning, making it suitable for maintaining data quality and history.

- **Aggregations**: Aggregations are typically performed in the gold layer, which is the final layer of data refinement. Aggregations can be done using the Spark DataFrame API.

In summary, this high-level overview outlines the key considerations before diving into the data engineering process. It emphasizes the need for continuous data streaming, a three-layer data architecture, scheduled processing, thoughtful transformations, efficient upsert mechanisms, and a clear plan for aggregations. Now that we have a plan in place, let's move on to data ingestion.

Ingesting the data

Before we move on to our ingestion code, there is some setup you will have to do to create a source from which to ingest. There are multiple ways to set up a Kafka service to provide a source for our process, but we chose to use Azure Event Hubs. However, you should use whichever service is most convenient for you. If you decided to use Azure Event Hubs, you will need to set up the service by following the instructions at the following link: `https://learn.microsoft.com/en-us/azure/event-hubs/event-hubs-quickstart-kafka-enabled-event-hubs`.

Once you have an Event Hubs/Kafka service created, you'll create a namespace and topic that will be used in this example. You'll also have to load data into that topic so that our ingestion process can consume the data. The code for this is located on our GitHub repository in the `Chapter 13 data_generator` folder.

The code will be excluded from the text of this book as it's written in Python. The main reason for this is that packages used to generate synthetic data are written in Python. If you're interested in how we generated data in this book please see the following project on Databricks Labs: `https://databrickslabs.github.io/dbldatagen/public_docs/index.html`.

Let's start with writing our ingestion process from an Apache Kafka topic and writing it to a Delta Lake table using Apache Spark Structured Streaming. Make sure to get your policy connection string from Azure Event Hubs. You can find your policy in **Shared access policies** in the left navigation of the **Azure Event Hubs** service. Select the policy and copy either the **Connection string-primary key** value or the **Connection string-secondary key** value. It will be in this format:

Endpoint=sb://<namespace>.servicebus.windows.net/;SharedAccessKey-Name=<policyName>;SharedAccessKey=<key>;EntityPath=<topic>.

Please refer to the following code:

```
val readConnectionString =        "Endpoint=sb://<namespace>.servicebus.
windows.net/;SharedAccessKeyName=policy1;SharedAccessKey=<key>;En-
tityPath=dewithscala"
val topicName        = "dewithscala"
val ehNamespaceName = "<namespace>"
val ehSasl =
    "org.apache.kafka.common.security.plain.PlainLoginModule" ++
    " required username='$ConnectionString' password='" ++ readCon-
nectionString ++ "';"
val bootstrapServers = s"$ehNamespaceName.servicebus.windows.net:9093"
```

The preceding code defines configuration parameters such as the Kafka connection string, the topic name, the Event Hubs namespace name, the **Simple Authentication and Security Layer** (**SASL**) configuration for Kafka, and the Kafka bootstrap servers. The bootstrap server and port are defined by Azure.

Let's take a look at the following code now:

```
val df = spark.readStream
    .format("kafka")
    .option("subscribe", topicName)
    .option("kafka.bootstrap.servers", bootstrapServers)
    .option("kafka.sasl.mechanism", "PLAIN")
    .option("kafka.security.protocol", "SASL_SSL")
    .option("kafka.sasl.jaas.config", ehSasl)
    .option("startingOffsets", "latest")
    .load()
```

This code uses Apache Spark Structured Streaming to create a streaming DataFrame (df) that reads data from the Kafka topic specified by topicName. It configures various Kafka-specific options such as security settings, timeouts, and the starting offset for reading data. The starting offset can be set to earliest or latest. Latest will only read messages from the topic that you haven't already read. Earliest will get all messages available on the topic.

Now, the following code processes the data from Kafka, casting the key and value columns to strings, and then writes the data to a Delta table:

```
df.selectExpr("CAST(key AS STRING)", "CAST(value AS STRING)")
    .as[(String, String)]
    .writeStream
```

```
.format("delta")
.outputMode("append")
.option("checkpointLocation", s"$target/_checkpoints/")
.option("path", s"$target/bronze/data/")
.start()
.awaitTermination()
```

It specifies the output mode as `append`, indicating that new data will be appended to the table. Checkpoints are used to maintain the streaming state, and the path for storing Delta data is provided. Finally, the streaming job is started and set to await termination, which means it will run until manually stopped.

Our code demonstrates a typical setup for streaming data ingestion from Kafka into a Delta Lake storage layer using Apache Spark Structured Streaming, with the necessary configuration and settings to ensure data reliability and security.

Let's move on to transforming our data in our Silver layer.

Transforming the data

Our Silver layer code will process our device data, flattening, transforming, and deduplicating the data from our Bronze layer.

Refer to the following code:

```
val reprocess: Boolean = args(0).toBoolean
val bronzeSource: String = "./src/main/scala/com/packt/dewithscala/
chapter13/data/bronze/data/"
val target: String = "./src/main/scala/com/packt/dewithscala/
chapter13/data/silver/"
```

This code defines a `reprocess` Boolean variable based on a command-line argument and sets file paths for the Bronze and Silver data sources, as shown here:

```
val bronzeData: DataFrame = spark.read.format("delta").
load(bronzeSource)
```

Here, the process loads data from the Delta Lake Bronze layer located at the `bronzeSource` path into a DataFrame named `bronzeData`.

Next, the following code defines a schema for parsing JSON data from the `value` column of `bronzeData`:

```
val jsonSchema: StructType = StructType(
    Seq(
       StructField("device_id", StringType),
       StructField("country", StringType),
```

```
        StructField("event_type", StringType),
        StructField("event_ts", TimestampType)
    )
  )
```

It specifies the structure of the data with fields such as `device_id`, `country`, `event_type`, and `event_ts`.

Now, the following snippet processes and transforms the data in `bronzeData`:

```
val updateSilver: DataFrame = bronzeData
    .select(from_json(col("value"), jsonSchema).alias("value"))
    .select(
      col("value.device_id"),
      col("value.country"),
      col("value.event_type"),
      col("value.event_ts")
    )
    .dropDuplicates("device_id", "country", "event_ts")
```

It extracts fields from the JSON data in the `value` column and removes duplicate rows based on the `device_id`, `country`, and `event_ts` columns, creating a DataFrame named `updateSilver`.

Next, the following code checks the value of the `reprocess` variable:

```
reprocess match {
  case true =>
    updateSilver.write
      .format("delta")
      .mode("overwrite")
      .save(s"${target}silver_devices")
  case _ => {
    val silverTarget = DeltaTable.forPath(spark, s"{$target}silver_
devices")
    silverTarget
      .as("devices")
      .merge(
        updateSilver.as("update"),
        "devices.device_id = update.device_id AND devices.country =
update.country AND devices.event_ts = update.event_ts"
      )
      .whenNotMatched()
      .insertAll()
      .execute()
  }
}
```

If `reprocess` is `true`, it overwrites the entire Silver layer. If `reprocess` is anything else, it updates the Silver layer using Delta Lake's `merge` operation, merging data from `updateSilver` into the existing Silver layer based on the specified conditions.

All in all, this code takes data from a Bronze layer, applies transformations, and updates a Silver layer while considering whether to reprocess or update incrementally based on the value of `reprocess`. It leverages Delta Lake to manage data updates and transformations efficiently.

Creating a serving layer

The final step in our pipeline will be a process to write to our serving layer, referred to as the Gold layer.

Refer to the following code:

```
private def writeDelta(df: DataFrame, tableName: String) = {
    df.write
      .format("delta")
      .mode("overwrite")
      .save(s"${target}${tableName}")
}
```

This code defines a reusable function, `writeDelta`, that takes a DataFrame, `df`, and a table name, `tableName`, as arguments. It writes the DataFrame to a Delta Lake table with the specified table name, overwriting the existing data if it already exists.

Next, have a look at the following code:

```
val silverSource: String = "./src/main/scala/com/packt/dewithscala/
chapter13/data/silver/ silver_devices"
val target: String = "./src/main/scala/com/packt/dewithscala/
chapter13/data/gold/"
val silverData: DataFrame = spark.read.format("delta").
load(silverSource)
```

In the preceding code, file paths for the Silver and Gold layers are defined. Our code loads data from the Delta Lake Silver layer located at `silverSource` into a DataFrame named `silverData`.

Now, we process the data from `silverData` to count event types by date:

```
val case1Df: DataFrame = silverData
    .groupBy(to_date($"event_ts").alias("event_date"), $"event_type")
    .agg(count($"event_type").alias("event_count"))
  writeDelta(
    case1Df,
    "event_by_date"
  )
```

This code groups the data by the date portion of the `event_ts` column and the `event_type` column and then calculates the count of each event type for each date. The result is written to a Delta Lake table named `event_by_date` using the `writeDelta` function.

Next, we need to write code to find the latest device state:

```
private val windowSpec =
    Window.partitionBy("device_id").orderBy(desc("event_ts"))

private val dfWindowedRank = silverData
    .withColumn("dense_rank", dense_rank().over(windowSpec))

val case2Df: DataFrame = dfWindowedRank
    .filter("dense_rank = 1")
    .drop("dense_rank")

writeDelta(
    case2Df,
    "latest_device_status"
)
```

This code creates a window specification for partitioning by `device_id` and ordering by descending `event_ts`. Then, it calculates a dense rank within each partition based on the window specification. The DataFrame is filtered to keep only rows where the dense rank is 1, representing the latest device state. The result is written to a Delta Lake table named `latest_device_status` using the `writeDelta` function.

We now have a working streaming process, so let's move on to orchestration in the next section.

Orchestrating our streaming process

We used Argo in our last batch process for orchestration in *Chapter 12*, so let's use Databricks Workflows to show another way to schedule our process in a cloud environment. Please refer to *Chapter 2* for using the Community Edition of Databricks.

Use the knowledge gained from previous chapters to build your Spark jar and deploy it to a location that Databricks can access. This can be a cloud storage account or your **Databricks File System** (**DBFS**).

Go to your Databricks workspace and look for **Workflows** in the left navigation:

Figure 13.3 – Databricks navigation

Here are the steps to create a new workflow to orchestrate your pipeline:

1. In your **Databricks** left navigation, click on **Workflows**. The first step in our process will be to create a job to run our streaming process. Create a new workflow by clicking on the **Create job** button. Edit the task and select **Spark Submit**, then input your jar location, as well as class names and packages. Refer to the following screenshot example:

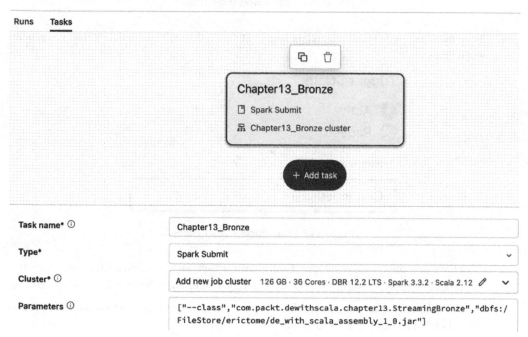

Figure 13.4 – Databricks streaming task in a workflow

2. Next, we'll use a special trigger to make sure that one and only one process is running continuously. In the right area of the job, locate the **Schedule & Triggers** section and click on **Add trigger**:

Figure 13.5 – Databricks Schedules & Triggers

3. Select the **Continuous** trigger type from the drop-down list:

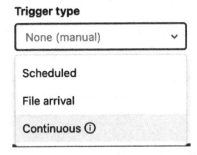

Figure 13.6 – Databricks trigger types

4. Next, make sure you select the **Active** trigger status as this will immediately start the process when you save it:

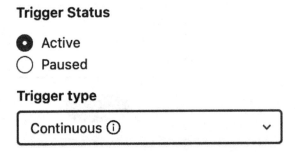

Figure 13.7 – Databricks trigger status

5. Click **Save**, and your process will start. **Continuous** is a special type of trigger that will ensure that this process is always running. This is an ideal trigger since our process is a streaming pipeline.

6. Next, we want to create another pipeline that is scheduled to run every 15 minutes to process our data from bronze to Silver to Gold:

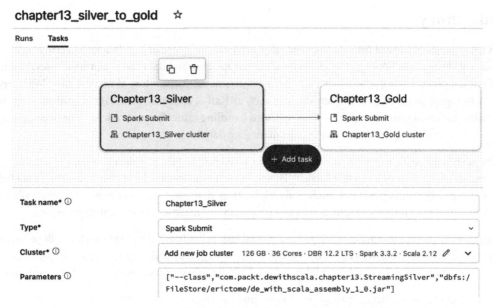

Figure 13.8 – Databricks streaming tasks for silver and gold

Go back to the main **Workflow** page, and create another job. This time, we'll create two tasks for our **StreamingSilver** and **StreamingGold** objects. Each will be set to **Spark Submit** task types and will use their own job cluster. See the example in *Figure 13.8*.

7.   Similarly to the streaming bronze pipeline, edit the **Schedule & Triggers** section, but this time, select **Scheduled** for a trigger type:

Figure 13.9 – Databricks silver to gold trigger

8.   Next, in **Schedule**, select **Every 15 Minutes** starting at **0 minutes past the hour**. The job will be triggered every 0, 15, 30, and 45 minutes of every hour.

9.   Last, make sure you have **Trigger Status** set to **Active** and save the trigger.

Our streaming process will now be streaming in bronze data continuously from Kafka and processing that data from silver to gold every 15 minutes! Now, let's summarize this chapter and all we've learned.

Summary

In this chapter, we dived into a comprehensive exploration of streaming data engineering tasks and real-world use cases. We began by understanding our use case and data and planning the development of our data engineering process specific to the requirements and context of our use case. We learned how to ingest streaming data from sources such as Kafka, ensuring that data is continuously and reliably streamed into our pipeline. This included handling critical aspects such as configuring Kafka consumers, securing the data transfer, and managing data loss.

The next step was transforming the data. We discovered how to take raw data from our source, process it, and shape it into a more usable format. This transformation involved not only converting data types but also performing operations such as deduplication, aggregation, and timestamp manipulation. These transformations are essential for preparing data for analytical or reporting purposes.

After transforming the data, we explored the crucial task of loading it into a serving layer. By leveraging the power of Delta Lake, we efficiently managed data storage and updating processes. We learned how to write data to Delta Lake tables, making it available for downstream analytics and consumption.

This comprehensive journey through understanding use cases, ingesting streaming data, transforming it, and loading it into a serving layer has equipped us with valuable knowledge and practical skills for tackling real-world data engineering challenges, and this chapter and the previous one are applications of all the material covered in this book. We hope you enjoyed this book as much as we enjoyed writing it!

Index

Packtpub.com

Subscribe to our online digital library for full access to over 7,000 books and videos, as well as industry leading tools to help you plan your personal development and advance your career. For more information, please visit our website.

Why subscribe?

- Spend less time learning and more time coding with practical eBooks and Videos from over 4,000 industry professionals

- Improve your learning with Skill Plans built especially for you

- Get a free eBook or video every month

- Fully searchable for easy access to vital information

- Copy and paste, print, and bookmark content

Did you know that Packt offers eBook versions of every book published, with PDF and ePub files available? You can upgrade to the eBook version at packtpub.com and as a print book customer, you are entitled to a discount on the eBook copy. Get in touch with us at customercare@packtpub.com for more details.

At www.packtpub.com, you can also read a collection of free technical articles, sign up for a range of free newsletters, and receive exclusive discounts and offers on Packt books and eBooks.

Other Books You May Enjoy

If you enjoyed this book, you may be interested in these other books by Packt:

Cracking the Data Engineering Interview

Kedeisha Bryan, Taamir Ransome

ISBN: 978-1-83763-077-6

- Create maintainable and scalable code for unit testing
- Understand the fundamental concepts of core data engineering tasks
- Prepare with over 100 behavioral and technical interview questions
- Discover data engineer archetypes and how they can help you prepare for the interview
- Apply the essential concepts of Python and SQL in data engineering
- Build your personal brand to noticeably stand out as a candidate

Data Engineering with dbt

Roberto Zagni

ISBN: 978-1-80324-628-4

- Create a dbt Cloud account and understand the ELT workflow
- Combine Snowflake and dbt for building modern data engineering pipelines
- Use SQL to transform raw data into usable data, and test its accuracy
- Write dbt macros and use Jinja to apply software engineering principles
- Test data and transformations to ensure reliability and data quality
- Build a lightweight pragmatic data platform using proven patterns
- Write easy-to-maintain idempotent code using dbt materialization

Packt is searching for authors like you

If you're interested in becoming an author for Packt, please visit `authors.packtpub.com` and apply today. We have worked with thousands of developers and tech professionals, just like you, to help them share their insight with the global tech community. You can make a general application, apply for a specific hot topic that we are recruiting an author for, or submit your own idea.

Share Your Thoughts

Now you've finished *Data Engineering with Scala and Spark*, we'd love to hear your thoughts! Scan the QR code below to go straight to the Amazon review page for this book and share your feedback or leave a review on the site that you purchased it from.

`https://packt.link/r/1804612588`

Your review is important to us and the tech community and will help us make sure we're delivering excellent quality content.

Download a free PDF copy of this book

Thanks for purchasing this book!

Do you like to read on the go but are unable to carry your print books everywhere?

Is your eBook purchase not compatible with the device of your choice?

Don't worry, now with every Packt book you get a DRM-free PDF version of that book at no cost.

Read anywhere, any place, on any device. Search, copy, and paste code from your favorite technical books directly into your application.

The perks don't stop there, you can get exclusive access to discounts, newsletters, and great free content in your inbox daily

Follow these simple steps to get the benefits:

1. Scan the QR code or visit the link below

https://packt.link/free-ebook/9781804612583

2. Submit your proof of purchase

3. That's it! We'll send your free PDF and other benefits to your email directly

Made in the USA
Monee, IL
28 January 2024

52468389R00168